T0378125

Exiting the Fragility Trap

SERIES IN HUMAN SECURITY

Series editors: Geoffrey Dabelko, Brandon Kendhammer, and Nukhet Sandal

---

The Series in Human Security is published in association with Ohio University's War and Peace Studies and African Studies programs at the Center for International Studies and the Environmental Studies Program at the Voinovich School of Leadership and Public Affairs.

Technologies of Suspicion and the Ethics of Obligation in Political Asylum, edited by Bridget M. Haas and Amy Shuman

Exiting the Fragility Trap: Rethinking Our Approach to the World's Most Fragile States, by David Carment and Yiagadeesen Samy

Exiting the Fragility Trap

Rethinking Our Approach to the

World's Most Fragile States

David Carment and Yiagadeesen Samy

OHIO UNIVERSITY PRESS | ATHENS

Ohio University Press, Athens, Ohio 45701
ohioswallow.com
© 2019 by Ohio University Press
All rights reserved

To obtain permission to quote, reprint, or otherwise reproduce or distribute material from
Ohio University Press publications, please contact our rights and permissions department at
(740) 593-1154 or (740) 593-4536 (fax).

Printed in the United States of America
Ohio University Press books are printed on acid-free paper ⊚ ™

29 28 27 26 25 24 23 22 21 20 19   5 4 3 2 1

Library of Congress Cataloging-in-Publication Data
Names: Carment, David, 1959- author. | Samy, Yiagadeesen, author.
Title: Exiting the fragility trap : rethinking our approach to the world's
    most fragile states / David Carment and Yiagadeesen Samy.
Description: Athens : Ohio University Press, 2019. | Series: Series in
    human security | Includes bibliographical references and index.
Identifiers: LCCN 2019028379 | ISBN 9780821423905 (hardcover) | ISBN
    9780821446867 (pdf)
Subjects: LCSH: Political stability--Developing countries--Case studies. |
    Legitimacy of governments--Developing countries--Case studies. |
    Nation-building--Developing countries--Case studies. | Developing
    countries--Politics and government--Case studies.
Classification: LCC JF60 .C37 2019 | DDC 320.9172/4--dc23
LC record available at https://lccn.loc.gov/2019028379

For William, Anna, and Milana

—David Carment

For Allee, Keshana, and Shayana

—Yiagadeesen (Teddy) Samy

Contents

List of Illustrations   ix

Acknowledgments   xi

Abbreviations   xiii

Introduction   State Fragility in a Time of Turmoil   1

Chapter 1   A Typology of Countries, with a Focus on the Fragility Trap   31

Chapter 2   Elites and the Trap
  Drivers of Change   63

Chapter 3   The Fragility Trap
  Yemen and Pakistan—The MIFFs   81

Chapter 4   In and Out of Fragility
  Mali and Laos—Landlocked and Unstable   112

Chapter 5   Fragility Exit
  Bangladesh and Mozambique—A Fine Balance   145

Chapter 6   Explaining the Fragility Trap and What to Do about It   176

Notes   191

References   201

Index   225

Illustrations

FIGURES

1.1 Afghanistan, fragility, 1980–2014 48

1.2 A fragility trap model 51

1.3 Mozambique, fragility, 1980–2014 57

3.1 Yemen's fragility ranking, 1980–2014 83

3.2 Yemen's ALC trends, 1980–2014 84

3.3 Pakistan's fragility ranking, 1980–2014 94

3.4 Pakistan's ALC trends, 1980–2014 96

4.1 Mali's fragility ranking, 1980–2014 114

4.2 Mali's ALC trends, 1980–2014 115

4.3 Laos's fragility ranking, 1980–2014 127

4.4 Laos's ALC trends, 1980–2014 128

5.1 Bangladesh's fragility ranking, 1980–2014 147

5.2 Bangladesh's ALC trends, 1980–2014 148

5.3 Mozambique's fragility ranking, 1980–2014 162

5.4 Mozambique's ALC trends, 1980–2014 163

TABLES

I.1 Examples of indicators for ALC 14

1.1 Top forty fragile states, 2014 40

1.2 Ten most fragile states, by ALC component, 2014 41

1.3 Fragility trap countries, 1980–2014 49

1.4 Correlates of fragility, 1980–2014 52

1.5 Fragility as a function of various traps: trapped countries 53

1.6 Typology of countries   55

1.7 Correlates of fragility, 1980–2014   58

1.8 Fragility as a function of various traps   59

Acknowledgments

Building on twenty years of research on fragile states, this book really is a labor of love. It reflects our prior knowledge on the subject along with new insights on research design and analysis. It represents the kind of interdisciplinary, policy-relevant, multimethod approach that the Norman Paterson School of International Affairs, where we are both based, has become famous for in its teaching and publications. Transforming all this complexity into the written word would not have been possible without the support of several organizations, individuals, and funding agencies. We are greatly indebted to many of the school's excellent PhD students whose painstaking research and consummate writing skills contributed greatly to the completion of this volume. Joe Landry, an expert on fragile states in his own right, contributed significantly to our thinking about the fragility trap concept, to data collection and analysis, and to the Mozambique and Bangladesh case studies. Scott Shaw was responsible for much of the background research on Mali and Laos. Scott's ideas on "isomorphic mimicry," the rent economy, elite capture, and backsliding shine through in several chapters. Rachael Calleja contributed greatly to the background research on Pakistan and Yemen along with Christopher Ostropolski. Mark Haichin was a significant help in providing thorough literature reviews on legitimacy traps and unconsolidated democracy. Together with Rachael, Mark assisted with the creation of the various graphics that appear in this volume. Simon Langlois-Bertrand was hugely important in collecting and analyzing the data. We are also deeply indebted to Dr. Peter Tikuisis, whose work on fragile states' typologies was an inspiration for our own work and whose contributions to the Country Indicators for Foreign Policy (CIFP) project has been a significant addition, including his creation of a CIFP-based minimalist data set. In addition to these individuals, David Carment would like to thank the Centre for Global Cooperation Research, Duisburg, where he was a fellow in 2014–15 and where much of the preliminary work was completed. Hugely important as well was the World Institute for Development

Economics Research (WIDER), where Carment was a visiting scholar in 2017. WIDER's support toward the completion of this manuscript was instrumental. Sage guidance from WIDER staff members Rachel Gisselquist, Tony Addison, and Finn Tarp along with many of the visiting and resident institute fellows helped significantly. Yiagadeesen Samy would like to thank Carleton University's special grants program, which allowed us to hire research assistants to help with data collection and analysis. He is also indebted to the various scholars who have shaped his thinking, both theoretical and empirical, about the nature and persistence of fragility, especially in sub-Saharan Africa. Finally, Carment and Samy would also like to thank the Social Sciences and Humanities Research Council of Canada for its support in funding this research.

Abbreviations

ALC	authority, legitimacy, and capacity
ANC	African National Congress
AQAP	al-Qaeda in the Arabian Peninsula
AQIM	al-Qaeda in the Islamic Maghreb
BNP	Bangladesh Nationalist Party
CFA	Communauté Financière Africaine (African Financial Community) within the West African Economic and Monetary Union
CIFP	Country Indicators for Foreign Policy
CPIA	Country Policy and Institutional Assessments (World Bank)
DAC	Development Assistance Committee
DFID	Department for International Development (UK)
EIU	Economist Intelligence Unit
FATA	Federally Administered Tribal Areas
GDP	gross domestic product
GNI	gross national income
FAO	Food and Agriculture Organization of the United Nations
FE	fixed effects
FI	Fragility Index
Frelimo	Frente de Libertação de Moçambique
FSI	Fragile States Index

GWOT	Global War on Terrorism
HRW	Human Rights Watch
ICG	International Crisis Group
IISS	International Institute for Strategic Studies
IMF	International Monetary Fund
IS	Islamic State
Lao PDR	Lao People's Democratic Republic
LCMD	Lao Citizens Movement for Democracy
LICUS	Low Income Country under Stress
LPRP	Lao People's Revolutionary Party
MDG	Millennium Development Goal
MIFF	middle-income fragile or failed state
MNLA	National Movement for the Liberation of Azawad
MQM	Muhajir Qaumi Movement
MRG	Minority Rights Group International
MUJAO	Movement for Oneness and Jihad in West Africa
NGO	nongovernmental organization
ODA	official development assistance
OECD	Organisation for Economic Co-operation and Development
OLS	ordinary least squares
ONUMOZ	United Nations Operation in Mozambique
PDRY	People's Democratic Republic of Yemen, or South Yemen
PML-N	Pakistani Muslim League
PPP	Pakistan People's Party

Abbreviations

RE	random effects
Renamo	Resistência Nacional Moçambicana
RLG	Royal Lao Government
SDG	Sustainable Development Goal
SEM	State Evolution Model
SME	small and medium-sized enterprise
TI	Transparency International
UCDP/PRIO	Uppsala Conflict Data Program at the Peace Research Institute Oslo
UNDHA	United Nations Department of Humanitarian Affairs
UNDP	United Nations Development Programme
USAID	United States Agency for International Development
WFP	World Food Programme
WIDER	World Institute for Development Economics Research
YSP	Yemen Socialist Party

Introduction

State Fragility in a Time of Turmoil

It is frequently assumed that developing states experience sustained progress over time as their economies grow, their institutions consolidate, and poverty diminishes. But for many, this is simply not the case. Some of the so-called fragile states suffer from quick reversals, while others improve in certain areas and weaken in others. Those fragile states whose stagnation is so tenacious despite generous aid programs and substantial and costly interventions are considered to be stuck in a "fragility trap." States that are persistently fragile pose an unmet challenge to policymakers, theorists, and analysts because they show little indication of how they might exit from their political, economic, and social malaise. Conventional aid policies do not appear to work as effectively in these countries. Caught in a low-level equilibrium, trapped states appear to be in a perpetual political and economic limbo that can last for years and, in several cases, decades. By definition, those stuck in a trap are characterized by weak policy environments, making engagement in them a long-term challenge. Their structural complexity means policy entry is difficult.

The persistence of fragility raises questions about the idea of managing transitions out of fragility. This is an issue raised by the Development

Assistance Committee (DAC) of the Organisation for Economic Co-operation and Development (OECD), or OECD DAC, in a report on fragile states (OECD 2015) and by Gisselquist (2015), in an assessment of fragility persistence. The idea that state fragility is solely a transitory phenomenon associated with, for example, a postconflict peace process is empirically untrue. For example, research on fragile, closed, and unstable states (Bremmer 2006; Tikuisis and Carment 2017) shows that they move both forward and backward in terms of their political and economic development so that stability and openness are never secure. Indeed, Bremmer (2006) shows that it is easier, when economic resources and growth are in doubt, for a leader to create stability by closing the country than to build a civil society and establish accountable institutions.

Chauvet and Collier's (2008) study on failing states provides one explanation for this behavior. They found the average duration of a failing state is a lengthy fifty-four years because external financing for resource exports and foreign aid tend to encourage rents and thereby retard reforms. Along similar lines, Andrimihaja, Cinyabuguma, and Devarajan (2011) argue that aid resources focused on poor property rights enforcement, corruption, insecurity, and violence are needed to propel states stuck in the fragility trap toward better economic outcomes. But such policy options are rarely successful because the incentives for leaders of trapped states to embrace reforms that affect their personal interests are too weak. Elite capture of the state and the benefits it accrues mean there are few incentives for ruling regimes to enact political and economic reform. Thus, we believe that reversals and traps occur not just because of highly authoritarian regimes. There are those states that fail to achieve sufficient capacity to meet the needs of their population yet are caught in a legitimacy trap with little inclination to exit. Then there are those states that are perpetually economically weak and often plagued by violence, perhaps shifting slightly with changes in effectiveness and leadership but not sufficiently to escape fragility. Such conditions can be exacerbated by high economic inequality or low development and recessions. Finally, there are those states with strong authority and democratic aspirations but without sufficient capacity to break free of fragility. In brief, challenges to and degradations in authority and capacity deriving from poor economic policy or failure to manage societal tensions appear to be key reasons why countries remain stuck in a fragility trap.

Further, the vexatious nature of fragility traps has motivated researchers and policymakers to recast their thinking about the causes of fragility, their inherent complexity, and the interdependence between aid and other forms of third-party assistance (Gisselquist 2015; Brinkerhoff 2014). In previous research on the causes of fragility (Carment, Prest, and Samy 2010), the authors argue that the inherent ambiguity in the fragility concept allowed policymakers to adopt it to their own agendas, a point reinforced by Grimm (2014) and Lemay-Hébert and Mathieu (2014), among others. While this conceptual flexibility lent itself to a diversity of policy programs and policy initiatives, we now see that the resulting lack of coherence has not generated the kinds of effective policy responses needed to fix the world's most fragile states (Brinkerhoff 2014). The inherent difficulty is in understanding the nature of the "trap" in which the most extreme cases are stuck. The following metaphor by Kingwell (2007) and quoted in Carment, Prest, and Samy (2010) is helpful to understand the extent of this problem:

> Fragility belongs to a class of properties, or qualities, philosophers call dispositional. A dispositional property differs from a static one in being lodged in potential rather than actuality. An antique china teacup is always fragile and it is also always white but its whiteness is bodied forth at every moment whereas its fragility depends on what will happen under certain future circumstances. (Kingwell 2007, F7)

The basic assumption of this metaphor is the scope and extent of the equilibrium in which such states are stuck and the impacts that "future circumstances" will produce on decreasing or improving a state's level of fragility. These future circumstances may be fortuitous and promising, such as a change in government or an economic windfall, or they may be a severe shock, such as a drought, an earthquake, or a neighboring civil war. The ability to withstand or manage negative effects is often referred to as "resilience" (Briguglio et al. 2009). Since fragility traps are a function of pernicious and often lethal "feedback loops" and equilibria, we argue that successful transitions from fragility involve a specific sequence of policies intended to improve a state's authority, legitimacy, and capacity through, among other things, compliance with the law and incorporation of peoples into a functional economy. (See, for example, Lambach, Johais, and Bayer [2015] and Call [2008] for extensions on this approach.) To be sure, sequencing is not without its challenges and controversies, particularly for those states emerging from conflict or with little or no experience in democratization.

For example, recognizing that countries in transition face a higher risk of conflict due to their institutional weakness, Mansfield and Snyder (2007) suggest that donors should prioritize strengthening recipient institutions prior to providing broader democracy promotion and support. While such "sequencing" is intended to maximize the likelihood of successful transitions by "rationalizing" democratization through securing institutional strength prior to transformation, Carothers (2007) argues that a "gradual" approach to building democracy, which encourages donors to contribute to supporting democratic principles and values in current contexts, could help develop democracy from current conditions rather than waiting for the conditions needed under sequencing.[1]

FRAGILITY AND CHARACTERISTICS OF STATENESS

Thus, to break free of the bad equilibrium in which states may find themselves, it is important to focus on those elements of statehood that can pull the country forward, akin to an all-wheel-drive vehicle in snow that shifts traction to the wheels that have the best grip while letting the others do less work. Applying the available power to wheels that spin freely without traction will only make it more likely that the vehicle remains mired. In this vein, we will show that shifts out of fragility are not obtained through economic transformation or capacity alone and especially if economic gains do not lead to positive changes in authority and legitimacy. To make this argument, we rely on our theoretical and conceptual foundations from past research. As noted elsewhere, fragility is a measure of the extent to which the actual practices and capacities of states differ from its idealized image (Carment, Prest, and Samy 2010). Based on our conceptualization, fragility is a matter of degree, not kind. It is a measure of the extent to which the actual institutions, functions, and political processes of a state accord with the strong image of sovereign state, the one reified in both theory and international law. By our definition, all states are to some extent fragile. This is, we believe, a closer representation of reality than an arbitrary line, however drawn, between failed and stable, weak and strong, or resilient and vulnerable. While conflict-affected states are by definition fragile, some but not all fragile states are mired in deep-rooted conflict and violent transitions (Tikuisis et al. 2015).

The core structural elements of stateness that we use in this book are represented by authority (A), legitimacy (L), and capacity (C). Collectively

Introduction

known as ALC, they are our key organizing concepts for evaluating the change of states over time (Carment, Prest, and Samy 2010). Authority is defined as the extent to which a state possesses the ability to enact binding legislation over its population, to exercise coercive force over its sovereign territory, to provide core public goods, and to provide a stable and secure environment to its citizens and communities. The definition of authority thus derives in part from Max Weber's definition of the state as having a monopoly on violence. Legitimacy refers to the extent to which a particular state commands public loyalty to the governing regime and generates domestic support for that government's legislation and policy. Such support must be created through a voluntary and reciprocal arrangement of effective governance and citizenship founded upon broadly accepted principles of government selection and succession that is recognized both locally and internationally. Capacity considers the extent to which a state can mobilize and employ resources toward productive ends. States that are lacking in capacity are generally unable to provide services to their citizens and cannot respond effectively to sudden shocks such as natural disasters, epidemics, food shortages, or refugee flows.

OPERATIONALIZING ALC

The Country Indicators for Foreign Policy (CIFP) data set that we use in this volume provides an annual fragility index that goes back to 1980. CIFP's overall fragility index is calculated from more than eighty indicators that are spread across the three main characteristics of stateness—authority, legitimacy, and capacity—and six clusters of state performance (demography, economics, environment, governance, human development, and security and crime), with gender as a crosscutting theme.

In the case of authority, some of the indicators used to operationalize the concept are straightforward. They are fundamentally meant to represent effective governance—namely, the ability of states to deliver core public goods such as public security, law and order, and economic stability. We distinguish core public goods from other social services, such as education and health (discussed further below under capacity). For example, measures related to conflict intensity, rule of law, or political stability speak directly to the ability of governments to control disruptions within their territories and thus exercise authority. The control of territory, which prevents under- and ungoverned spaces from arising, is fundamental for state authority, rather than anarchy, to emerge. Consider, for instance, the tribal territories between Pakistan and Afghanistan or in Yemen for several decades, where lack of control over territory has resulted in the emergence of terrorist groups and secessionist movements. One of the challenges of state building in places such as Afghanistan is the fact that the central government has no effective control over its territory outside of Kabul and a few other large cities.

Incidents of (or fatalities resulting from) terrorism, military expenditure, or the external debt of a country are all factors that have an impact on the ability of a country to provide security within its borders. This lack of security may, for example, lead to refugee flows across borders, as we have seen in the cases of the ongoing migrant crisis resulting from the Syrian conflict and the refugee flows across the African continent toward European countries. Whether the ability of countries to avoid conflicts is related to the issue of authority or other factors is contested in the literature. For example, Collier et al. (2003) note that several root causes of conflict are prevalent throughout the literature—namely, ethnic and religious tensions, lack of democracy, and economic inequalities. However, they also argue that the "key root cause of conflict is the failure of economic development" (53). For them, poor countries that stumble into conflict are likely to experience perpetuated conflict or become "trapped" in further conflict, with more unequal and ethnically diverse societies having a higher risk of lengthy conflicts. This tendency to equate conflict with underdevelopment or fragility with underdevelopment is arguably too simplistic. For example, many low-income countries, such as Malawi and Tanzania, have been able to avoid civil conflicts and are quite resilient. On the other hand, there is now an increasing interest in political settlements and elite pacts as being at least as important as the technical challenges of international development (Pospisil and Menocal 2017), but this has yet to be fully translated into policy actions.

Authority is also not always considered on its own merit. For instance, in its work on supporting state building in situations of conflict and fragility, the OECD conflates authority and capacity as "state capability and responsiveness"—namely, the provision of security, justice, economic management, and service delivery (OECD 2011). The report argues that the state has four important functions: (1) to provide security, enforce the law, and protect its citizens, (2) to make laws, provide justice, and resolve conflict, (3) to raise, prioritize, and expend revenues effectively and to deliver basic services, and

Introduction

(4) to facilitate economic development and employment. While the first two relate to the exercise of authority, the last two are arguably related to capacity. For example, basic services include not only rule of law and security but also social services such as education and health, which have more to do with capacity than authority. We discuss measures related to capacity further below.

Since authority is about effective governance, several indicators to operationalize authority by the CIFP project draw from the World Bank's Worldwide Governance Indicators (see http://info.worldbank.org/governance/wgi/index.aspx#home). These include political stability, which refers to "perceptions of the likelihood that the government will be destabilized or overthrown by unconstitutional or violent means, including politically-motivated violence and terrorism," and regulatory quality, which refers to "perceptions of the ability of the government to formulate and implement sound policies and regulations that permit and promote private sector development." Similarly, the level of corruption in a country is another indicator of authority because it measures the ability of that country to regulate and prevent the abuse of public office for private gain. In sum, when borders are secure, collective violence and terrorism are under control, corruption is not predominant, core public goods (such as rule of law and security) are provided to populations, and economic stability ensures that growth and development are taking place, all of these features are indicative of countries with strong authority.

However, there are other indicators to measure authority, which, though important, may be less straightforward. Consider, for example, measures related to the ease of paying taxes from the World Bank's Ease of Doing Business Indicators. While taxation is about governments raising revenue to finance public goods and services, there is a significant literature that examines how taxation can contribute to governance and state building (see, e.g., Bräutigam, Fjeldstad, and Moore 2008). Viewed from the perspective of state building, tax collection is more than just economic resources, though. It is about the state having control over its territory to extract an optimal amount of revenue for the provision of public goods and services in return (Prichard 2010; African Capacity Building Foundation 2015). Finally, other measures related to infrastructure such as roads, electricity, and telephones are not necessarily the ones that come to mind when thinking about authority. And yet while they contribute to growth and development, they also act as networks that allow states to exercise better control over their territories.

In terms of operationalizing legitimacy, a straightforward indicator proposed for measuring legitimacy is the regime type of the state in question. Some have argued that certain types of government, such as dictatorships, are perceived as less legitimate than others and are forced to rely more on coercion of the population as a result (Badie, Berg-Schlosser, and Morlino 2011). To these authors, regime type could theoretically be used as a stand-in for legitimacy. The issue, however, is that this is little more than an ideal type and is unlikely to be an accurate representation of state legitimacy in reality (Badie, Berg-Schlosser, and Morlino 2011). Perhaps the best-known such measure of regime type is the Polity IV data set, which scores states between +10 for fully institutionalized democracies and −10 for fully autocratic states (Marshall and Cole 2014). Another well-known measure of the extent of democratic freedoms across the world is published annually by Freedom House and rates countries according to their political rights and civil liberties. Both the Polity IV and Freedom House indicators are used by CIFP to measure legitimacy.

Others have taken a narrower approach in using regime type to measure legitimacy, focusing on certain behaviors associated with particular regimes. Parkinson (2003), for example, proposes the use of representation as a measure of legitimacy, though this is problematic in that the applicability of such a measure is restricted to democratic states. Grävingholt, Ziaja, and Kreibaum (2015) instead use state repression as an indicator for state legitimacy, with greater levels of repression being indicative of less legitimacy due to such measures typically being costly and thus avoided when possible. This proposed measurement of legitimacy is itself a broad category, encompassing indicators such as the use of violence by the state to maintain power, restriction of the media, and the number of citizens who seek asylum in other states (Grävingholt, Ziaja, and Kreibaum 2015). Attempting to determine legitimacy by regime type alone, however, appears problematic, given that some autocratic states can stave off potential fragility and failure from popular unrest through means beyond coercion. Schwarz and de Corral (2013), for example, note that several Middle Eastern states have been able to prevent the loss of legitimacy via the use of natural resource revenues to buy off various societal groups.

Accountability mechanisms are also referenced in the literature as possible measures of legitimacy. In the case of CIFP, we use the voice and

Introduction

accountability indicator from the Worldwide Governance Indicators of the World Bank as one indicator of legitimacy. Weatherford's (1992) article on methods to measure political legitimacy, for example, cites the accountability of leaders to the people they govern as a major system-level component of legitimacy. Accountability mechanisms that could be used to measure legitimacy include legislatures, courts, and elections, with their ability to hold leaders to account serving as a way to measure the legitimacy of a state (Mulgan 2011). It is noted, however, that the main flaw in using accountability mechanisms and other system-level components to measure legitimacy is that it focuses more on formal governing structures than the subjective aspects of legitimacy (Weatherford 1992). Levi, Sacks, and Tyler (2009) highlight corruption and accountability as a way of measuring legitimacy, specifically the perception of administrative competence among citizens. For the former, they propose using the salaries of government officials and the potential rewards for citizens to attempt bribing them as an indicator, while the latter is to be measured by the government's ability to detect and punish corruption via the enforcement and monitoring of laws consistently and equitably (Levi, Sacks, and Tyler 2009). Gilley (2006) likewise proposes using corruption in measuring legitimacy, specifically by surveying citizens regarding their attitudes on corruption and their views of government officials.

Some authors have proposed using the integrity and quality of elections as a way of determining legitimacy within a state. As stated previously, elections could be considered a type of accountability mechanism in democratic states because poor performance or perceived corruption by the government can lead to it being removed from power by voters (Mulgan 2011). Norris, Frank, and i Coma (2014) assemble the Perceptions of Electoral Integrity data set to measure electoral integrity, specifically noting how questionable results can generate illegitimacy for governments and undermine them. The data set, which is based on various standards of electoral integrity, considers a total of forty-nine indicators measuring various aspects of the electoral cycle, such as campaign financing and the vote count. Several authors have also used electoral integrity to measure state legitimacy in case studies, such as Dizolele and Kambale in their 2012 article on the questionable results of the 2011 elections in the Democratic Republic of Congo, which noted how they undermined the government's legitimacy. The main issue with attempting to measure legitimacy using the integrity of elections, however, is that it is of little use in states where elections are not held, limiting the efficacy of such a measure to democratic states and those that hold sham elections.

Perhaps one of the more commonly referenced measures of state legitimacy is the willingness of citizens to obey the commands of the government. This ties directly to the commonly accepted definition of legitimacy as the recognition of a government's commands as justifiable (e.g., Gilley 2006; Levi, Sacks, and Tyler 2009). One proposed way of measuring this willingness, albeit indirectly, is through the quality of public goods and services provided by the government to its citizens, with better performance being considered an indicator of greater legitimacy (Levi, Sacks, and Tyler 2009). Other authors, such as Turper and Aarts (2017), propose using citizen trust in government institutions as a measure, citing it as a key indicator of legitimacy in democratic states. They note, however, that the single-item measurements and composite score models typically used to measure political trust are flawed in their own ways, potentially limiting the viability of such a measure. Some authors also suggest using consistent adherence to procedural justice by the government to measure citizen willingness to obey since it establishes that the government is willing to act in accordance with the law rather than circumventing it when convenient (Levi, Sacks, and Tyler 2009; Fisk and Cherney 2016). Fisk and Cherney (2016) also posit in their research on government legitimacy that service delivery and its influence on citizen perceptions could be used as an indicator, though their findings in Nepal suggest that it is not as correlated as procedural justice is. Authors such as Lemay-Hébert and Mathieu (2014) further highlight the OECD's measures of legitimacy, which include adherence to legal processes and service delivery as input and output legitimacy, respectively.

Finally, it is important to point out that some authors propose the use of multiple indicators for measuring state legitimacy, which aligns with the approach taken by the CIFP project. While more challenging to implement than individual indicators due to the difficulties in acquiring sufficient data for each indicator, this approach is perceived as especially useful due to lending greater accuracy to analyses. Weatherford (1992), for example, proposes a model for measuring political legitimacy that would combine the political components studied at the macro level, such as government responsiveness and external efficacy, with personal indicators from microlevel studies such as political interest and political efficacy. Lamb (2014) similarly argues that accurately measuring legitimacy (or the lack thereof) requires a multidimensional approach rather than focusing solely on individual views or public attributes at the expense of the other. The United States Agency for International Development (USAID) model for studying state fragility takes a different approach, evaluating legitimacy in political, security, economic, and social outcomes with indicators such as the nature of political participation and level of support for militant groups using interviews, polls, and surveys (USAID 2005). Carment, Prest, and Samy (2008) similarly use a model based on a number of indicators for legitimacy, such as the Polity IV score for level of democracy, gender, and human empowerment measures, and press freedom. In chapter 2, we will more closely examine how legitimacy affects the capacity of states to develop over time, in particular public support for leaders and elites—both national and regional.

Most, if not all, definitions of fragility point to the lack of capacity—namely, the use of resources toward productive outcomes—as one important aspect of fragility. Brinkerhoff (2010, 66) defines capacity as follows: "Capacity deals with the aptitudes, resources, relationships and facilitating conditions necessary to act effectively to achieve some intended purpose. Capacity can be addressed at a range of levels, from individuals all the way up to entire countries." Although state building is now increasingly recognized as being critical, much of the focus of international actors is about building capacity and service delivery. Measures such as gross domestic product (GDP, both total and in per capita terms) and reserve holdings can thus be used to operationalize capacity because they speak to the amount of resources that states have. Further, they are available for most countries and thus helpful for comparative analysis. But even something like reserve holdings may be misleading if countries keep higher levels of reserves as a strategy to undervalue their exchange rates rather than a means to self-insure against future crises.

In his discussion of capacity development, Brinkerhoff (2010) talks about how donors have increasingly considered the environment within which capacity development takes place, which inherently poses a problem for fragile contexts. Indeed, an important change that has happened since the early 2000s is that donors have begun to focus their aid on countries with a strong track record of good performance.[2] This so-called selectivity or ex post conditionality requires that governments implement certain agreed reforms before becoming eligible for aid. For example, the US Millennium Challenge Corporation was established as an independent US foreign assistance agency in 2004. It partners with and provides aid to poor countries that are committed to good governance, economic freedom, and investments in their citizens. Countries become eligible for aid compacts (grants) based on an assessment of their performance on several indicators that include civil liberties and political rights, accountability, government effectiveness, rule of law, corruption, trade policy, and fiscal policy. Not surprisingly, some of the most fragile countries in the world have not benefited from aid under this program.

Several of the countries that we consider trapped in fragility, such as Afghanistan, the Central African Republic, the Democratic Republic of the Congo, Somalia, and South Sudan, are low-income countries with poor policy environments.[3] These are countries that do poorly on human development indicators and are unable to provide basic services such as health and education to their populations. Indicators such as GDP and GDP per capita and those related to the provision of basic services—namely, education completion rates, health expenditure, and the Human Development Index of the United Nations Development Programme (UNDP)—are thus used to measure capacity. This is not to say these countries have not experienced economic growth. However, to the extent that growth and development may not always be inclusive or trickle-down, other measures such as education and health indicators, life expectancy, and infant mortality are important complements to income measures. In fact, the point of creating the UNDP's Human Development Index—which combines per capita income with life expectancy and education—was to shift the focus away from a narrow conception of development based on income to a broader one that recognized the multidimensionality of the development process. Over time, this elastic definition of development has been stretched to include other dimensions such as gender and inequality.

However, it is also true that per capita incomes can explain much of the variation that is observed in the availability of social services such as health and education across countries. In other words, notwithstanding the problems that result when growth and development are not inclusive enough, improvements in per capita incomes are essential for the poor and the services that they can afford.[4] Indeed, sustained economic growth—that is, continued improvements in incomes—is the most effective way to deal with extreme poverty and ensure that people have access to basic services.[5] In this regard, the Millennium Development Goals (MDGs) led to significant

Introduction

increases in aid toward poverty reduction and the social sectors and away from the hard sectors such as infrastructure. As the first MDG of halving poverty was achieved before the 2015 deadline, the emphasis in recent years has shifted to "shared prosperity" (World Bank 2014). Inequality, which was not among the eight MDGs, is now one of the seventeen Sustainable Development Goals (SDGs). However, Dollar and Kraay (2002) and Dollar, Kleineberg, and Kraay (2016) have shown that even the poorest quintiles benefit from income growth overall. Unfortunately, there are significant gaps in data on inequality for fragile countries.

Other measures related to capacity focus on external factors in the form of foreign aid, remittances, foreign direct investment, and countries' trade balance (and openness to trade) can add to resources that are mobilized domestically. There are important distinctions from the latter (e.g., taxes collected) and external finance such as foreign aid and remittance flows. Taxes imply a fiscal contract between governments and citizens whereby there is an expectation that governments will provide public goods and services in return for the taxes collected from citizens. On the other hand, foreign aid and remittance flows can be characterized as "unearned revenue" and may in fact create disincentives for governments to mobilize resources domestically, especially during an economic downturn. However, even if they can create disincentives to raise revenue locally and a situation of overdependence, external finance such as foreign aid is important for small economies that do not have large internal markets and face difficulties either raising revenue locally or attracting other sources of external finance.

Table I.1 provides examples of indicators used by the CIFP project to operationalize the ALC construct. This list is by no means exhaustive, but it indicates the range of indicators that can be used to measure various characteristics of stateness. Tikuisis et al. (2015) argue that a disadvantage of using several indicators is that they may describe similar state characteristics and lead to biases as a result of oversampling. They propose the use of a minimalist construct based on data availability and unambiguous correspondence with authority, legitimacy, and capacity. As a result, their minimalist State Evolution Model (SEM) considers only a few variables to categorize states, which are highlighted in table I.1. A minimalist approach is also helpful because the data requirements are less demanding. In the next chapter, we choose correlates that build on the ALC construct to test the correlation of various traps with the fragility trap.

TABLE I.1. EXAMPLES OF INDICATORS FOR ALC

Authority	Legitimacy	Capacity
Conflict intensity	Press freedom	Education—primary completion female
Dependence on external military support	Gender Empowerment Measure	Education—primary completion total
External debt—percentage of GNI	Gender Related Development Index	Foreign aid—percentage of expenditures
Government effectiveness	Human rights—empowerment	Foreign aid—total and per capita
Infrastructure—electricity	Human rights—physical integrity	GDP per capita
Infrastructure—telephones	Level of democracy	GDP total
Level of corruption	Participation in international political organizations	Health expenditure—percentage of GDP
Military expenditure—percentage	Permanence of regime type	Human Development Index
Paying taxes	Restrictions on civil liberties	Infant mortality
Political stability	Restrictions on political rights	Life expectancy—total
Terrorism—number of fatalities	Voice and accountability	Literacy total
Terrorism—number of incidents		Remittances as portion of GDP
		Reserve holdings—total

WHY FOCUS ON THE FRAGILITY TRAP?

In applying the fragility index and ALC construct to an evaluation of states stuck in a fragility trap, we ask three core questions: (1) Why do states stay stuck in a fragility trap? (2) What lessons can be gleaned from states that have successfully transitioned from fragility to effectiveness and resilience? (3) In what ways do targeted and context-specific policies and interventions support fragile states' transitions toward resilience and sustainable exits from the fragility trap? In seeking answers to these questions, there are a number of criticisms that such an endeavor might precipitate and that we must confront before we embark on this study. The first is that it is hardly original to argue that states do not constantly modernize in teleological terms. It has been over fifty years since theories of modernization put forward by Rostow (1960), among others, were held in check by Huntington (1968), who reoriented the discussion in opposition to the unilinear assumptions of modernization theory (Fukuyama 2006). Huntington's examination of institutional breakdown as a consequence of rapid social mobilization showed how states decay or reverse their trajectory. Since then we have witnessed numerous contributions over the last three decades from Migdal (1988, 2001), Jackson (1990), Rotberg (2003, 2004), and Mata and Ziaja (2009), among numerous others who, through their writings, have opened up the theoretical discussion regarding chronic fragility.

Second, we have seen a backlash against the idea of the fragile or failed state as policy prescription. Consider that an article in *Foreign Affairs* (Mazarr 2013) argued that the concept of state failure was no longer useful to policymakers because the so-called Global War on Terrorism (GWOT) was essentially over and that the results from comprehensive interventions in failed states over the last decade were generally unsatisfactory. But these criticisms were largely directed at a very narrow and specific understanding of fragility amid the development of a particular single-ranked index of country performance vaulted onto the policy stage with the introduction of the Fund for Peace "Failed States Index" (FSI) in 2005. Almost exclusively, those states that ranked high on the FSI list were those experiencing, emerging from, or entering into large-scale conflict.[6] Kaplan (2014), among others, has been critical of such methodologies because they are not sufficiently nuanced and are overdetermined by conflict.[7]

Along with these more mainstream policy and empirical criticisms are the debates over the securitization of development, or the security-development nexus (Buur, Jensen, and Stepputat 2007; Stern and Öjendal 2010; Duffield 2005). This school of thought questions the linkages between security and development as they are seen through Western policymaking lenses. Some argue that the focus on this nexus is another tool of the international hegemonic communities that can be used to further security interests and funnel much-needed aid money toward "hard" approaches to intervention in fragile states. It also questions the use of the term "security-development nexus," arguing that it is not clear exactly what is meant by it and that it is used inconsistently and for different purposes (Stern and

Öjendal 2010). We take these points seriously when considering the development of our theory, analysis, and conceptual framing of the problem. We understand that we must locate the fragility trap within a larger set of assumptions of how states develop over time. We are sensitive to the need for nuance and disaggregation, avoiding overdetermination in conceptualizing the fragility trap primarily as a function of conflict. We are also aware that fragility traps cannot be solely defined through a security lens.

Notwithstanding these criticisms, we believe a focus on the fragility trap is warranted on both theoretical and policy grounds. From a policy perspective, there are numerous challenges to states stuck in a fragility trap, including risks of ethnic conflict, challenges to economic development, and regional instability. Leaders must ensure they have institutions to provide adequate services to the population, and they must always find ways to properly channel ethnic, social, and ideological competition that will otherwise erode the effectiveness of weak institutions even more. They must find a way to overcome the cumulative effects of poverty, overpopulation, rural flight, and rapid urbanization as well as environmental degradation, which can otherwise overwhelm a vulnerable state's legitimacy.

In more basic terms, our need to understand the fragility trap promotes a disaggregated analysis of fragility. From a theoretical perspective, these challenges are both conceptual and causal. We know that examining fragility is more nuanced than just considering whether it does or does not exist. As noted, fragility can be viewed as the inverse of resilience. But what actually defines state resilience? Is it the resilience against economic shocks, against humanitarian disasters, or against political violence? Perhaps it is a composite of these, which still presents an analytical challenge. It would be prudent, then, to examine the fragility trap along separate dimensions of stateness in an effort to bring increased rigor and clarity to the identification of state structural factors that are causal to a specific dimension of fragility. Such an approach, if successful, would show that the core characteristics of the fragility trap are interlinked and generate negative spillover effects across domains of state performance. A key but underemphasized element in the conceptual discussion on fragility traps is the legitimacy that upholds existing divisions of labor and political order. Societal perceptions and expectations are essential determinants of how a population views and reacts to state policies. A state that does not fulfill the most basic obligations of statehood means that leadership does

Introduction

not have the means and credibility to compel internal order and deter or repel external aggression.

Weaknesses in legitimacy also derive from a leadership that does not, or cannot, provide sufficiently for the people to attract minimal domestic support. For example, when the central state starts to deteriorate, leading to the fractionalization of society, loyalties can shift from the state to traditional communities that seem to offer better protection, employment opportunities, and public services. Thus, compliance with state laws can degenerate when state institutions lose legitimacy in the eyes of large segments of the population, resulting in lost economic productivity.

There are other important reasons to focus on fragility traps. For one, states in a fragility trap are quantitatively and qualitatively distinct from those that are not. Indeed, while it has been argued that states close to this tipping point can benefit more from foreign aid (Andrimihaja, Cinyabuguma, and Devarajan 2011), using aid resources to tackle endemic problems such as poor property rights enforcement, corruption, insecurity, and violence may not be sufficient to propel states stuck in the fragility trap toward better economic outcomes. Since this policy insight is simply a theoretical premise without sufficient empirical validity to support it, an objective of this volume is to assess how specifically bad policies keep states stuck in traps while better policies help shift them away from fluctuations and tipping points. This matters because donors are hesitant to allocate aid dollars precisely because of such volatility and lack of traction. For example, many of the countries stuck in the fragility trap are aid darlings (e.g., Afghanistan) yet have shown little to no improvement in their condition. Indeed, the 2009 European Report on Development came to the conclusion that from 1979 to 2009, fragility levels of the bottom thirty-five countries had not improved. Clearly the fragility trap exists, and thinking about these trapped countries requires further theorizing and empirical evaluation.

Another reason to focus on fragility traps is that over the past decade, the majority of research has focused on the causes of fragility. Absent from this very large and well-documented research are studies of fragility persistence. Conversely, we still do not completely understand why states that were once considered fragile have successfully recovered and have become stable, while others remain fragile for long periods of time. Finally, the tendency to focus on causes of fragility using ex post facto analysis has lent itself to reactive rather than anticipatory policy responses. Exit and prevention strategies are often missing or weak in the overall policy envelope. With sufficient forewarning, donors and other international actors can contribute to supporting and facilitating political and institutional processes in order to strengthen the basis for resilience and to prevent a country from lapsing back into fragility and potential failure. This might include political settlements, by working to underpin the responsiveness of the state to effectively fulfill its principal functions in providing key services or by supporting legitimate forms of societal political pressures that will determine how a state should function.

WHAT IS A TRAP? CONCEPTUAL AND THEORETICAL UNDERPINNINGS OF SEVERAL TRAPS

Scholars have long recognized the existence of traps wherein states are unable to achieve economic growth, provide essential services, and control the use of force within their borders. The seminal interpretation of this concept has been outlined by economists as the "poverty trap," which describes various self-reinforcing mechanisms whereby individuals or countries that start out poor are likely to remain poor (Azariadis 1996; Azariadis and Stachurski 2005). Consider, for example, the textbook neoclassical growth model, which predicts convergence in incomes across countries. The observation of divergence in incomes in the data has led to a search for possible explanations. Accordingly, theories of conditional convergence argue that some countries may face intrinsic characteristics—distance from seaports, natural resource endowments, institutional legacies resulting from colonial history—that prevent them from attaining higher income levels.[8] Another explanation is related to the issue of thresholds and multiple equilibria. Instead of a unique equilibrium for a country, it can find itself in a low- or high-level equilibrium, depending on its ability to cross a minimum threshold level of income per capita at which there are increasing returns. Such multiple equilibria growth models allow for the possibility of poverty traps and provide an argument for coordinated public intervention in the form of a big push (e.g., significant increases in aid flows) to enable countries to reach a high-level equilibrium.

Broadly speaking, the main identified causes of such traps include lack of technology adoption, market failure, and institutional failure. Poverty traps occur when poorly functioning markets and institutions perpetuate themselves through a positive feedback-cycle mechanism because the incentive structures are distorted by imperfect information, high transaction costs, and pervasive corruption. Moreover, institutions are difficult to reform from the outside, and change often has to come from within (Weaver 2008; Chauvet and Collier 2008). Institutional structures are heavily "path dependent," a fact that also feeds into the perpetuation of the poverty trap because they are resistant to (in this case, positive) transformation (David 1994). Often institutions and their rules are created and maintained by those in power; in a sense, they are a political construction, where those in power have the incentive to stay there and a disincentive to promote reform (North 1995). It is also important to note that poverty traps do not have to be limited to the state level and that within countries local variations of the same phenomenon exist (Jalan and Ravallion 2002).

Another important trap is the so-called conflict trap, which occurs "if the long-term risk of conflict in a country or region increases considerably after the first conflict onset" (Hegre et al. 2011, 3).[9] Countries in the conflict trap tend to be stuck there for a very long time, they generate spillovers to other countries, and they have a high chance of returning to conflict even after the first one has ended (Hegre et al. 2011). Collier et al. (2003) identify several channels through which a conflict trap arises. First, civil wars halt economic development through their impacts on growth and per capita incomes; the loss of human and physical capital as a result of war has devastating consequences for countries as a result of lost production. Countries become trapped when war causes poverty, and low income contributes to tension. Low growth means high unemployment and thus plenty of angry young men ready to fight.[10]

In addition to the poverty trap and the conflict trap, fragile countries may face a capability trap that prevents them from carrying out basic functions such as service provision, maintenance of law and order, and security (Pritchett and de Weijer 2010; Pritchett, Woolcock, and Andrews 2010, 2013). Empirical research focusing on "capability traps" have largely drawn on the effects of donor communities (Pritchett, Woolcock, and Andrews 2010, 2013) or are based on limited interpretations of state development equivalent to economic growth (Andrimihaja, Cinyabuguma, and Devarajan 2011) or governance (Rotberg 2004). In a valuable interpretation of the capability trap, Pritchett, Woolcock, and Andrews (2013) and Andrews, Pritchett, and Woolcock (2017) argue that the key reasons for failures of interventionists come from the kinds of aid delivered to the most fragile states and the subsequent lack of an optimal response that undermines the development of strong institutions and public administration strategies. They argue that states adopt either "isomorphic mimicry" to maintain international legitimacy despite structural dysfunctionality or "premature load bearing," which allows failure to exist while creating the illusion of implementing effective developmental policies and the trappings of modernization.

Some studies have identified mechanisms by which states can artificially prop up their institutions so that the institution looks and feels like an ideal model; however, the actual functionality and resilience is left lacking (Pritchett, Woolcock, and Andrews 2010, 2013). Closely related is the idea of premature load bearing, wherein newly formed state institutions are expected to achieve much more than is possible in a short period of time. Western development agencies commonly use results-based management approaches to decide where and how much aid to allocate, resulting in unrealistic expectations that are not met. This is because states adapt to the expectations placed on them as Pritchett, Woolcock, and Andrews's idea of isomorphic mimicry shows. Indeed, Bermeo (2016) shows that fragile state reversals and "regressive" trends in governance are partly due to the fact that abuses have become subtler. Outright military coups have become less common, and those coups that do occur often attempt to frame their actions in the context of an effort to restore or improve democracy. Democratic backsliding, moreover, often takes place in those very democratic institutions, such as elections and majority rule. Bermeo (2016) makes the case that a great deal of these trends can be explained by the improvement and implementation of international observation.

Such strategies, according to Pritchett, Woolcock, and Andrews (2010, 2013), allow states to buy time to enable reforms to work, to mask nonaccomplishment, or to actively resist or deflect internal and external pressures for improvement. Further, they suggest that it is dangerous to conflate institutional form with institutional function. Systemic isomorphic mimicry occurs when organizations implement policies or programs that mimic the institutional forms of functional states and expect them to operate in the developing state in the same manner. The illusion of development is rewarded and overshadows its lack of functionality. Pritchett, Woolcock, and Andrews (2010, 2013) warn that this can lead to premature load bearing, which occurs when unrealistic expectations overwhelm the capabilities

Introduction

of institutions and ultimately undermine indigenous efforts and systemic change in the developing state. Thus, weak administrative capability is the main cause of slow or stagnant development. Baliamoune-Lutz and Mc-Gillivray (2008) reinforce this point by showing the "modernization theory" bias that assumes institutions can be imported into countries to facilitate rapid development. Clearly, there are fundamental differences between the internal political and economic orders of these types of capability-trapped states. Further, implementing development policy that does not consider the specific incentive structures that help provide order can be ineffective or further exacerbate core structural problems. While these preliminary studies of potential explanations of the capability trap and its causes are certainly useful, many of the conclusions are drawn on the basis of anecdotal evidence and specific examples of how these principles may play out in practice. Likewise, when it comes to the economic modeling of fragility referenced above, only three variables are empirically tested, leaving out a great deal of valuable information and oversimplifying the phenomenon.

A final and related trap is one we call the "legitimacy trap," which describes the weakness of societal values to legitimize the actions of the state, leading to a perpetuation of weak institutions and rule of law. In contrast to capability traps driven largely by donor expectations regarding institutional capacity and development, legitimacy traps conjure up ideas of societal consent and participation in systems of good governance (local, regional, and global) and effective leadership. The legitimacy trap carries a normative dimension about the kinds of outcomes and processes that are most appropriate to ensure stable political orders. Different political orders have different forms of legitimating processes, but the assumption is that each will derive stability from constructive, ongoing, and effective bargaining between the state and society. Formally, as defined earlier, legitimacy is the extent to which a state commands public loyalty to a form of governance in order to generate domestic support for that government's legislation and policy, through a voluntary and reciprocal arrangement of effective governance and citizenship founded upon broadly accepted principles of government selection and succession that are recognized both locally and internationally.

As others have argued, this implies that institutional design is crucial to legitimacy. States in which the ruling regime lacks either broad and voluntary domestic support or general international recognition suffer from a lack of legitimacy and poor institutional design. Other studies referencing legitimacy point to political interference, rent seeking, elite capture, and lobbying as the key culprits in propagating extreme fragility (Asongu and Kodila-Tedika 2013). One can think of legitimacy first as a process that engenders viable and lasting state-society relations, such as a just and fair legal system that improves the likelihood of compliance with the law, and secondly as an outcome from which society derives some lasting benefit, such as security or education. The basic institutional mechanisms of a state may reflect mechanisms that are deemed necessary for facilitating a realization of those effective outcomes, while processes may relate to programs and policies that a state is willing to undertake in order to attain effective outcomes. Attitudinal and cultural perceptions of these processes and outcomes capture a related kind of state-society legitimacy because they represent a shared belief in a particular type of political order. When organized around forms of identity, community, class, or gender, these shared beliefs resonate within and impact the overall effectiveness of the political order.

Differences in how a political system should be ordered, for example, will generate crises of legitimacy, internal struggles, and sometimes violence. Compliance with the law typically declines when state institutions lose legitimacy in the eyes of large segments of the population, but that is not always the case. Clearly, in many countries the idea of legitimate political orders is simply rhetorical window dressing; governments routinely base their legitimacy on a variety of other grounds, invoking ideology, external threats, or even the divine right of kings to justify their exercise of authority. Similarly, the protection of human rights, as enshrined in such documents as the Universal Declaration of Human Rights, presents a meaningful normative metric with which state performance may be measured.

Again, such documents are clearly aspirational in nature; few, if any, (especially fragile) states have the capacity, let alone the will, to implement global ideals of human rights. Similar arguments may be made with respect to respect for political rights and civil liberties, the treatment of disempowered populations, and environmentally sustainable policies. For example, there is strong evidence that globally, and particularly in fragile states, women (as a group) are more vulnerable and marginalized than men (as a group) across numerous political indicators of legitimacy (voice and representation), social indicators (enrollment in primary and secondary educationa institutions, literacy, health), and economic indicators (wages, income, labor force participation, land rights).

As Pritchett, Woolcock, and Andrews (2010, 2013) argue, legitimacy is also derived from international recognition to the extent that there are international standards, norms, and rules by which states are expected to behave. In this regard, legitimacy is distinct from legality insofar as an outcome or a process can be considered legitimate without being legal. Consider, for example, the World Bank's approach of measuring governance as a set of traditions consisting of both formal and informal institutions that determine how authority is exercised in a particular country for the common good, thus encompassing the process of selecting, monitoring, and replacing governments; the capacity to formulate and implement sound policies and deliver public services; and the respect of citizens and the state for the institutions that govern economic and social interactions among them.

The World Bank framework does not conflate effective or good governance with "legitimate" political processes such as democracy, although that is often what the literature does. The two ideas are related, and understanding both is essential. In other words, the most effective governance outcomes may not be achieved in the presence of democratic structures. Certainly, the relationship between democracy and good governance is not absolute, where nondemocratic and hybrid regimes are capable of achieving good governance in the absence of democratic political processes. In this regard, policymakers must be sensitive to the need for measures of legitimacy that incorporate participatory processes and state-society relations while not equating them completely with democracy.

The legitimacy trap underpins our understanding of why state-society relations are so weak in fragile states. Yet it is a largely underemphasized, if not neglected, aspect of development policy and theory. Assessments of fragile states are particularly prone to this problem wherein the majority of donors have either focused on economic capacity or governance. Indicator-based analyses, in particular, typically reflect this dichotomy while underemphasizing questions of legitimacy. In part, that neglect is a function of the methodological difficulty of measuring legitimacy—especially when it comes to evaluating inclusivity and horizontal inequalities within a society. In part, it reflects an undue emphasis on growth as a solution to underdevelopment.

In reality, it cannot be assumed that a strong state is coterminous with strong state-society relations, just as it cannot be assumed that a fragile state necessarily has weak state-society relations. Similarly, a state's legitimacy is closely tied to its treatment of minorities and the effectiveness of its policies toward poverty, inclusivity, and inequality. Narrow policies favoring one group are seen to be less legitimate than broad distributive ones. A less legitimate state does not merely respond to crises produced by uneven political and economic opportunities but is also itself the dominating force providing differential advantages to regions and peoples. Similar to Bremmer's (2006) idea of open and closed systems, there are instances of fragility where the state is underconsolidated—a situation where the state is not effective in the performance of its duties—and cases where the state is overextended—where it becomes a threat to its inhabitants.

In reviewing these various interpretations of what might keep fragile states trapped, we see merit in each, in particular those that emphasize weak capabilities and legitimacy since the two are interlinked. To be sure, not all fragility trap countries are conflict-ridden ones or those mired in extreme poverty or ones that might suffer from chronic legitimacy problems. Rather, fragility trap states exhibit a combination of these factors that place them at the bottom, including economic underdevelopment, a lack of political authority, and poor legitimacy. Further, in many of these descriptions, directions of causality are difficult to tease out, meaning that research examining the fragility trap should use a combination of both macrolevel comparisons and microlevel qualitative case studies (Carment and Samy 2012). This type of mixed-methods analysis will allow for a better understanding of how structural factors interact with exogenous shocks and agency-driven processes.

An additional caveat is that while the fragility trap is evocative of Collier's (2007) conflict trap, not all states trapped in extreme fragility are affected by conflicts, just as most, but not all, countries in conflict are fragile by definition (Carment, Prest, and Samy 2010). The fragility trap is not purely about economic development either. Not all poor people live in fragile states. According to recent studies, four-fifths of people living on less than $2 a day, an internationally accepted poverty line, live in middle-income countries, not poor ones (Sumner 2012). However, notwithstanding the claim that poverty is distributed across both low- and middle-income countries, it is estimated that by 2025 most absolute poverty will once again be concentrated in low-income countries. While middle-income countries will continue to make progress against poverty, the distribution of the global poor is growing in fragile states. That is because the number of poor people in fragile states has stayed flat since 1990 at about five hundred million and will continue at roughly that level until 2025. So while there may be more poor people in middle-income countries, those numbers will decrease over time. Additionally, by 2025, there will be twice as many poor people in fragile states relative to those in middle-income countries. For the same reasons that economic growth lifted China and India out of extreme poverty, foreign aid may be less relevant to middle-income countries as opposed to solutions developed through their own domestic policies. Most important, if absolute poverty levels in fragile states persist, then rather than being irrelevant, foreign aid will be essential for those states stuck in a fragility trap.

Related to the above point, there are those states that were recently or are now at the bottom of fragility rankings but which are defined as middle-income. This group includes some large states such as Angola, Iraq, Pakistan, and Nigeria and smaller ones such as Papua New Guinea and Yemen.[11] These states are often described as middle-income fragile or failed states (MIFFs). The MIFFs account for over two hundred million of the world's most impoverished people. Taking into account MIFFs as part of the fragility trap problematic raises important questions about how fragility is conceptualized and measured but also how to engage them. MIFFs pose a problem for donor engagement because they do not always need as much aid or the kind of aid targeting poor states. Their problems are mostly ones of distribution, political legitimacy, and governance. While some MIFFs perform well economically because they are resource rich, not all do, raising the question of why that particular type of state performs poorly despite reasonable economic performance.

Another reason for the persistence of fragility traps is clearly related to Pritchett, Woolcock, and Andrews's (2010, 2013) identification of "isomorphic mimicry," or the prevailing development orthodoxy to reward countries that are seen to be performing well or are thought to have good policy environments, with no clear direction on how to engage those characterized by perpetually poor policy environments. Conversely, high concentration of aid to a few aid darlings among the most fragile states (OECD 2015) means that some fragility trap states are vastly overfunded with respect to their capacity to absorb these funds, leading to premature load bearing. Fragility trap states with weak policy environments and poor institutional characteristics face a real challenge in effectively absorbing large amounts of aid over short periods of time. Studies have shown that the macroeconomic impact of aid on growth declines with fragility and that this effect is especially important in low- and lower-middle-income countries. Conversely, the aid orphans among the most fragile states are resource constrained as they cannot rely (as much as nonfragile states can) on other sources of financing, such as remittances and foreign direct investment.

One of the general conclusions we draw from an assessment of these various traps is that core structural elements of stateness represented by ALC provide key organizing concepts for evaluating the change within states over time. Indeed, as pointed out by Kaplan (2014) and reinforced by Grävingholt, Ziaja, and Kreibaum (2012), when state fragility is conceptualized as a multidimensional phenomenon, one does not lose policy-relevant information, compared to a situation where a single composite index is used. In brief, authority matters because leaders must ensure they have institutions to provide adequate services to their populations and protect them. Legitimacy matters because leaders must find ways to properly channel ethnic, social, and ideological competition that could otherwise erode the effectiveness of institutions. Capacity matters because leaders must find a way to overcome the devastating effects of poverty, overpopulation, rural flight, rapid urbanization, environmental degradation, and so forth. For example, the loss of legitimacy in state institutions in some segments of the population can result in noncompliance with the rule of law. Consequently, social and political order can break down, along with the loss of national cohesion and recognition of a common authority. As Faust, Grävingholt, and Ziaja (2013, 7) noted, what is needed is a bridge between single-score rankings "and the anarchic picture emerging when every country context is considered as qualitatively different." That such approaches are possible has recently been demonstrated in formal modeling (Besley and Persson 2011) and through data-driven clustering (Carment, Prest, and Samy 2010; Grävingholt, Ziaja, and Kreibaum 2012; Tikuisis, Carment, and Samy 2013).

THE WAY FORWARD

In chapter 1, we construct and test a fragility trap model to explain why some states are stuck, while others are not. We focus on the duration of the trap over a thirty-five-year period and the key causes of its persistence over time, drawing on operationalized interpretations of the four traps identified above. To test our model, we conduct statistical analysis based on an overarching framework organized around the three clusters of ALC. We then exploit the time series nature of our data set to conduct

Introduction

a comparative analysis of fragile state types. We argue that changes over time—or transitions—are a function of the sequencing of changes in key structural features of "stateness." For states that successfully exit fragility, not only do we expect to observe improvement in these key features, we also expect a specific kind of causal sequence to occur. Understanding the underlying causal features of this sequence of changes will contribute to a general framework and theory of fragility dynamics. Using a threefold typology of states—those that are stuck in a fragility trap, those that have successfully exited, and those that fluctuate between a successful exit and fragility—we examine where they fit with respect to some of the results on the determinants of state fragility. This methodology is consistent with current theoretical insights regarding exits from fragility described by Marshall and Cole (2014) and Naudé, Santos-Paulino, and McGillivray (2011, 8), who argue that "it is not unreasonable to conclude that all states are fragile to various degrees, in various domains and over different periods of time."

In chapter 2, we first examine why elites are important to understanding fragility dynamics. Then we turn to theoretical explanations of the kinds of elite behavior we observe in fragile states. We consider the importance of legitimacy and how its absence ultimately undermines those elites whose actions contribute to perpetual fragility. This chapter emphasizes state-society relations, specifically the role of legitimacy in underpinning the behavior of political, social, and economic elites. A focus on legitimacy is important for a number of reasons. First, previous studies found that legitimacy is rarely factored into aid allocation decisions (Carment, Prest, and Samy 2008). Second, its absence correlates strongly with weaknesses in the institutional processes that uphold rules, norms, and enforcement characteristics that collectively determine economic performance. Third, findings on the Arab Spring and democratic backsliding show that a lack of legitimacy is a key driver of instability and stagnation even when economic performance and state security are strong (Tikuisis and Carment 2017).

This chapter also considers the most salient causes of stagnation and reversal in light of our need to identify drivers of change that inform our case study comparisons. A focus on elites is important for three reasons. First, as fragile states undergo constant contractions and expansions in effectiveness and capacity, elites play an important role in implementing policies that effect those changes. Second, and related to the first, despite their importance, elites are often taken as a given in much of fragile states research, especially with its focus on structural transformation. Third, we assume the pursuit of elite interests may bring benefits to their own group but may also produce counterproductive outcomes for the state when its government proves incapable of adaptation. In some cases, that adaptation may entail a contrary policy change that alienates sectors of society or, worse, leads to the collapse of the state itself.

In chapters 3, 4, and 5, we juxtapose the threefold typology derived from our large sample analysis in chapter 1 against the main points in chapter 2 and apply them to six contrasting case studies. This comparison is an appropriate means to provide further support for our claims regarding the utility of sequencing fragile state transitions and fragility traps. Methodologically, there are two key strengths to this approach. First, theory building from cases often results in the generation of novel insights due to the constant association of seemingly incongruous evidence between different case types (Eisenhardt 1989). We will highlight the differences among the three types of fragile states through a structured comparative approach, by isolating and comparing common variables such as the ALC clusters and an identical time period for each. Second, a typology is more often than not empirically testable through quantitative means because measurable constructs have already been used to develop it to begin with. However, detailed cases can be held up for comparison in order to determine whether our theoretical claims hold true more generally (Eisenhardt 1989).

With these advantages in mind, we examine the sequencing dynamics present in a selected country of each type in more detail. Specifically, we look at two country-cases in each chapter: Yemen and Pakistan (type 1, countries trapped in fragility), Laos and Mali (type 2, countries that have moved into and out of fragility), and Bangladesh and Mozambique (type 3, countries that have exited fragility) as exemplars of each particular type. The selected cases are exemplars of the class of fragile states we wish to examine, a technique that is referred to as the "typical-case approach" (Gerring 2007, 91). The approach relies on the notion that the case selected is representative of the broader set of cases within the given category and is used to prove causal mechanisms that may provide evidence for or against a given theory (Seawright and Gerring 2008). By using this typological framework built on statistical analysis of the cases, we reduce the potential for case selection bias. The idea is to provide both enough control and enough variation on the dependent variable so that observations on the cases can be comparatively

Introduction   29

assessed in order to provide insight into each country type (George and Bennett 2005, 83). The specific countries to be examined were also selected based on the principle of maximizing geographical diversity and the range of fragility outcomes in order to improve the overall generalizability of the findings (Flyvbjerg 2006). Finally, there were also considerations made regarding data availability and the viability of information from secondary sources for in-depth case examination.

In chapter 3, we compare Pakistan and Yemen. Yemen, a country of twenty-five million inhabitants on the southern tip of the Arabian Peninsula, has been stuck in a fragility trap for over thirty-five years. It has ranked in the top forty most fragile countries for its entire postunification history and has been ranked among the top twenty most fragile countries more than two-thirds of that time. CIFP's rankings have placed Pakistan in the top twenty fragile states in the world in most years during the past two decades. On the one hand, as Pakistan's inability to control internal conflict, environmental degradation, and a highly unequal society increase over time, the legitimacy of the government continues to erode, and challenges from within increase. Yemen chose to not initially participate in the GWOT, suffered the consequences, and has since fallen into collapse. Pakistan, in contrast, was a full partner in the GWOT. Its economy has since stabilized, while its political fortunes remain uncertain.

In chapter 4, our two cases are Laos and Mali, countries that have moved into and out of fragility for over thirty years. They are both affected by environmental impacts and regional volatility, and because they are landlocked are dependent on their neighbors for economic prosperity and political stability. The picture of Mali's stability from 1980 to the present is of a country that continually "exits" fragility, only to reenter it further down the road. In fact, this is a pattern followed by many countries, including Laos. What these countries show is that stability is both achievable and easily reversed. In Mali's case, we witness forms of "isomorphic mimicry" and elite "rent seeking" in which elites take on the trappings of Western institutions to generate international support while failing to incorporate and develop fundamental strengths over time.

In chapter 5, we consider our successfully exited cases. They are Bangladesh and Mozambique, both of which have been fragile for much of their existence. Yet, unlike the other fragile states examined in this volume, both have managed to improve their performance over time. Since their calamitous and inauspicious beginnings, both Mozambique and Bangladesh have been beset by assassinations, internecine political infighting, and corruption. Yet their economic situations have improved despite ongoing aid dependence in the case of Mozambique and deep corruption in the case of Bangladesh. To be sure, both have significant structural problems that continue to hamper their economic growth and political development. In particular, in the case of Mozambique, structural economic weaknesses are beginning to reveal themselves, and the political situation has been volatile in the last few years. But in comparison to other countries examined in previous chapters, their exit from fragility is more clear-cut if not spectacular.

In comparing the successfully transitioned states against those that remain fragile and stuck in a trap, the concluding chapter (chapter 6) puts forth an explanation on why states fail to exit the fragility trap. We juxtapose this conclusion against those states that have successfully done so. Here we provide generalizable results, especially as they relate to how policies can support viable exits from the fragility trap. The chapter concludes by making the case that we must move beyond such exclusive definitions and understandings of fragility traps defined by the presence of large-scale violence or economic underdevelopment. There is a real need for closer and better monitoring of specific countries whose negative trends could be reversed through strategically timed and fairly narrow and specific policy interventions.

Chapter 1

A Typology of Countries, with a Focus on the Fragility Trap

In this chapter, our main objectives are to identify countries that are caught in a fragility trap and to understand why they have not seen much progress over time. To accomplish these tasks, we not only consider the most difficult cases but also more successful ones that have been able to become increasingly resilient over time. Indeed, while most, though not all, of the countries stuck in fragility are faced with cycles of repeated violence and have remained fragile for very long periods, others have emerged from fragility and become more resilient over time (Pritchett and de Weijer 2010; World Bank 2011). We are interested in finding out if the causes associated with trapped states are unique to them or are also found among other types of states. If we find, for example, that those states that built resilience and are no longer fragile have distinct underlying causal mechanisms in comparison to trapped states, we will have a stronger basis for explaining the fragility trap. If, however, we find similar causal patterns across the three types (those that are trapped, those that move "into" and "out" of fragility, and those that have "exited" fragility), we would need to identify why that is the case and revise our assumptions regarding the importance of legitimacy and authority accordingly (see the introduction).

Ultimately, our goal is to develop a model for why countries are stuck, not only by examining cases that fit that profile but also by teasing out the lessons from states that have become more stable over time, even if only for short periods in some cases. Accordingly, we develop and use well-defined criteria to build a typology of states that reflects two sets of criteria. First, it seeks to identify the underlying causes of fragility, not merely contemporary conditions, and, second, it is dynamic and captures key "state transition" trajectories. More generally, understanding the underlying structural features in the sequence of changes across the three types and more specifically where there are differences among them will motivate our discussion in chapter 2 and the subsequent case studies in chapters 3, 4, and 5. Our sequencing analysis will determine whether and how a fragile state has been able to build resilience, which sectors of state performance are typically more fragile than others, what the shared vulnerabilities across fragile states are, and differences among the entry points for policy engagement for the three types of states.

But coming up with a typology is challenging because state fragility remains a contested concept. Policymakers have embraced the term, but academics continue to debate its relevance.[1] Building a useful theoretical framework is challenging because, like Tolstoy's unhappy family, each fragile state is unique in its own way, often leading researchers to rely solely on case studies or nonstate frameworks of analysis. But a purely comparative or historical approach to examine fragile states has its downside in that by itself it does not yield an integrated framework that can be helpful for building policy and theory. The approach that we take here is a mixed one in the sense that we examine a broad range of cases in order to determine whether some common underlying trends can be observed, and we subsequently consider specific cases in more depth. A second reason for the lack of theorizing has perhaps to do with the urgency of showing results on the policy front, especially by donor governments and their frustrated constituencies, leading to pressures to bypass or not pay sufficient attention to theoretical frameworks. Instead of a long-term proactive strategy that addresses the root causes of fragility and conflict, donors often react to volatile situations and look for quick wins. A third is that researchers from various disciplines, such as economics and political science in particular, have for far too long worked in isolation and thus adopted narrow conceptions of what functioning states should look like and what characteristics they should possess.

It is therefore not surprising that the lists of fragile states produced by various organizations can sometimes be quite different in terms of how they rank countries. However, because many of these lists tend to draw from overlapping data sources, they are highly correlated. For example, the correlation between the Fragile States Index (FSI) of the Fund for Peace and the Fragility Index (FI) of the CIFP project for 2014 was 0.95 ($N = 178$). Among the top twenty countries ranked by the FSI and FI, sixteen of them showed up on both lists. In 2014, both indices ranked South Sudan, Somalia, and the Central African Republic first, second, and third, respectively, but rankings are increasingly different as one goes down each list. However, there has been an effort at the OECD level in recent years to generate a list of fragile countries that combines the information from various lists including CIFP's.

Building on the discussion in the introduction, there are several reasons why a focus on countries trapped in fragility is necessary. First, the term "fragility trap" tends to be used loosely and is undertheorized. Empirically, the challenges are compelling, and there is no consensus about which countries are trapped in fragility and which ones are not. Reliable estimates and projections of states stuck in a fragility trap vary. Cilliers and Sisk (2013) forecast that ten African countries (the Comoros, the Central African Republic, the Democratic Republic of the Congo, Guinea-Bissau, Madagascar, the Republic of Congo, Somalia, Sudan / South Sudan, and Togo) face the prospect of remaining in a fragility trap beyond 2050. Sub-Saharan African countries tend to be in the worst shape, with at least twenty-six "more fragile" countries, including the ten that are trapped, identified by Cilliers and Sisk (2013). Consider that in the 1990s Burkina Faso and Burundi were at very similar levels in terms of growth and ranked closely in the World Bank's Country Policy and Institutional Assessments (CPIA, http:// datatopics.worldbank.org/cpia/). After conflict in Burundi, however, there was a major divergence, and fragility has persisted in Burundi for nearly two decades and is projected to worsen in the coming years. Burundi is expected to exit fragility and start building more resilience by or before 2030, while Burkina Faso is not among the twenty-six countries classified as more fragile (Cilliers and Sisk 2013).[2] This example indicates that once a state falls into a low-growth equilibrium whether due to conflict or some other factor, it is extremely difficult to emerge sustainably. However, Cilliers and Sisk (2013) never clearly define what a fragility trap is, instead conflating it with a conflict trap, security challenges, or weak governance structures.

According to data from the CIFP project, more than half of the forty fragile states in 1980 are still classified as fragile in 2015. And of those, about twenty of the most fragile states remain stuck at the bottom. With a focus on Africa, Andrimihaja, Cinyabuguma, and Devarajan (2011) found that not only do the continent's fragile states grow more slowly than nonfragile states, but also the probability that a fragile state in 2001 was still fragile in 2009 was 0.95. According to the authors, corruption, political instability and violence, insecure property rights, and unenforceable contracts conspire to create a "slow-growth-poor-governance equilibrium trap" into which these most fragile states fall and which they denote as a fragility trap. Andrimihaja, Cinyabuguma, and Devarajan (2011) is the only paper that we are aware of that formally models the fragility trap. It argues that foreign aid can be helpful for weak governments as long as it targets the root causes of instability, insecurity, and corruption. Accordingly, another important objective of the current chapter is to understand how the fragility trap can be reconciled with the various existing traps from the extant literature and better characterized.

Second, while existing research on state fragility has tended to focus on its determinants (Bertocchi and Guerzoni 2012; Carment, Prest, and Samy 2010), much less is known about why fragility persists over time (Carment et al. 2015). This is in part related to data availability. Most fragility indices cover the recent past, and they do not go back far enough in time to be able to clearly identify countries that have stagnated and the reasons behind their lack of progress. Third, fragile countries, including those that are among the worst performers, have become some of the biggest recipients of foreign aid and other forms of intervention over time. The OECD (2015) estimates that more than half of official development assistance (ODA) was allocated to countries that it classified as fragile and that per capita ODA to fragile countries has doubled since 2000. However, the problem is that one can find both "aid darlings" and "aid orphans" among fragile countries, which supports the view of Andrimihaja, Cinyabuguma, and Devarajan (2011) that donors tend to hold back aid in difficult environments. Yet it is not clear in some cases that these countries have made any progress, and even where

A Typology of Countries, with a Focus on the Fragility Trap 35

improvements have taken place, quick reversals remain a strong possibility. Understanding why and how countries emerge successfully from fragility may thus inform us about the types of interventions that are more likely to succeed.

In order to conduct the analysis in this chapter, we use data on state fragility—and its various dimensions—from the CIFP project (www .carleton.ca/cifp). CIFP's evaluative framework relies on multiple levels of information: structural data, events monitoring, and qualitative assessments (e.g., using survey data and expert opinions). Since our objective in the current chapter is to examine state transitions over the long term, we will consider structural data only. The CIFP structural data set is unique in its coverage, both across countries and over time, as it includes most countries in the world since 1980 until 2014.[3] The CIFP data set is the only one that we are aware of that goes back over several decades and that also disaggregates fragility along several dimensions. Since fragility is persistent (Carment, Prest, and Samy 2010), the CIFP data set allows us to examine movements over long periods of time that may not be visible with shorter time series data. If one wants to characterize those countries that are stagnating and trapped in fragility, these countries must by definition be among the worst performers over several decades or a sufficiently long period of time. Another benefit of the CIFP data set is that its multidimensional approach to fragility based on ALC is more helpful than one that focuses only on single composite indices.

Other indices such as the FSI and the Marshall-Goldstone State Fragility Index (Marshall and Goldstone 2007) are less suitable for examining the evolution of states because of their limited temporal coverage (i.e., since the mid-2000s). In the case of the FSI, the problem is magnified by its bias and proprietary nature of indicator selection, making it difficult to know which aspects of fragility are emphasized. The World Bank also classifies fragile countries according to the CPIA scores, but these are publicly available only since 2005 and the country coverage is limited.[4] Furthermore, the indicators used for the CPIA are about the quality of a country's policies and institutional arrangements, which, although directly or indirectly related to fragility, do not consider other aspects such as security and conflict. CPIA is more a country-rating than a country-ranking system. It is interesting to note that the 2013 report of the Independent Evaluation Group—which evaluates the activities of the World Bank—recommended that the World Bank rethink how it classifies fragile countries, as a result of the emergence of new drivers of fragility and conflict. The quality of the assessment conducted by the World Bank is also questionable because all of the CPIA indicators are the product of staff judgment rather than based on objective data.

Attempts at creating state typologies have not always been successful. For example, in a much earlier study capturing the diversity of failed state environments, Gros (1996) specifies a qualitative taxonomy of five different failed state types: chaotic, phantom, anemic, captured, and aborted. These various types derive their dysfunction from different sources, both internal and external, and consequently require different policy prescriptions. In another case, building from a compilation of work drawing on disparate research agenda, Rotberg (2004) derives a slightly less negative ranking that includes fragile, weak, failing, failed, collapsed, and recovering states. However, neither of these taxonomies, drawn mostly from case-based evidence, represents an effort to construct mutually exclusive categories quantitatively, nor do they provide a clear demarcation that unambiguously separates categories of state functions from one another.

Consider the problems inherent in a single ranking of state performance by the World Bank using its LICUS (Low Income Country under Stress) and CPIA frameworks. While these may resonate from a policy perspective, they are not without their critics on conceptual and theoretical grounds (Faust, Grävingholt, and Ziaja 2013). For one, a single-ranking index like the FSI is overdetermined, typically identifying states that are already in the midst of conflict. A second and related criticism of single-ranking indexes is that it is extremely difficult to derive meaningful policy implications from them. For example, *Third World Quarterly* (see Grimm [2014] among others) devoted an entire issue to questioning the utility of country rankings because of their overly simplistic and unhelpful portrait of donor-recipient country problems. In their detailed assessment, Baliamoune-Lutz and McGillivray (2008, 2) described the World Bank's subjective CPIA ranking as "fuzzy" since it does not provide a "crisp, clean and unambiguous" score that can be "compared with terribly high degree of precision." This view is reinforced by Faust Grävingholt, and Ziaja (2013), who argue that many of the findings developed by Collier et al. (2003) and others using World Bank rankings are indefensible upon closer scrutiny. In response to these criticisms, calls for a more nuanced context-driven approach to address these ranking deficiencies have been made by Carment, Prest, and Samy (2010), Grävingholt, Ziaja, and Kreibaum (2012), and Cilliers and Sisk (2013).

Call (2008) notes that the FSI, in particular, fails to provide sufficient discrimination to be of any practical value. As Call remarks (2008, 1495), "The consequence of such agglomeration of diverse criteria is to throw a monolithic cloak over disparate problems that require tailored solutions." More recently, Coggins (2014) argues that the FSI uses categories that remain undefined, that its indicators are not transparent, and that the ranking of certain states defies logic. This is exemplified by Faust, Grävingholt, and Ziaja (2013, 6): "Performing in different constellations Colombia and Mozambique, for example, close neighbors on the 2012 Failed States Index (84.4 and 82.4 points each), lag behind in different state functions." As observed by Bakrania and Lucas (2009), Faust, Grävingholt, and Ziaja (2013), and Brinkerhoff (2014), conceptual ambiguity makes it more difficult to derive effective policy responses. This includes picking up the pieces when situations deteriorate, dealing with regional spillover effects, and helping to create a long-term policy environment in which poverty reduction, property rights, and good governance can become feasible. Apart from the need to better understand the type and amount of resources to allocate at any given time and place, donors also need to understand the likely consequences of such allocation in advance.

In brief, ambiguity on what differentiates fragility trap states from others makes it difficult to identify priority problems and to prescribe suitable interventions. Indeed, applying a tailored approach is one of the key requirements advocated by Blair, Neumann, and Olson (2014). Such an approach demands a deeper appreciation of state conditions beyond just a single ranking of performance. This requirement for a more meaningfully systematic and coherent approach to the categorization is echoed by several others (Goldstone 2009; Cilliers and Sisk 2013; Furness 2014; Brinkerhoff 2014; and Marshall and Cole 2014).

The rest of the chapter unfolds as follows. In the next section, we make a case for the use of a multidimensional approach to examine fragile states and present the latest fragility data from the CIFP project. The following section, "Operationalizing and Measuring the Fragility Trap," operationalizes the fragility trap in terms of combinations of other traps and their relationships with authority, legitimacy, and capacity. In "Extracting

Fragility Trap Countries from CIFP's Data," we use the CIFP data set to identify fragility trap countries, and the following section, "Correlates of the Fragility Trap," examines correlates of fragility for these countries. "A Typology of Countries" identifies two additional types of countries: those that have moved into and out of fragility and those that have exited fragility. In "The Evolution of States across Various Typologies," we extend our analysis of the correlates of fragility for trapped countries to the two additional types identified in the preceding section. The final section summarizes our findings.

CIFP: A MULTIDIMENSIONAL APPROACH

Carment, Prest, and Samy (2010) propose a fragile states framework that consists of an overall fragility index and three different dimensions of stateness—authority (A), legitimacy (L), and capacity (C)—which they refer to as the ALC framework (see introduction). They argue that the determination of a resilient or vulnerable state rests upon conceptualizations and measures that are relative. Some states may be strong (or resilient) by one measure and weak by others. The proper referents for understanding state fragility and state-building processes are thus not only a state's own past, present, and future performance in absolute terms but also its performance relative to other states at any given point. The rate of change, which is understood by examining a state's relative performance as opposed to absolute performance, whether progressive or regressive, tells us whether a state is moving toward increasing fragility or improvement. In other words, structural characteristics and measures of performance are useful for understanding state fragility only if there are appropriate reference cases from which to compare. And since these reference points are themselves evolving over time, it is important to understand that "fragility" is a relative term and has meaning only with respect to state performance at specific points in comparison with a given state's peers.

This ALC approach is in fact a synthesis of different theoretical foundations and three policy-inspired research streams—namely, development, conflict, and security/stability (Carment, Prest, and Samy 2010). The development stream—represented by capacity—drew support from the World Bank, the OECD, and bilateral organizations such as the United Kingdom's

A Typology of Countries, with a Focus on the Fragility Trap 39

Department for International Development (DFID) and was the result of the poor track record of structural adjustment and market-friendly reforms conducted in various developing countries. It led to terminology such as "difficult partners," "difficult environments," and LICUS. The conflict stream—represented by authority—is a product of early-warning and conflict-prevention tools developed in the 1990s as the world shifted from interstate to intrastate conflicts in the final years of the Cold War and continuing thereafter with the negative experiences of countries such as Rwanda, Sierra Leone, and Somalia. The security/stability stream—represented by legitimacy—focused on threats that weak and failed states pose to their neighbors and the international community, such as support of al-Qaeda by the Taliban regime in Afghanistan before 9/11.

In order to calculate composite indices for ALC for a particular country, various indicators are converted to a nine-point score based on the performance of that country relative to a global sample of countries. A higher score means that a country is performing poorly relative to other countries. Averages over a five-year time frame are calculated for global rank scores in order to minimize the likelihood of wide fluctuations in yearly data affecting country performance. A similar approach is adopted when countries are classified according to six clusters of state performance (demography, economics, environment, governance, human development, and security and crime) and gender as a cross-cutting theme.

Table 1.1 shows the 2015 fragility ranking using CIFP's data set (based on 2014 data and the framework by Carment, Prest, and Samy [2010]) for the top forty fragile states and the various dimensions of fragility described above. Countries with a fragility score of 6.5 and above are considered serious, and this is true for the top twenty countries. South Sudan, the worst performer, has a score above 7.5, which is considered very serious and approximating a failed, collapsed, or failing state. Not far behind are Somalia, the Central African Republic, Sudan, and Afghanistan. These countries do worse on authority and legitimacy (all above 7.0 and sometimes even higher than 8.0) relative to capacity scores. Although many of the worst performers in that table have been stuck at the top of the fragility rankings for many years, not all of them are. The Central African Republic, for example, was not among the most fragile countries for much of the 1980s and 1990s, and its situation started deteriorating in the early to mid-2000s.

TABLE 1.1. TOP FORTY FRAGILE STATES, 2014

Rank	Country	Fragility	Authority	Legitimacy	Capacity	Governance	Economics	Security and crime	Human development	Demography	Environment	Gender
1	South Sudan	7.76	8.24	7.34	7.27	7.86	6.15	8.64	7.95	8.46	–	4.93
2	Somalia	7.27	7.65	7.68	6.24	7.86	6.86	7.75	6.25	5.93	9.00	6.55
3	Central African Rep.	7.20	7.46	8.01	6.43	7.99	7.24	6.47	7.48	6.29	6.62	6.78
4	Sudan	7.11	7.97	7.38	6.16	7.69	6.71	8.49	6.31	5.81	7.48	6.67
5	Afghanistan	7.08	7.83	7.17	6.25	7.43	6.56	8.28	6.37	6.78	7.99	6.83
6	Yemen	7.08	7.72	7.42	5.71	7.76	7.10	8.21	5.48	6.47	6.07	7.78
7	Congo, Dem. Rep.	7.02	7.83	7.50	5.84	7.53	5.86	8.03	7.13	7.17	8.60	6.66
8	Chad	6.95	6.76	7.52	6.80	7.49	6.56	5.42	7.63	7.15	8.28	7.17
9	Iraq	6.81	7.56	6.91	5.85	7.29	6.04	8.56	6.30	6.37	4.94	7.01
10	Ethiopia	6.81	6.86	7.25	6.42	6.76	6.08	6.90	7.27	7.52	7.16	6.04
11	Syria	6.78	7.51	7.28	5.23	8.27	6.79	8.72	4.29	5.48	4.86	6.49
12	Eritrea	6.72	6.31	7.84	6.34	7.66	7.13	4.00	7.59	6.77	6.81	5.21
13	Burundi	6.71	6.43	6.69	7.09	6.83	6.81	5.72	6.58	7.32	8.00	4.89
14	Nigeria	6.63	7.14	6.21	6.31	6.25	5.91	7.15	7.27	7.76	6.75	7.06
15	Guinea	6.62	6.30	6.87	6.84	6.82	7.24	4.21	7.82	6.44	6.98	6.39
16	Mali	6.58	6.72	6.81	6.27	6.24	6.23	7.85	6.51	6.13	7.83	7.94
17	West Bank and Gaza	6.56	6.14	–	6.75	7.29	6.06	6.82	6.41	7.10	–	8.16
18	Uganda	6.54	6.81	6.26	6.41	6.23	5.61	7.14	6.94	8.23	6.04	4.96
19	Guinea-Bissau	6.53	5.90	6.80	7.10	7.06	6.63	3.58	7.67	6.97	8.11	5.53
20	Pakistan	6.49	7.48	5.92	5.78	6.26	6.05	8.65	5.61	6.52	6.52	6.30
21	Niger	6.34	5.84	6.54	6.75	6.05	6.48	5.36	6.65	6.55	8.39	7.72
22	Haiti	6.31	5.60	7.20	6.55	6.87	6.47	3.93	7.31	5.61	8.28	6.78
23	Cameroon	6.30	6.34	6.46	6.13	6.49	5.74	5.39	6.94	7.10	7.36	5.89
24	Liberia	6.29	5.83	6.85	6.45	6.50	6.65	4.15	7.14	6.27	7.39	6.80
25	Zimbabwe	6.27	6.01	6.65	6.29	6.90	6.22	4.65	7.12	5.73	6.99	4.99
26	Gambia	6.24	5.36	7.54	6.33	7.10	6.45	3.17	6.33	7.17	7.73	6.91
27	Congo, Rep.	6.21	5.96	7.07	5.94	7.18	5.81	4.18	7.04	6.65	6.36	6.61
28	Kenya	6.21	6.52	5.75	6.17	5.79	5.96	5.74	6.83	7.51	5.98	5.84
29	Angola	6.17	5.90	6.54	6.25	6.66	6.33	3.06	7.58	7.21	6.24	4.20
30	Djibouti	6.16	5.27	6.90	6.86	6.84	6.46	4.87	6.83	4.50	7.75	6.82
31	Myanmar (Burma)	6.12	6.13	7.17	5.35	7.30	5.60	6.21	5.65	4.81	7.41	4.78
32	Mauritania	6.09	5.54	6.64	6.37	6.49	6.83	4.22	6.38	5.30	7.31	6.82
33	Tajikistan	6.07	5.54	6.25	6.50	6.96	6.83	4.32	5.74	5.68	4.96	5.21
34	Comoros	6.04	4.98	6.37	7.10	6.05	6.97	3.11	7.56	6.19	6.84	8.29
35	Mozambique	5.99	5.39	6.15	6.56	5.59	5.91	4.42	7.49	6.15	7.81	6.21
36	Côte d'Ivoire	5.98	5.47	6.79	6.00	6.24	5.30	4.09	7.08	7.27	6.85	7.96
37	Korea, North	5.96	5.69	7.50	5.12	7.87	6.48	3.61	5.67	4.36	–	4.12
38	Togo	5.96	5.18	6.45	6.51	6.27	5.96	3.19	7.08	6.31	7.78	5.98
39	Sierra Leone	5.96	5.22	6.36	6.56	5.90	6.14	3.11	7.30	6.83	7.84	6.55
40	Libya	5.94	6.99	6.35	4.32	7.43	5.59	8.19	4.48	2.29	4.72	5.32

A Typology of Countries, with a Focus on the Fragility Trap   41

Looking across the various dimensions, it is also clear that countries are fragile for various reasons. For example, Yemen and Iraq are ranked sixth and ninth overall, respectively, but they tend to have much better capacity scores compared to their performance on authority and legitimacy. Table 1.2 shows the top ten most fragile states in terms of authority, legitimacy, and capacity in 2014 using CIFP's data set. It provides evidence of the utility of the multidimensional ALC methodology because, except for South Sudan, which shows up under each category, countries tend to be fragile for different reasons. Similarly, when looking at the various clusters such as economics, security and crime, and human development, one can see significant variation among the countries in table 1.1. The worst performers face very serious governance and security and crime challenges, but the situation changes as we go down the list. Guinea (ranked fifteenth), for example, does poorly in the economics cluster but relatively well on security and crime.

TABLE 1.2. TEN MOST FRAGILE STATES, BY ALC COMPONENT, 2014

Authority	Legitimacy	Capacity
South Sudan	Central African Republic	South Sudan
Sudan	Eritrea	Guinea-Bissau
Congo, Dem. Rep.	Somalia	Comoros
Afghanistan	Gambia	Burundi
Yemen	Chad	São Tomé and Príncipe
Somalia	Congo, Dem. Rep.	Djibouti
Iraq	Korea, North	Guinea
Syria	Yemen	Timor-Leste
Pakistan	Sudan	Chad
Central African Republic	South Sudan	West Bank and Gaza

Note: Countries are ranked from 1 to 10 from top to bottom.

While state fragility as a concept continues to be debated, a consensus has begun to emerge in recent years that seems to favor a multidimensional approach to identifying fragile states (Carment, Prest, and Samy 2010; Call 2011; Grävingholt, Ziaja, and Kreibaum 2015; OECD 2015). For instance, Call (2011) disputes the utility of universal rankings of fragile or failing states, arguing instead in favor of discrete categories of analysis. In particular, he identifies three gaps (capacity, security, and legitimacy) that can be used to analyze the challenges faced by countries and that can be useful for policymakers, which echoes the ALC approach proposed by Carment, Prest, and Samy (2010). Call (2011) recognizes that these gaps may overlap but argues that they are sufficiently distinct to lead to different policy prescriptions. In particular, there is a capacity gap when state institutions are unable to deliver a minimum level of public goods and services to the population. There is a security gap when states are unable to provide minimum levels of security in the presence of organized armed groups. Finally, there is an internal legitimacy gap when most of the political elite and society do not accept the rules that regulate the exercise of power and the accumulation and distribution of wealth.

However, as recently pointed out by Grävingholt, Ziaja, and Kreibaum (2015), Call's (2011) approach is problematic because it does not consider the relative nature of each gap and instead assumes that they either exist or do not exist based on an arbitrary choice of thresholds. Grävingholt, Ziaja, and Kreibaum (2015) argue that when state fragility is conceptualized as a multidimensional phenomenon such as along the ALC components, one does not lose vital and relevant information compared to a situation where a single index is used. They use the same terminology as Carment, Prest, and Samy (2010), but they measure the ALC components using a limited number of indicators, in the same spirit as the minimalist construct adopted by Tikuisis et al. (2015). This enables them to identify specific groups of countries that are weak in particular dimensions and provides an argument for considering fragility as a multidimensional concept, which can then be used to generate different policy responses.

Another example of the multidimensional nature of fragility is provided by the OECD's recent fragile states report (OECD 2015). It argues that one of the problems with the MDGs agenda was that it did not include measures to deal with fragility, to build capacity, and to focus on social and economic resilience. On the other hand, the recently adopted SDGs now explicitly focus on the promotion of peaceful and inclusive societies for sustainable development, on the provision of access to justice for all, and on building effective, accountable, and inclusive institutions (goal 18). The OECD fragile states report (OECD 2015) thus argues that rather than using a single categorization of fragile states, various measures of risk and vulnerability need to be considered. Five clusters or dimensions of fragility indicators are proposed: violence; access to justice for all; effective, accountable, and inclusive institutions; economic inclusion and stability; and capacities to prevent and adapt to social, economic, and environmental shocks and disasters (i.e., resilience). A few countries—the Central African Republic, Chad, the Democratic Republic of the Congo, Côte d'Ivoire, Guinea, Haiti, Sudan, Swaziland, and Yemen—are vulnerable across all the five dimensions of fragility, but more countries are weak in some dimensions, suggesting that fragility affects many countries in various forms.

OPERATIONALIZING AND MEASURING THE FRAGILITY TRAP

The multidimensionality of fragility means that we must examine the emergence of fragility traps in relation to other traps. Building on the ALC construct identified above, we argue that a fragility trap model can be conceptualized as resulting from either one or a combination of various other traps that are related to authority, legitimacy, and capacity. In the preceding chapter, we provided the conceptual underpinnings of the various traps that are potentially linked to the fragility trap. We briefly review the mechanisms behind these traps in this section but focus more on how they have been operationalized and empirically verified. Our ultimate objective is to figure out how strong the linkage is between the fragility trap and these various other traps. In the subsequent section, we identify a list of countries that are stuck in a fragility trap based on their fragility scores and rankings.

As noted in the introduction, the first of these traps is the poverty trap (Azariadis 1996), whose existence has been debated by economists for quite a while. For example, Kraay and McKenzie (2014) review various types of mechanisms that can give rise to poverty traps and conclude that they are rare and restricted to remote areas.[5] According to them, the cross-country evidence shows that stagnant income levels predicted by poverty traps are quite rare and even low-income countries tend to experience positive growth rates. They are thus skeptical that a big push in the form of aid or loans as advocated by Sachs (2005) is needed. Easterly (2006) compares per capita income growth rates for the poorest fifth of countries over fifty years and finds that their growth rate was not zero, nor does he find evidence of stationary income for the poorest countries. However, we are not aware of studies that have considered the performance of very fragile countries specifically. The latter constitute a fairly small group, and they have been (or are) generally low-income countries. Poverty and lack of capacity restricts the ability of their governments to deliver public goods and services. It is thus not unreasonable to consider poverty traps as a possible determinant of fragility traps.

Second, as noted in the introduction, some fragile countries have—or are—experiencing conflict. It seems natural to thus examine conflict traps as leading to fragility traps. Collier et al. (2003) argue that once countries fall into civil wars, the risk that conflicts will happen again increases significantly. We can thus speak of a "conflict trap" if the first conflict onset increases the risk of long-term conflict significantly. The likelihood that a country will experience civil war depends largely on whether it has faced a civil war before. Evidence of such a trap would thus be found in both the duration and recurrence of conflicts. According to Collier (2007), conflicts have a higher likelihood of occurring in low-income countries, in environments where growth is either slow or even stagnant and declining, and in countries that are heavily dependent on primary commodity exports such as oil and diamonds. In the case of the latter, the so-called natural resource curse or natural resource trap refers to the notion that resource-rich countries will not grow as fast as countries that have lower quantities of natural resources and was popularized by Sachs and Warner (1995). There are several reasons that a natural resource trap could occur. First, discovery and exports of natural resources lead to an appreciation of country's currency (the so-called Dutch disease) and make other exporting sectors less competitive. Second, the volatility in commodity prices allows governments to spend carelessly without focusing on economic growth during commodity price booms, and spending is not reduced when prices decline. Third, resource rents lead to a deterioration in governance and public institutions and make countries more vulnerable to conflicts. Resource revenues allow government to buy votes by bribing community leaders instead of making sound investments and delivering public goods and services. To the extent that resource wealth is "unearned" revenue, it reduces the needs for taxation and breaks the fiscal contract between governments and their citizens.[6] However, we know that there are countries such as Mozambique or El Salvador that have been able to recover from civil wars and avoid them for many years.[7] Similarly, as in the case of the conflict trap, there are exceptions (e.g., Botswana) when it comes to the resource curse in developing countries, and several statistical studies have found no evidence of the resource curse (see the survey by Frankel in

2010). For example, Bruunschweiler and Bulte (2009) dispute the claim that natural resource abundance leads to conflict, by arguing that the measure of resource dependence is endogenous; once endogeneity is accounted for, resource dependence is no longer significant in conflict regressions, and conflict increases the dependence on resource extraction.

Third, as described in the introduction, Pritchett and de Weijer (2010) and Pritchett, Woolcock, and Andrews (2010) argue that fragile states are caught in a "big stuck" or "capability trap" that prevents them from implementing basic functions that include provision of services, maintaining law and order, and security. The authors do not explain why the capability trap exists but instead attempt to explain how countries are able to continue to get away with not acquiring capability. According to them, the capability trap creates an interesting dynamic whereby situations of apparent reform are presented to attract flows of development resources even when the reforms may not be yielding actual improvements. This implementation failure, according to the authors, has to do with "isomorphic mimicry" whereby structures exist in form rather than function and with "premature load bearing" (see also the introduction) whereby unrealistic expectations impose too much pressure on local structures and weaken capability. In order to illustrate the presence of capability traps, Pritchett, Woolcock, and Andrews (2010) use indicators drawn from various sources that measure the ability of the state to deliver—namely, the quality of government, government effectiveness, progressive deterioration of public services, and optimum use of resources by government (i.e., resource efficiency)—as evidence of a lack of state capability. There is thus a similarity between their approach and the governance trap of Collier (2007), but Pritchett, Woolcock, and Andrews (2010) are careful to avoid broad measures of governance that include political factors because it is their view that states can be highly capable without being democratic.

Fourth, Takeuchi, Murotani, and Tsunekawa (2011) argue that the process of state building—namely, how effective and legitimate states are formed—should be the main mechanism to overcome fragility, similar to what is proposed by the OECD/DAC principles for engaging in fragile states (OECD 2007). They consider two types of fragile states. First, capacity trap countries, similar to capability trap countries, are considered to be those unable to provide security and social services and have thus failed to build legitimacy. Initially lack of security prevents the government from delivering social services, which weakens legitimacy and then capacity. This creates a vicious circle between lack of capacity and the establishment of legitimacy. Second, legitimacy trap countries have a high capacity to provide security and services but suffer from weak legitimacy as a result of high inequalities and authoritarian management. Being successful and initially achieving relatively high legitimacy subsequently act as a disincentive for states to respond to new challenges and delegitimize them.

In order to measure the capacity and legitimacy of states, Takeuchi, Murotani, and Tsunekawa (2011) use the political stability indicator (as a measure of the capacity of the state to maintain public order) and the voice and accountability indicator from the World Governance Indicators of the World Bank. A country that is in a capacity trap would have seen a stagnation or deterioration of both indicators over time, while those in a legitimacy trap would have seen an improvement in capacity but not in legitimacy (voice and accountability). According to Takeuchi, Murotani, and Tsunekawa (2011), examples of countries that are in a capacity trap are Afghanistan, Sudan, Iraq, and the Democratic Republic of the Congo, while countries in a legitimacy trap include Cambodia and Rwanda. Compared to the ALC framework proposed by Carment, Prest, and Samy (2010), which distinguishes between authority and capacity, here capacity includes both political stability and the provision of social services. There is also a "feedback loop" between capacity and legitimacy as described above.

We believe that legitimacy is crucial to explaining failures to exit fragility traps. That is because these traps occur when a state fails to establish strong legitimacy even in the face of improved capacity. The risk states face is a closure of the political system even when growth is achieved. More specifically, a legitimacy trap describes the weakness of societal values to legitimize the actions of the state, leading to a perpetuation of weak institutions and rule of law. Legitimacy traps conjure up ideas of societal consent and participation in systems of good governance (local, regional, and global) and effective leadership. The legitimacy trap carries a normative dimension about the kinds of outcomes and processes that are most appropriate to ensure stable political orders. But it also implies a fair and equitable distribution of resources for public welfare. Different political orders have different forms of legitimating processes, but the assumption is that each will derive stability from constructive, ongoing, and effective bargaining between state and society.

EXTRACTING FRAGILITY TRAP COUNTRIES FROM CIFP'S DATA

To understand why countries are trapped, we need clear criteria for selecting those that have been stuck for several years and show no signs of improvement over time. Using the CIFP structural data set, countries trapped in fragility were selected based on the number of times (more than half) that they appeared in the top twenty fragile countries in the world over the thirty-five-year period from 1980 to 2014 and based on fragility scores whose long-term trajectory did not show signs of improving. In other words, both the ranking and fragility scores of countries were considered. By selecting countries on the basis of how often they rank among the worst performers and a deterioration in performance based on actual fragility scores, we shield ourselves from the likelihood that the ranking of countries is affected by the fact that others are doing better than they are while they are also improving rather than doing worse. As a result, our selection criteria allow us to capture the persistence of fragility over time, which is ultimately what one would expect for countries that are trapped.

As an example of a country stuck in a fragility trap, consider the case of Afghanistan, as shown in figure 1.1. Its overall fragility rank has varied from first to eighth over a thirty-five-year period, meaning that it always ranked in the top twenty. Its fragility score has deteriorated over time and has been at or higher than 6.5 (serious) since 1988, reaching a peak of 7.5 (very serious) in 2000. After the US-led coalition led to the fall of the Taliban regime in late 2001, the country's situation improved, but the gains that were made quickly disappeared over the next few years. When we examine the ALC components for Afghanistan, both authority and legitimacy have deteriorated significantly in the last few years, but the deterioration in capacity is less pronounced. Despite receiving significant amounts of aid from Western donors in the last fifteen years, the results have been far from satisfactory. The state and its institutions continue to depend heavily on external financing and technical support to function properly. Many of its policies are not supported by the majority of the population because decisions are made by a central government that is often not in touch with subnational-level actors and local populations. The ongoing war involving the Afghan government, coalition forces, the Taliban, and various terrorist networks and a general lack of security further prevent institutions from delivering on their core functions.

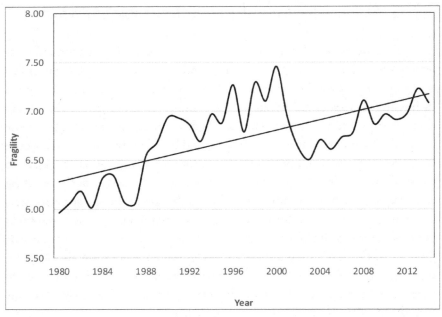

Figure 1.1 Afghanistan, fragility, 1980–2014

Table 1.3 shows the list of countries identified as being trapped in fragility based on the above criteria.[8] These countries have seen their fragility scores deteriorate over time (as in the case of figure 1.1 for Afghanistan), and they have at one point or another had a score of 6.5 or above. They have also been ranked among the top twenty fragile countries at least twenty-five times over a thirty-five-year period. Out of the ten countries listed in table 1.3, seven are in Africa, two are in Asia, and one is in the Middle East. All the trapped countries have experienced conflict in their recent past or continue to experience conflicts and organized violence. Except for Pakistan, Sudan, and Yemen, which are lower-middle-income countries, the seven other countries trapped in fragility are low-income countries; there are thirty-one low-income countries in the world according to the most recent World Bank classification. Interestingly, in its Δranking for 2015, the Fund for Peace Fragile States Index also ranks most of these countries among the worst performers. Uganda, ranked twenty-third, is the "least fragile" case among those listed in table 1.3 according to the FSI. Ranked 103rd and 117th out of 168 countries by Transparency International's Corruption Perceptions Index in 2015, Ethiopia and Pakistan are the least corrupt of the group. All the others are among the most corrupt in the world.

A Typology of Countries, with a Focus on the Fragility Trap   49

TABLE 1.3. FRAGILITY TRAP COUNTRIES, 1980–2014

Country	Number of times in top twenty	Number of times fragility score > 6.5	Fragility score and rank in 2014
Afghanistan	35	27	7.08, 5th
Burundi	32	18	6.71, 13th
Chad	25	13	6.95, 8th
Dem. Rep. of Congo	26	18	7.02, 7th
Ethiopia	31	14	6.81, 10th
Pakistan	29	8	6.49, 20th
Somalia	28	14	7.27, 2nd
Sudan/South Sudan	30	17	7.11, 4th / 7.76, 1st
Uganda	28	2	6.54, 18th
Yemen	25	12	7.08, 6th

When we look at the performance of the fragility-trapped countries in terms of the ALC framework, their performance on authority is worse on average, followed by legitimacy and then capacity. In terms of the six clusters of state performance, the worst average score is on human development, followed by demography and then governance. These countries perform very poorly on gender, with an average score of 7.30 for the entire sample over time.

CORRELATES OF THE FRAGILITY TRAP

We now examine which of the various traps identified in the section on "Operationalizing and Measuring the Fragility Trap" matter the most for the countries identified in table 1.3. Our analysis proceeds in two steps. First, we examine correlations between proxies for the various traps and CIFP's fragility index for both trapped and nontrapped countries. Second, we systematically check whether the ten countries listed in table 1.3 fit the description of these various traps by examining their performance over time. Our analysis does not consider the natural resource trap as a direct driver of fragility because it is expected to affect either institutions and conflict (the conflict trap) or income and poverty (the poverty trap). We build on the approach taken by Naudé, Santos-Paulino, and McGillivray (2011), who identify four causes of fragility: conflict, low development status, vulnerability, and the lack of a developmental state.

In our case, conflict intensity is related to the conflict trap, low development status (through per capita income and absolute poverty) is related to the poverty trap, and lack of a developmental state is related to the capability and legitimacy traps. We do not consider vulnerability to be as relevant here because our focus is more on countries that are trapped, whereas vulnerability, especially to natural hazards, tends to be associated with small island developing states. To be sure, vulnerability can contribute to fragility but is not considered to be a root cause of the fragility trap. Furthermore, the extent to which countries are resilient or less vulnerable is partly a function of strong institutional foundations, which should be captured by capability and legitimacy.

As shown in figure 1.2, the following variables are considered as proxies for each of the traps: per capita income and absolute poverty for the poverty trap; conflict intensity from the Uppsala Conflict Data Program at the Peace Research Institute Oslo (UCDP/PRIO) data set, which measures the level of fighting (minor or war) that a state-based conflict reaches in each year, for the conflict trap; government effectiveness from the Worldwide Governance Indicators of the World Bank for the capability trap; and voice and accountability from the Worldwide Governance Indicators of the World Bank for the legitimacy trap. We consider absolute poverty in addition to per capita income when we examine the specific country cases because it is possible that growth is not as pro-poor in fragile environments that are by definition unstable and lack legitimacy. The government effectiveness variable measures perceptions of the quality of public services, the quality of the civil service and the extent to which it is independent from political pressures, the quality of policy formulation and implementation, and extent to which government is committed to policies. The voice and accountability variable measures perceptions of the extent to which citizens can participate in the selection of government, as well as freedom of expression, freedom of association, and a free media. Both the government effectiveness and voice and accountability variables range from −2.5 to 2.5, with higher values corresponding to better governance scores.

A Typology of Countries, with a Focus on the Fragility Trap

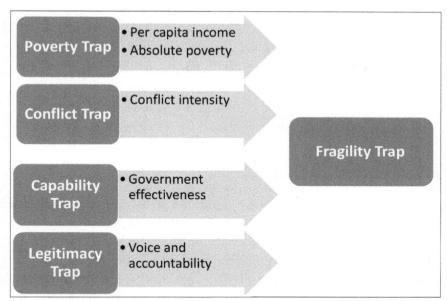

Figure 1.2 A fragility trap model

Correlations between these variables and CIFP's fragility index—for the overall sample of nonadvanced countries,[9] for the overall sample of nonadvanced countries excluding trapped countries (i.e., nontrapped countries), and for the fragility trap countries—are shown in table 1.4. All of these correlations are significant at the level of 1 percent, and there are no surprises as far as the signs go, except in the case of GDP per capita for trapped countries. In the broader sample of all nonadvanced economies, there is an expected negative and significant relationship between per capita income and fragility—that is, lower incomes are associated with higher fragility. However, in the case of countries trapped in fragility, it is interesting to note that higher fragility is associated with higher per capita incomes, meaning that despite increases in income in these countries over time, they have remained fragile (or, alternatively, that fragility has not prevented these countries from improving their income levels). This simple and preliminary correlation exercise shows that the poverty trap explanation is quite weak, a point also made by Easterly (2006) and Kraay and McKenzie (2014) for broader samples of countries. When we test whether as a group the mean income growth rate for the trapped countries is zero, we statistically reject the hypothesis of zero mean over the period 1980 to 2014.

TABLE 1.4. CORRELATES OF FRAGILITY, 1980–2014

Variable	All nonadvanced countries	Nontrapped countries	Trapped countries
GDP per capita	−0.47	−0.47	0.22
Conflict	0.34	0.28	0.19
Government effectiveness	−0.77	−0.76	−0.67
Voice and accountability	−0.67	−0.63	−0.60

Note: All correlations are significant at the 1 percent level.

The conflict variable remains significant across the various samples. However, it is weakly correlated at 0.19 with fragility when the trapped countries are considered, which is surprising, given that many of these countries tend to be affected by ongoing conflicts and instability. This result can be explained by the fact that not all of the countries have had high-intensity conflicts over the full period under examination. On the other hand, the government effectiveness (capability) and voice and accountability (legitimacy) variables remain significant and highly correlated with the fragility index for the overall sample, nontrapped countries, and countries trapped in fragility. They both indicate that deteriorations in capability and legitimacy are significantly correlated with poor fragility scores. To further test which of these traps correlate the most with the fragility index for countries that are trapped, we estimate the following regression using panel data for the period 1980–2014:

$$fragility_{it} = \alpha_0 + \alpha_1 \ln(gdppc_{it-1}) + \alpha_2 conflict_{it-1} + \alpha_3 governmenteffectiveness_{it-1} + \alpha_4 voiceandaccountability_{it-1} + u_i + v_t + e_{it}$$

where i indexes countries and t indexes time, the various independent variables are as defined above and lagged one period, u_i and v_t are country and time-specific effects, and e_{it} is the normal disturbance term. The Hausman test provided strong evidence against the null hypothesis that there is no misspecification in the case of random effects for the different models estimated. As a result, fixed effects (FE) estimates with period dummies are reported (column [2] in table 1.5), as well as panel-corrected standard errors that account for both cross-section heteroscedasticity and autocorrelation. We also show how the estimates vary using ordinary least squares (OLS) and random effects approaches (RE)—see columns (1) and (3) of table 1.5.

TABLE 1.5.
FRAGILITY AS A FUNCTION OF VARIOUS TRAPS: TRAPPED COUNTRIES

Explanatory variables	(1) OLS	(2) FE	(3) RE
Constant	5.466**	5.295**	4.909**
	(34.584)	(9.395)	(17.094)
ln(GDPPC)	0.093**	0.122	0.191**
	(3.502)	(1.263)	(4.146)
Conflict	0.036*	0.045*	0.033
	(2.079)	(2.235)	(1.575)
Government effectiveness	−0.376**	−0.268**	−0.371**
	(−8.764)	(−3.221)	(−4.586)
Voice and accountability	−0.148*	−0.243**	−0.172*
	(−2.423)	(−3.413)	(−2.368)
#Observations	121	121	121
#Countries	9	9	9

Note: Except where indicated otherwise, the figures in parentheses are the robust t-statistics.
*(**) indicates 5(1) percent level of significance. Coefficients on time and country dummies not reported.

The results are shown in table 1.5 and largely confirm what was observed from the simple correlations in table 1.4. The poverty trap story does not hold for the countries trapped in fragility once country-fixed effects are accounted for. The legitimacy and capability traps are the most significant, followed by the conflict trap. There are two caveats here that are worth pointing out. First, the sample size is inevitably small because it examines only the countries that are trapped (excluding Somalia because of gaps in data). Second, the time period considered includes only sixteen years because of lack of data for the government effectiveness (capability) and voice and accountability (legitimacy) variables.

How about the performance of the individual trapped countries over time? With respect to per capita income, we find very weak evidence of a poverty trap. There are many gaps in data on per capita incomes for Somalia, and it cannot be examined. South Sudan, being a new country, cannot be considered either. However, for all the other countries, per capita incomes have generally increased over time. The only exception is the

Democratic Republic of the Congo, whose per capita income in 2014 is lower than the 1980 level. Even in this extreme case, per capita incomes have increased since 2001 after the disastrous decades of the 1980s and 1990s. When we examine data on absolute poverty, most of the trapped countries have seen the number of people living on less than $1.90 per day decline over time, as well as a decline in the headcount ratio.[10] Burundi and the Democratic Republic of the Congo are the only two countries where the number of people living in absolute poverty has increased; however, the head-count ratio has decreased in each case. Overall, we find very weak evidence of a poverty trap when we examine individual trapped countries.

With respect to the conflict trap, the clearest example of a country trapped in conflict is Afghanistan, where the intensity of the conflict situation has remained almost the same over the entire thirty-five-year period (see also previous section). Other countries that fall into that category include Pakistan and Somalia (over the long term) and South Sudan and Yemen (more recently). Even if most of the trapped countries have been affected by conflict in the past three and a half decades, the intensity of conflict has varied over time, and countries such as Burundi and Chad have been relatively peaceful in recent years. Perhaps the most surprising example is that of the Democratic Republic of the Congo, which saw a collapse in economic performance in the 1980s and early 1990s without conflict playing a significant role during those years.

When it comes to capability (measured by the government effectiveness variable), all of the countries trapped in fragility have numbers in the negative range, with very poor scores in cases such as Afghanistan, the Democratic Republic of the Congo, Somalia, and South Sudan. Seven out of the ten countries have seen no improvement or a deterioration in their performance over time since the early 2000s, the period for which we have consistent data.[11] Burundi, Ethiopia, and Uganda have recorded modest improvements in their government effectiveness scores. A similar observation can be made with respect to legitimacy (measured by the voice and accountability variable): all of the trapped countries have legitimacy scores in the negative range, and only a few (such as Afghanistan—surprisingly—and Uganda) have seen some improvement over time, while most have seen their scores deteriorate.

A TYPOLOGY OF COUNTRIES

In this section, we broaden our categorization of states to consider those that moved into and out of fragility and those that have exited. The first column of table 1.6 is the same list of countries identified as trapped earlier. To select countries that have moved into and out of fragility, we once again use fragility rankings and scores over time. These are countries that moved into and out of the top forty ranked countries and whose fragility scores were relatively flat over the long term. In other words, when improvements in the situations of these countries occurred, they did not last very long. A third category of countries that has exited fragility was also selected. Specifically, we consider countries that were among the most fragile countries in earlier periods and were able to exit the top forty rankings for a period of ten years or more. The fragility scores of the selected countries also indicate that their long-term trajectory showed a clear pattern of improvement over a sufficient number of years. While there is always a danger that these countries may see their situations deteriorate, we are interested in understanding why they remained resilient for several years despite being fragile in earlier periods.

TABLE 1.6. TYPOLOGY OF COUNTRIES

Fragility trap	In and out	Exit
Afghanistan	Cameroon	Algeria
Burundi	Comoros	Bangladesh
Chad	Equatorial Guinea	Benin
Dem. Republic of Congo	Guinea-Bissau	Cambodia
Ethiopia	Laos	Guatemala
Pakistan	Mali	Malawi
Somalia	Mauritania	Mozambique
Sudan / South Sudan	Rwanda	Nicaragua
Uganda	Senegal	
Yemen		

In terms of the ALC framework, countries from the "in" and "out" categories tend to do better on authority on average, followed by legitimacy and capacity. In other words, despite recording improvements in authority scores, they have not been able to move out of the top forty rankings more permanently because of a lack of improvement in legitimacy and capacity. These findings are confirmed when we examine their performance at the cluster level: poor on human development and economics (which both measure capacity), relatively poor on governance (which serves as a proxy for legitimacy), and much better on security and crime (as a proxy for authority). Their performance on gender is also quite weak, though not as weak as countries trapped in fragility.

An interesting case from the second type of countries selected is that of Equatorial Guinea. Although being an oil producer and one of the richest countries in sub-Saharan Africa in per capita terms, it has moved into and out of the top forty rankings since the mid-1980s. In fact, there is a significant difference between its ranking on per capita gross national income and human development (UNDP 2016), which shows that improvements in per capita income have not been matched by corresponding improvements in other indicators of development such as health and education. Its poor record on legitimacy (as a result of performing poorly on civil liberties and political rights), among other criteria, has prevented it from building the sort of resilience that would allow it to remain more stable over time. We should note that there are several cases of countries that even if fragile, are not included among states moving into and out of fragility, once again because of our selection criteria.

As a group, the countries in the exit category tend to do slightly better on authority than on legitimacy, but their capacity scores are not as strong. This is understandable, given that three of these countries (Benin, Malawi, and Mozambique) are classified as low-income countries by the World Bank, while four others (Bangladesh, Cambodia, Guatemala, and Nicaragua) are lower middle-income countries. Only Algeria is an upper middle-income country from that group. The analysis by cluster shows that these countries do poorly on human development (hence their poor showing on capacity) and much better on security and crime (hence their good showing on authority). They also do quite poorly on gender even if better than the countries trapped in fragility.

As an example of a country from the exit category, consider the case of Mozambique, a state we examine in detail in chapter 5. Mozambique was ranked among the most fragile countries (in the top ten) during the 1980s, a period that coincided with the civil war in that country. Although the choice of Mozambique may seem odd, given sporadic fighting since 2013 by militants of the political organization Renamo, it is nonetheless an interesting case because it has avoided another full-scale civil war for several years. With the end of the civil war in 1992, the country was able to move out of the top forty fragile countries since the mid-1990s and until 2012. Its overall fragility score improved significantly during that period (see figure 1.3), driven by improvements in capacity followed by legitimacy and authority, respectively. Guatemala is in a similar, if not better, situation, having overcome the legacy of a thirty-six-year old civil war that ended in 1996. Since then, the country has remained permanently out of the top forty fragile countries in the world and seen significant improvements in authority scores over time.

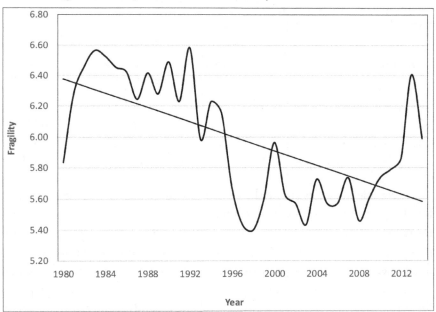

Figure 1.3   Mozambique, fragility, 1980–2014

THE EVOLUTION OF STATES ACROSS VARIOUS TYPOLOGIES

In this section, we extend our empirical analysis to compare states that moved into and out of, and have exited, fragility with those that are trapped. Since states are trapped for various reasons discussed earlier, it logically follows that the ones that have exited, temporarily or permanently, would have been able to overcome some of these barriers. The second column of table 1.7 reports the same results presented earlier so that readers are able to compare with the two other groups of countries in the third and fourth columns. The correlation between per capita income and fragility is negative for countries that have exited fragility, which is what one would expect: as incomes improve, fragility scores decline, and countries become more stable. This result is different from the trapped countries and those that moved into and out of fragility. In these cases, fragility scores and per capita income are positively correlated, which means that the fragility situations of these countries deteriorated despite improvements in income. All the other variables (conflict, government effectiveness, and voice and accountability) behave as expected for both countries that have exited, and moved into and out of, fragility.

TABLE 1.7. CORRELATES OF FRAGILITY, 1980–2014

Variable	Trapped countries	In and out countries	Exit countries
GDP per capita	0.22	0.16	−0.40
Conflict	0.19	0.36	0.51
Government effectiveness	−0.67	−0.29	−0.10
Voice and accountability	−0.60	−0.31	−0.19

In table 1.8, we estimate the same regression as before using panel data for the period 1980–2014 to test which of the various traps are significant for the two new types of countries identified in the earlier section on the typology of countries. For ease of comparison, we include the estimates using fixed effects for trapped countries from column (2) of table 1.5. Compared to states that are trapped in fragility, the conflict trap is highly significant for both those that have moved into and out of, and those that have exited, fragility. The poverty trap story is once again not very compelling, being significant only at the 5 percent level for countries that have exited fragility. However, the capability and legitimacy traps are less significant for countries that have exited fragility when compared to those that are trapped. In the case of countries that have moved into and out of fragility, the poverty and legitimacy traps are not significant. The capability trap is significant but is positively correlated with fragility—that is, improvements in capability are associated with deteriorations in fragility.

A Typology of Countries, with a Focus on the Fragility Trap

TABLE 1.8. FRAGILITY AS A FUNCTION OF VARIOUS TRAPS

Explanatory variables	(1) Trapped	(2) In and out	(3) Exit
Constant	5.295**	5.407**	8.168**
	(9.395)	(7.700)	(7.092)
ln(GDPPC)	0.122	0.014	−0.451*
	(1.263)	(0.122)	(−2.356)
Conflict	0.045*	0.298**	0.464**
	(2.235)	(7.756)	(5.303)
Government effectiveness	−0.268**	0.243**	−0.186*
	(−3.221)	(3.751)	(−1.863)
Voice and accountability	−0.243**	−0.178	−0.230*
	(−3.413)	(1.537)	(−2.036)
#Observations	121	140	127
#Countries	9	9	8

Note: Except where indicated otherwise, the figures in parentheses are the robust t-statistics.
*(**) indicates 5(1) percent level of significance. Coefficients on time and country dummies not reported.

Taken together, the findings in the case of countries that move in and out imply that fragility tends to persist when countries are unable to make significant progress on legitimacy followed by capacity. The fact that conflict remains highly significant for countries that have moved into and out of fragility means that these countries have trouble controlling territory and people, which may in turn make them less resilient despite economic growth. We surmise that even moderate levels of conflict intensity are preventing these countries from exiting fragility permanently. There is thus a difference in terms of why countries are stuck in fragility when compared to why they exit permanently or temporarily. Legitimacy matters the most for trapped countries and slightly less so for countries that have exited fragility, while the conflict trap matters the most for the other two typologies. In essence, for those countries that have successfully exited fragility, they are able to tolerate modest levels of conflict because they have more effective authority and legitimacy. In contrast to those countries that continually move in and out, low capacity and to some extent uneven authority have a derogatory influence. The key here appears to be weakness in legitimacy in trapped states.

The objective of this chapter was to first identify a set of countries trapped in fragility using CIFP's data set in order to understand why they have not seen much improvement in their situations over time. We were able to show that there is small group of countries that has been stuck in the top twenty fragile states for several years during a thirty-five-year period with fragility scores often higher than 6.5, which we consider to be serious cases. These are countries that have experienced various levels of conflict during their turbulent history and that are also among the largest recipients of foreign aid and other types of interventions. We then examined which factors from the extant literature on the existence of different traps (poverty trap, conflict trap, capability trap, and legitimacy trap) are highly correlated with the fragility scores of this particular group of countries.

We find strong evidence of capability and legitimacy traps as important correlates of fragility-trapped countries, evidence of the conflict trap as a contributing factor, and no evidence of the poverty trap story (when country fixed effects are taken into account). We were able to reach this conclusion after comparing the group of countries trapped in fragility with those that are not and after examining the ten cases of countries that we identified as being trapped in fragility. To the extent that fragility is multidimensional and that the fragility trap is the result of various traps (poverty, conflict, capability, and legitimacy), our analysis indicates that countries are trapped for a combination of reasons that have more to do with government capability and legitimacy, relative to conflict and poverty. There are also differences in terms of how these various traps unfold across countries. In terms of CIFP's conceptual approach, these results indicate that authority (government effectiveness and to a certain extent conflict intensity) and legitimacy (voice and accountability) are the key structural characteristics that correlate the most with fragility for those countries that are trapped in fragility, while capacity (income per capita and poverty) is not significant. In particular, improvements in capacity do not guarantee that countries will be able to escape the fragility trap, especially when corresponding improvements are not happening to authority and legitimacy. However, capacity becomes important once countries are able to exit the fragility trap.

We then extended our analysis to build a threefold typology of states by including those that have successfully exited fragility, those that fluctuate between a successful exit and fragility, and those that are stuck in a fragility trap. We find that countries that exit fragility over long periods of time have been able to avoid a recurrence of large-scale conflict; examples include Algeria, Guatemala, and Mozambique. However, this is only possible when they are able to concurrently build legitimacy, which we found was significant for countries that remain trapped. We surmise that for exiting states there is a staged sequence in which building legitimacy lends itself to enhanced capacity over time. Although we might have expected the capability trap to be more significant in the case of countries that exit fragility, it is the ability of these countries to avoid conflicts and therefore build legitimacy that seems to matter the most. Simply put, exited states are not the mirror image of those that are trapped. This claim is strengthened by our observation that countries can remain trapped despite building strong capacity.

For countries that move into and out of fragility, the conflict trap is significant. Surprisingly, even as the governments of these countries became more capable, their fragility scores did not improve permanently because they are unable to exercise control over people and territories. However, at this point we cannot conclude that conflict is a cause of their ongoing dips in fragility as it is not perpetually intense, nor is it constant. It is likely, for example, that conflict only emerges as result of endogenous shocks or when the states exhibit low carrying capacity. Overall and linking our findings back to the ALC construct, legitimacy and authority are important factors behind the evolution of states, while capacity appears to be less important. Again, we are not arguing that capacity is irrelevant or inconsequential but simply that it does not vary as much as we thought it would across the three types and therefore is unhelpful in explaining why countries are stuck, permanently or temporarily.

Given the findings from this chapter, we believe that an in-depth analysis of four issues is justified. First, we want to know more specifically how weak legitimacy interacts with fragility to generate outcomes that drive a country into a trap and keep it there. In the next chapter, we will do exactly that with a focus on elite decisions and state-society interactions, with a specific focus on how a lack of legitimacy relates to weakened authority, undergoverned spaces, elite capture, and rent-seeking behavior. Second, we want to know why it is that despite reasonable capacity, performance states remain trapped for decades. How is it possible, in other words, that trapped states do not share the virtuous cycles of political and economic development that many nontrapped states do? We will examine this question in relation to our first set of pairwise comparisons in chapter 3. Third, we want to know why is it that the conflict trap appears to be holding back some states, apparently causing them to move into and out of fragility over long periods of time. Is conflict a cause of these fluctuations or a symptom of a larger set of economic and political processes? To answer that question, we will examine our second set of pairwise comparisons of "in and out states" in chapter 4. Finally, we want to know if our hunch about the two-stage exit from fragility is an accurate description of how states exit. In other words, do states that exit from fragility get their political and social house in order before realizing long-term sustainable growth? To answer this question, we will examine two exited states in chapter 5.

Chapter 2

Elites and the Trap

Drivers of Change

This chapter considers complementary explanations for evaluating fragile state transitions, with an explicit focus on drivers of change and causes of fragility persistence. The typology from the previous chapter identified the core structural causes of the fragility trap. We detailed structural indicators of fragility to explain the variance between those fragile states that are trapped, those that successfully exit, and those that move into and out of fragility. By examining the role of elites, leaders, and change agents in this chapter, we focus on a complementary theoretical explanation of why fragility traps persist. The complementary causal explanations in this chapter provide the context necessary for the comparative case studies that follow in subsequent chapters. Our central focus is on how national, regional, and local elites work to keep a fragile state trapped. To this end, we must be open to the possibility that for the many fragile states, reversals are not only possible but likely. Further, in moving beyond a purely structural analysis, we can consider how elites affect change and how those changes are underpinned by legitimizing forces and state-society relations (Leftwich 2010). We are compelled to consider how elites bargain with each other, how credible their agreements are, and, most important, public expectations of the outcomes stemming from those agreements.

We first discuss why elites are central to understanding fragility dynamics. Then we turn to explanations of elite behavior in fragile states. After that we consider the importance of legitimacy and how its absence ultimately undermines reform efforts in fragile states (Abulof 2017). We consider the most salient causes of stagnation and reversal in light of our need to identify drivers of change. We conclude with a brief description of the findings from this chapter and their implications.

In examining the theoretical foundations of fragility dynamics, we emphasize two reasons why elites are important. First, principal-agent theory tells us that "change agents," such as the military, politicians, and regional power brokers, are often "delegated" by states (the principal) some element of authority in decision-making and resource allocation (Jensen and Meckeling 1976). If this delegation of authority is problematic in a fragile states context, it is because certain elites will ultimately know more about local political and economic conditions than central governments. This relationship raises a fundamental problem of information asymmetries in that elites with local knowledge enjoy a distinct advantage over central governments that implement policies, influence institutions, and control and distribute resources such as rents from aid and the extractive sectors (Dizolele and Kambale 2012). The idea of elites as "change agents" is therefore important for understanding how to achieve and sustain reforms in the face of fragility persistence. Principal-agent theory makes it clear that elites (agents) may have no interest in increasing the welfare of the state (Horowitz 2005). Indeed, contrasting and varying levels of capability, interests, and knowledge raise the possibility that certain elites in trapped states function outside of conventional institutions and act against state interests. Therefore, an analysis of the mechanisms and techniques used by local leaders to maintain their privileged position is useful. Though Rotberg (2012) and Leftwich and Wheeler (2011), among others, show it is possible to break through such rent seeking and local-level power brokerage, the resistance of elites to reform suggests that trapped states are stuck in an equilibrium where the incentives to oppose change are stronger than they are for states that have exited from fragility. (For a critical review, see Di John 2010.)

Second, and related to the first point, an elite's legitimacy is derived from its capacity to preserve the status quo (Badie, Berg-Schlosser, and

Morlino 2011a). Rotberg (2012) contends this equilibrium works to thwart the emergence of "transformative" leaders. Transformative leaders are those with visionary plans who are capable of unifying constituencies, mobilizing public and political support, and maintaining trust to turn plans into reality (Turper and Aarts 2017). These include governmental performance in delivering essential political goods, safety and security, rule of law and transparency, participation and human rights, and sustainable economic growth and development, along with human development such as education, health, and employment (Feeny, Posso, and Regan-Beasley 2015).[1] As Debiel et al. (2009) and Boege, Brown, and Clements (2009) show, fragility persistence depends on the strength and legitimacy of local and regional elites. For example, examining the interaction of local leaders with the state apparatus in Afghanistan and Somaliland, Debiel and his coauthors (2009, 43) find that deeply fragile states function under conditions of hybridity where "local actors and power-holders do not evade interaction with state institutions because they regard the state as a potential source of income, power, and legitimacy." Indeed, the authors assert that long-term state building is likely to fail if formal and informal sources of authority are strictly divided and highly institutionalized. That is because local leaders function within an informal economy in careful balance with national leaders and their own rent-seeking behavior (see also Nay 2013).

In regard to other kinds of elites beyond traditional, regional, or national leaders, studies by Menkhaus (2004) examining state collapse in Somalia are instructive. Menkhaus shows that central governments will be politically ineffective without accommodating local actors who control important levers of power.[2] Within the political and social domains, local elite behavior ultimately influences the robustness of the political system, its institutions, and state-society relations.

Lemay-Hébert (2009), for example, notes that the loss of legitimacy by central authorities in many fragile states occurs in parallel with institutional collapse. Under certain conditions, elite interactions create a self-reinforcing cycle, such as a decline in authority institutions, harming both government legitimacy and capacity (Ferreira 2017). This downturn can, in turn, negatively impact authority even further, ensuring that states stay trapped (Carment, Prest, and Samy 2010). As noted by historical institutionalism (Thelen 1999; Steinmo 2008), in advanced societies, institutional structures tend to slow the pace of change and constrain actors, preventing novel ways of pursuing an objective from being applied or implemented. However, in fragile states' situations, the ability of elites to adapt to change or conversely ignore it is less likely to be driven by institutional structures and more by the distribution of power and the ability of elites to distribute resources on that basis (Carothers 2002).[3] Vanhanen (1990) long ago argued that the long-term nature of a political system is decisively influenced and determined by power distribution, in particular by how much is concentrated in the hands of one group or distributed among many independent groups.[4]

DECAY, DISENGAGEMENT, AND UNDERGOVERNED SPACES

To develop a more comprehensive understanding of the role of elites and their interactions, we must confront a core problem raised by North (2007) and his coauthors in their discussion of limited-access orders. North and his colleagues argue that external interventions are unable to solve the problems of fragile states because policy prescriptions advocate for the implementation of institutions and procedures mirroring those of developed Western countries (Babbitt, Johnstone, and Mazurana 2016; Call 2011). Mitchell (2010) makes a similar point regarding the post–Cold War US emphasis on privileging security interventions in weak and fragile states such as Iraq. The heavy skewing toward security, surveillance, and policing produces outcomes that ultimately fail because "governance" becomes equated with developing effective coercive capacity while forgoing or even ignoring local indigenous governance systems.

These insights are similar to those developed by Pritchett, Woolcock, and Andrews (2010), who in turn echo arguments from Pye and Verba (1965) and others on political decay. Their arguments are important because of the emphasis on context, state-society relations, and fragility dynamics. For example, political development can be reversed or become stagnant when elite interests undermine economic and political inclusivity. Here we must consider a distinction between structural reversals as constituted by changes across systems and policy shifts that occur within a system. Between-system changes would include, for example, shifts between a traditional and postcolonial state or an upheaval brought about by revolution or a war of independence. Within-system changes occur more frequently over time as a result of policy decisions taken by elites.

When it comes to evaluating fragility traps and those states that have escaped them, we must be sensitive to both possibilities. In other words, both structural transformation and incremental changes are part of fragility dynamics. While Pritchett, Woolcock, and Andrews (2013) frame their understanding of within-system changes in terms of administrative weakness and failure to provide effective service delivery, North focuses more on the political organization of elites by comparing them to open-access orders. Open-access orders are those in which open competition in economics and politics, coupled with the rule of law and institutional oversight, maintain general harmony in society. In contrast, fragile states are typically limited-access orders, featuring political and economic spheres dominated by elite groups that cooperate to share rents, keep institutions weak, and limit violence. These insights regarding elite bargaining are similar to Rothchild's (1986) seminal studies of elite-driven hegemonial exchange in a middle African context and Lustick's (1979) study of control models focused on indicators of segmentation, dependence, and co-optation. In reflecting on these limited-access orders, Fatton (1995) argues that specific structures are selected to help perpetuate popular support for the status quo. Drawing a distinction between local, regional, and national elites, he notes that where there was a convergence of interests for reform, it was largely in support of a national project such as achieving independence. Over time, such cohesion becomes largely fragmented by economic interests and ethnic loyalties. Local and regional elites subsequently become disengaged from the national project. The consequence of this fragmentation is the formation of patron-client relations and the development of personal rule in which subjective authority and the power of patrons determine system stability (Jackson and Rosberg 1982).

But under coercive patron-client relations, as Ake (2000) argues, affected populations will ultimately disengage and operate privately within a moral economy where the support for reform is further muted (Scott 1976). The subsequent lack of interdependency between state and society in turn undermines the possibility of autonomic and legitimized development because elites lack fundamental accountability, in which the possibility of overturning the government is always present.

In a trapped state, that delinking between state and society occurs either through voluntary disengagement or forced departicipation.[5] Departicipation refers to a reduction or elimination of political involvement as a consequence of choice, apathy, or coercion. Departicipation originates from a deliberate dismantling of participatory structures such as reducing the autonomy of groups or as a voluntary response or coping mechanism in the face of an oppressive state.

In fragility analysis, the term "undergoverned spaces" has similar meaning. In spaces that are undergoverned, we expect both diminished symbolic and material engagement. The most evident would be the failure of a constitutional order to properly protect the autonomy (territorially, economically, or politically) of minority groups, with the result that those groups are underserviced and disengaged from the national political scene. Under some conditions, coerced participation is as delegitimizing as departication. Both reflect an unhealthy relationship between state and society.

Even when voluntary and induced as a coping mechanism in the face of repressive regime, the disengagement paradigm is ultimately counterproductive. Disengagement reduces the chances for liberalization; it contributes to profound inequalities, and it weakens the state by creating a truly nonformal economy often based on a reconstituted "economy of affection" (Hyden 1980). As Azarya and Chazan (1987) argue, although disengagement may provide the basis for establishing a popular mode of action against an oppressive state, it also has nihilistic features and is more likely to induce rebellion in the long run. Disengagement thus constitutes the kind of decay that Pye (1971) describes as a crisis of legitimacy. It is that juxtaposition regarding questions of whom the elite are accountable to and whether they enjoy the support of the population that will determine if a fragile state will succumb to backsliding and reversal (Lust and Waldner 2015).

In brief, departication, undergoverned spaces, and disengagement do not offer a sustainable and viable alternative to weakened legitimacy. Disengagement is primarily a coping mechanism in the face of interelite bargaining. Therefore, if we are to understand why states stay stuck in a fragility trap, we need to determine if elites have deliberately induced such processes through specific policies. For example, in states that have exited fragility, we would expect greater institutional responsiveness, greater accountability among elites, and greater responsiveness to the challenges of departication and undergoverned spaces.

Undergoverned spaces are particularly problematic in trapped states because they can obstruct the formation of national identities, intensify the salience of regional and ethnic differences, and reduce the prospects for a functioning open economy. As Keister (2014) and Patrick (2010) demonstrate, the term "undergoverned" does not mean these spaces are lawless but that they are governed through alternative local laws that Debiel et al. (2009) argue emerge under conditions of hybridity. Most important for our purposes, these spaces serve as a brake on change because they limit national growth and entrench the power of elites (both local and national) who benefit from their perpetuation. In those states that have hegemonial exchange, for example, there is at least a minimum of distributive justice to ensure nascent stability but absent an elite that has the capacity to deliver on redistribution, and the likelihood of decay becomes more probable with time. In the following sections, we build on these insights in order to clarify how elites drive states toward a trap.

HYBRIDITY, BACKSLIDING, AND STAGNATION

Beyond the presumed connection between political and economic development, another body of literature in which we may understand elite behavior is institutional underdevelopment. This relationship is often conflated with democratic development and its counterparts political decay, backsliding, and stagnation. So, while our analysis is concerned with more than just democracy and development, it is important we consider that relationship nevertheless. By doing so we can examine conventional perspectives on elite behavior and demonstrate their relevance to fragility analysis.

For our purposes, democracy should be understood in its broadest terms as a political system in which power is shared by competing groups, led by elites in which the degree of their competition and the degree of public participation are relatively high. Institutionally, it means a political system in which the government is responsible to the electorate, in which political opposition has legal opportunities to compete for power. According to a 2016 report by Freedom House, 59 out of 195 countries are considered "partly free" (Freedom House, 2016). These are countries that, despite moving out of authoritarianism through the adoption of varying degrees of political, social, and economic liberalization, have not fully transitioned to democracy or have reversed in some key areas as they begin to open up. Such regimes, notably found in Africa (Kenya, Mozambique, Zambia), postcommunist Europe (Albania, Ukraine), Latin America (Haiti, Mexico), and Asia (Malaysia, Indonesia, Pakistan), began transitioning with the "third wave" of democratization from 1974 and were expected to transform into full democracies. However, many remain "partially liberalized," having adopted varying degrees of democratization (see Vanhanen 2000).

These partially liberalized regimes "are neither clearly democratic nor conventionally authoritarian" (Diamond 2002). Myriad labels have been used to describe them, including "hybrid" (Diamond 2002; Wigell 2008), "semi-democracies" (Diamond, Linz, and Lipset 1989), "illiberal democracies" (Zakaria 1997), "electoral democracies" (Diamond 1999), "competitive authoritarian" (Levitsky and Way 2002), "semi-authoritarian" (Ottaway 2003a), "soft authoritarianism" (Means 1996), "electoral authoritarianism" (Schedler 1998, 2006), and "anocracies" (Marshall and Cole 2014). While the proliferation of terms reflects ambiguity on how to classify countries that occupy this "political gray zone" (Diamond 2002), the continued prevalence of partially liberalized regimes raises questions surrounding the factors that cause, deter, or prevent their transformation in cases where liberalization and transition began but political change did not occur or is reversed. As we noted previously, the literature tends to identify low levels of economic development, weak institutional capacity, and perpetual conflict as three key factors that explain why these states do not transition out of fragility.

Writing about the so-called third wave of democratization, Huntington (1993) suggests that democratic transitions were caused by five major factors: legitimacy problems in authoritarian regimes, economic growth, religious doctrine to oppose authoritarianism, changing policies of external actors (the European Union, the United States, the Soviet Union), and "snowballing" (the cumulative effects of antiauthoritarian diffusion from country to country) based on earlier transitions. Once transition began, it was expected to proceed in three sequential stages: an "opening" phase marked by political liberalization and cracks in the ruling regime, a "breakthrough" phase where regime collapse is followed by the emergence of a democratic system, and a "consolidation" phase in which democratic forms become democratic substance (Carothers 2002).

While there are several countries (such as Benin, the Dominican Republic, Ghana, Guyana, and Romania) where democracy survived despite continually high levels of poverty and inequality (Levitsky and Way 2002), other studies in this vein have suggested that for well-governed poor countries, the only way out of the traps that threaten their capacity to deepen democracy is through a "big push" of financial resources from donor agencies (Sachs 2005). Further, this body of literature notes that the path to transition need not necessarily reach democratic consolidation. According to O'Donnell and Schmitter (1986), the outcome of a transition is inherently uncertain, where transitions from democracy could lead to liberalized authoritarianism or illiberal democracy as well as full democracy. The literature on democratic consolidation suggests that democratic transitions could be slowed by rapid growth (Lipset 1959; Olson 1993), high rates of inflation (Hirschman 1986), extreme income inequality, inadequate constraints on executive power, ethnic fragmentation, and the insufficient provision of "public goods" (Kapstein and Converse 2008). In brief, this literature argues that fragile states can become trapped because their hybrid regimes have not yet transitioned, due for the most part to stunted economic development further constrained by a failure to effectively distribute power and resources.

A second causal linkage focuses on "backslides" from openness to regime failure and civil war, as was the case in Côte d'Ivoire and Guinea (Marshall and Cole 2014). States backslide when they become less democratic (the Eastern European model), when their democratic practices are subverted and replaced by military usurpers (the Latin American and sometime African models), or when they fail to consolidate and grow as democratic polities and revert to autocracy (the Middle Eastern model).

For example, Huntington (1993) warns that previous waves of democratization are followed by "reverse waves," which pull countries away from newfound democracy. Driven by weak democratic values among elites and society, economic setbacks, social and political polarization, and the breakdown of law and order due to insurgency and reverse snowballing, such reverse transitions pull countries into the "gray zone" between democracy and authoritarianism. While Huntington's wave approach has received a mixed reception, generating both support (Strand et al. 2012) and rejection (Doorenspleet 2005; Przeworski et al. 1996), Diamond (2015) contends that instead of a reverse "wave," the last decade has seen a "protracted democratic recession" that has ebbed freedoms in some regions but has not "reversed" democracy as Huntington predicted.

Though all of these arguments are plausible and intuitive, we find them all deficient in explaining why fragile states remain trapped. With myriad potential explanations—some focused on human agency, others on historical antecedents and institutional path dependence—the precise role of elites is absent. That is because these studies tend to underemphasize that a key reason for a state failing to transition is the deep connection between and the importance of the simultaneous development of political, social, and economic orders, with the three changing in connection to one another. Yes, a fragile state may stagnate for economic or political reasons. It may even backslide for political reasons. But what is not clear in all these explanations is why. More accurately, these arguments all underemphasize the importance of understanding state-society relations, specifically the role of legitimacy in underpinning the behavior of political, social, and economic elites (Weatherford 1992).

Thus, we turn to a third set of arguments that come most closely to assessing interactions between state and society. These causal explanations tend to focus on the continued prevalence of hybrid regimes in which elites benefit from maintaining the status quo. These are states that have not transitioned toward fuller liberalization or consolidated democracy and are stuck in a low-level equilibrium. The question this literature asks is, why have these regimes not transitioned out of hybridity? The answer is they are, in fact, not partway through a transition. Indeed, Ottaway (2003, 3) contends that hybrid regimes are deliberately designed to "maintain the appearance of democracy without exposing themselves to the political risks that free competition entails." The absence of transition is therefore due to deliberate elite preference to resist reform in manner similar to Pritchett's "isomorphic mimicry."

Political change requires elite adaptation. Adaptation can be achieved if leaders enjoy the support of the people while simultaneously demonstrating they can allocate resources effectively and efficiently without political loss. Absent effective leadership and efficient resource allocation, stagnation and reversal will occur. Copans (1991) goes further by suggesting that prerequisites for stable political development entail an elite culture that enjoys a common political language that is autonomous from the state apparatus. Where intellectuals are integrated into the state bureaucracy, development will be curtailed. That is because intellectuals play a vital role in transmitting social reality through a vernacular that links society with the state and helps to legitimize the actions of the state. This rationale suggests that populations are unlikely to commit to reform if they do not see tangible improvements in local conditions, contributing to potential unrest, instability, or exit.

There are many examples of elites enthusiastically perpetuating stagnation. Observers have pointed to Egypt as a hybrid country that is "stable and can be sustained indefinitely, if there is astute political leadership and if the resources exist to keep public demands at bay" (Menocal, Fritz, and Rakne 2008, 32). Similarly, Brumberg (2005) notes that adopting hybrid models that utilize liberalized economies and pluralistic political systems actually helped entrenched elites maintain control in the Middle East prior to the Arab Spring. Elite gaming is essential even when those elites are under pressure to reform. So, for example, through economic liberalization, governments promote linkages between the government and different economic groups to avoid becoming beholden to any particular faction. Politically, Brumberg suggests that by providing social groups with a degree of freedom, state control is maintained by playing groups against each other. In such cases, partial liberalization can be seen as a strategy not for democratization but to sustain authoritarian control.

However, while superficially resembling a characteristic of a strong state, such elite bargaining does not, in fact, reflect stability. For example, Menocal, Fritz, and Rakne (2008) find that hybrid regimes tend to be both unstable and unpredictable in the face of exogenous shocks such as environmental calamity or economic collapse. Indeed, Marshall and Cole (2014, 21) state that hybrid regimes "very often reflect inherent qualities of instability or ineffectiveness and are especially vulnerable to the onset of new political instability events such as outbreaks of armed conflict, unexpected changes in leadership, or adverse regime changes." Menocal, Fritz, and Rakne (2008) argue that such instability is caused by the absence of a "principled" commitment to the rules of democracy by elites and the public.

In this regard, Chauvet and Collier (2008) examine the effects of various kinds of institutional processes in fragile states that make them more or less susceptible to regression and destabilization. Though their study focuses on the efficacy of democratization in fragile states, their findings apply equally well to other institutional processes. Theirs is an assumption that while democratization in fragile states does not necessarily have a beneficial effect on their economies, it is nevertheless a net benefit to the state because it promotes reform. That is because, as Bratton's (2007) study of informal and formal institutions shows, confidence in the democratizing process generates a greater degree of legitimacy for the regime (as can be seen in states where there was a change of regime following an election).[6]

Why is legitimacy so important? In examining the pathways to state failure, Goldstone (2008) shows that state stability is related to state effectiveness (how well a state carries out basic functions, including providing security, promoting economic growth, making laws, and delivering services) and legitimacy (the degree to which state actions are considered "reasonable," based on domestic social norms). For Goldstone, states with both effectiveness and legitimacy (even authoritarian regimes) are typically stable, while states that possess either effectiveness or legitimacy but not both may be prone to failure. Of particular interest to discussions of partially liberalized regimes, for instance, Goldstone suggests that while newly emerging democracies tend to have some legitimacy (although this can also be eroded in cases with severe corruption), they are generally ineffective and unable to provide economic and physical security to the larger populace, though their clients may benefit disproportionately. In these cases, "democracies that are perceived as ineffective are often replaced by military regimes in coups" (291). The result is democratic collapse similar to that seen in Nigeria in 1983 (Goldstone 2008). In sum, elites in fragile states work assiduously to maintain an equilibrium and resist reform as long as they have the resources and some level of popular support to do so.

UNDERSTANDING LEGITIMACY

As defined in the introduction, legitimacy is the extent to which a state commands public loyalty to a form of governance in order to generate domestic support for that government's legislation and policy through a voluntary and reciprocal arrangement of effective governance and citizenship founded upon broadly accepted principles of government selection and succession that are recognized both locally and internationally (Gilley 2016). One can think of legitimacy, first, as a process that engenders viable and lasting state-society relations, such as a just and fair legal system that improves the likelihood of compliance with the law (or input legitimacy) and, secondly, as an outcome from which society derives some lasting benefit, such as security or education (or output legitimacy). For example, basic institutional input legitimacy of a state may reflect mechanisms that are deemed necessary for facilitating a realization of those effective outcomes, while processes may relate to programs and policies that a state is willing to undertake in order to attain effective output legitimacy. Attitudinal and cultural perceptions of these processes and outcomes capture a related kind of state-society legitimacy because they represent a shared belief in a particular type of political order. When organized around forms of identity, community, class, or gender, these shared beliefs resonate within and impact the overall effectiveness of the political order (Lamb 2014). This definition of legitimacy is subject to debate, with some authors opting for adherence to Max Weber's interpretation of persons subject to a given authority recognizing it as right and feeling an obligation to obey it, while others define legitimacy according to the need for authorities to use coercion to avoid being disobeyed (Uphoff 1989; Lottholz and Lemay-Hébert 2016).

The importance of legitimacy in underpinning elite behavior cannot be stressed enough. Capacity trap countries fail to provide security and social services, and the net result is a failure to establish legitimacy. Legitimacy trap countries demonstrate a higher capacity to provide security and services to the population but suffer from weakening legitimacy due to expanding inequalities and authoritarian management (Grimm and Leninger 2012). In both instances, a lack of legitimacy entails greater coercion and various resources to force the population to obey the government. This weakness stems from a number of causes, such as a lack of representation or an inability to provide basic services (Gisselquist 2015).[7]

Weak legitimacy is important for a number of other reasons. Legitimacy's absence correlates strongly with weaknesses in the institutional processes that uphold rules, norms, and enforcement characteristics that collectively determine economic performance (North 1995; Carothers 2007; Goldstone and Ulfelder 2004). Institutional processes provide the normative legitimacy to formal rules that encourage and incentivize particular action across society (North 1990, 2005). In a similar vein, the actions of political elites and institutions perceived as unreliable or ineffective by the state's citizens, and thus illegitimate, contribute to popular dissent that weakens the state (see also Bräutigam and Knack 2004; Carment, Prest, and Samy 2008). Ismail (2016), using a social contract approach, argues that citizens delegate power to the state due to their own lack of capacity. If the government does not appear to be willing or able to fulfill performance expectations such as public goods and order, the population will not consider it to be legitimate and will be more likely to disobey it.

Pritchett, Woolcock, and Andrews (2013) go further by arguing that the legitimacy of fragile states' institutions requires animated and sustained support to indigenous systems of political and economic order. As North (2005, 161) notes, in understanding the inherent links between state and society, efforts to put in place formal rules in the absence of social acceptance "is a recipe for disappointment, not to say disaster." Indeed, North et al. (2007) warn that institutional change will fail if reforms do not account for local challenges pertaining to distribution or violence.

Perhaps the simplest explanation of the relationship between legitimacy and elites is that governments that are seen as illegitimate are forced to expend greater resources toward means of repression and coercion, weakening themselves in the process (Migdal 2001, contra Marquez 2015). Conversely, when ruled by a legitimate government, citizens can be expected to be more likely to defer to its authority voluntarily, rather than needing to be forced to obey. As Mitchell (2010) and Levi, Sacks, and Tyler (2009) write, while it is possible for a government that lacks legitimacy to rule solely through coercion, this is ultimately less effective and more difficult, and they cite the costs involved in surveillance and punishment relative to legitimate rule.[8]

In writing about horizontal inequalities, Stewart (2009) shows that the exclusion of certain groups from political and economic benefits can deeply undermine legitimacy. A key driver of deep fragility in this case would be the prevalence of exclusion and horizontal inequalities. At the same time, later efforts to reform these inequalities via direct action can be stymied by that same lack of legitimacy, South African apartheid and its subsequent abolishment being an example of this (Stewart and Brown 2009). In that case and others, policies meant to remedy these inequalities fail because the state does not have sufficient legitimacy. Other authors focusing on states that rely on foreign aid, particularly in sub-Saharan Africa, have noted that these states depend more on international legitimacy than domestic sources and are less likely to provide effective institutions and services as a result (e.g., Moss, Pettersson, and van de Walle 2006; Baliamoune-Lutz and McGillvray 2008). A disproportionate dependence on international support may actually weaken elite legitimacy (Djankov, Montalvo, and Reynal-Querol 2008; Tavares 2003).

Such research shows that trapped states such as Afghanistan need the government to be considered legitimate in order for at least some stability to be achieved, which in turn allows for more effective governance (Barakat, Evans, and Zyck 2012). More broadly, Bertocchi and Guerzoni's (2012) study of state fragility in sub-Saharan Africa in the 1992–2007 period found that restrictions on civil liberties increased the likelihood of fragility, being more significant than variables such as internal armed conflict and ethnic fractionalization. Schwarz and de Corral (2013), however, note that the loss of legitimacy that is expected to occur alongside such repression has been mitigated to an extent in a number of Middle Eastern states by using oil revenues to essentially buy support.

Similarly, Schwarz and de Corral (2016) find that states that spent natural resource revenues on social welfare to prevent a loss in legitimacy can potentially undermine their efforts to stay in power if they implement economic reforms that benefit regime cronies more than the general population (citing Egypt as an example). Deckard and Pieri (2016) study this further in the Nigerian context, noting that the apparent ineffectiveness of the government in defending citizens from armed groups such as Boko Haram has served to delegitimize its legitimacy in the eyes of the population.

LEGITIMACY, ELITES, AND THE FRAGILITY TRAP

Legitimacy is crucial for states to exit the fragility trap, but it can also perpetuate fragility if narrowly construed and tied solely to producing narrow outcomes. Coercive states with strong patron-client arrangements may be able to withstand further weakening of their authority and capacity structures and may even be able to prevent and withstand destabilizing shocks for a short period. But over time they, too, will face legitimacy challenges. This is because leaders who take advantage of uncertainty in the political system to consolidate their power base and provide benefits primarily to their political supporters are more likely to seek improvements in the legitimacy structures that favor their interests (McMann 2016). We call this "elite capture," the process whereby resources designated for the benefit of the larger population are usurped by a few individuals of superior status—be it economic, political, educational, ethnic, or otherwise.

Elite capture occurs because, on the one hand, leaders have to establish a power base that is broad and inclusive enough to fend off potential challengers. On the other hand, in order to maintain support from within their narrow political base, leaders have to show they are unwilling to compromise on fundamental policy issues. This can result in increasing fragility if the narrower political base prevails and generates narrow benefits for themselves. According to Bueno de Mesquita et al. (2003) and Bueno de Mesquita and Smith (2012), the nature of the benefits to be distributed to the political base will vary with the nature of the government. Open-access orders need to reward their base with public goods that benefit large parts of the population, as even a narrow political base in such systems will be too large to win over with private benefits. Limited-access orders, on the other hand, are able to survive with a smaller support base and can therefore use private benefits to tie their welfare to that of the current leadership.

Unfortunately, a government of a trapped state that lacks sufficient resources to retain these supporters is likely to lose its narrow power base, thus becoming vulnerable to destabilizing challenges (for specific arguments, see Knutsen and Nygård 2015). In an argument similar to that of Takeuchi, Murotani, and Tsunekawa (2011), Bueno de Mesquita and Smith (2012) contend that legitimacy is compromised when the state can no longer deliver resources, satisfying neither the narrow nor the broad political base. Reinforcing this point, Levi and Sacks (2009) show that a decline in the provision of public goods is often followed by decreasing voluntary compliance.

In essence, elite capture that diverts government spending from public goods and services to the interests of certain elites reduces both state capacity and authority and ends up undermining legitimacy (McLoughlin 2015). In this regard, François and Sud (2006), for example, propose that legitimacy is ultimately derived from government performance and its ability to fulfill core state functions. They consider poor governance to be the main underlying cause of fragility due to how it generates mass dissatisfaction, which can potentially lead to outright support for rebels. The OECD's (2010) report on state fragility highlights this point by showing that elites of the most fragile states tend to divert spending toward their own interests instead of public goods, noting that they often have little real interest in improving the state's capacity (and by extension its legitimacy). Ginsburg's (2008) study of democratic transitions in Asia highlights that the provision of widely available social goods played a key role in generating legitimacy for governments, while states that limited the distribution of goods ended up suffering greater political instability.

In most trapped states, elites benefit from undermining the state when they engage in corrupt rent seeking. Clardie (2011) finds that increased military spending, which is meant to ensure that military leaders will be satisfied, draws resources away from other state functions, undermining state legitimacy and reducing popular support for the government due to reduced service delivery. Gisselquist's (2015) study of state fragility in sub-Saharan

Africa similarly notes that a lack of government accountability mechanisms weakens legitimacy just as much as a lack of capacity because the perception that the government is only working for the interests of a small portion of the population leads to widespread dissent. As noted by Buterbaugh, Calin, and Marchant-Shapiro (2017), elite corruption was a major cause of the loss of legitimacy that led to the 2011 Arab Spring, alongside the ineffectiveness of Middle Eastern governments in actually providing public goods and services.[9]

Low service delivery is thus noticeable in political systems where there is limited access to political and economic functions, as it allows elites to use the system to stay in power and generate rents (North et al. 2007). Such arrangements usually lack legitimacy because institutions are used for political control rather than popular governance. Sudden shocks to the political system end up leading to violence when elites or the general population are dissatisfied with new arrangements in the distribution of resources (North et al. 2007).[10]

This chapter focused on the importance of theoretical and empirical efforts to measure and interpret legitimacy in the context of understanding why fragile states weaken or remain stagnant. Like Takeuchi, Murotani, and Tsunekawa (2011), we argue that legitimacy is crucial to explaining failures to exit. When a state fails to establish strong legitimacy even in the face of improved capacity, the risk it faces is closure of the political system even when growth is achieved. Related behavior includes rent seeking and elite capture as well as failures to incorporate undergoverned spaces and narrowly defined local elite interests. We also stressed the importance of interactions between legitimacy and other proposed components of state fragility. These include, for example, how ineffective or corrupt state institutions end up being considered illegitimate by citizens.

By conducting this analysis, we are better positioned to do a context-specific analysis of fragility drivers and clusters over time. In subsequent case study chapters, we specify how drivers of fragility are reflected in ALC clusters and assess their relative importance in determining a state's trajectory and the capacity of elites to mitigate these drivers of fragility if exacerbated. Case studies allow us to determine the value of feedback loops between two or more of our ALC constructs. In drawing up a list of potential cases for comparison, we draw two from each of the three types of states identified in the introduction: states that remain deeply fragile and trapped (type 1), states that exit fragility only to fall back into it (type 2), and states that exit the fragility trap (type 3). For each of the case studies, we use CIFP data to track their fragility rankings and ALC performance over a thirty-five-year period. For ease of interpretation and brevity, we identify the main inflection points over time and their relationship to A, L, and C, and relevant ALC interactions, in order to identify potential feedback loops. In the subsequent three chapters, we consider two cases of each type: Yemen and Pakistan for type 1, Mali and Laos for type 2, and Bangladesh and Mozambique for type 3.

Chapter 3

The Fragility Trap

Yemen and Pakistan—The MIFFs

Pakistan and Yemen provide contrasting examples of extremely fragile states. In this chapter, we examine the two fragility trap cases separately. We then compare our findings in the last section in light of the key drivers and structural transformations identified. We focus on drivers of fragility and elite decision-making. Though both have failed to exit the trap, they have taken substantially different paths over the last thirty-five years. On the one hand, Yemen originally chose not to participate in the GWOT, suffered the consequences, and has since fallen into collapse. On the other hand, Pakistan was a full partner in the GWOT. Its economy has since stabilized, while its political fortunes remain doubtful, as the long-term fallout from the war takes effect.

To be sure, Yemen's and Pakistan's causes of fragility can be traced well beyond 2001 and its ancillary events (Brehony 2011; Carment, Prest, and Fritzen 2007). Pakistan's leaders have emptied the country of strong legitimate rule over the past four decades. Yemen has experienced multiple civil wars, of which the most recent multidimensional conflict and humanitarian crisis is a continuation. Despite being among the most fragile countries in the world, both Yemen and Pakistan are not among the poorest. On the one hand, though it is the poorest in the Arab region, Yemen was until recently classified by the World Bank as a middle-income country or, as we have described it in the introduction, a middle-income failed and fragile state (MIFF). Simply put, Yemen's dysfunction is not a capacity problem but a legitimacy and authority one.

Pakistan's strong economic performance in the face of continued governance challenges also renders it a MIFF. CIFP's rankings have placed Pakistan in the top twenty fragile states in the world for most years over the past two decades. Pakistan's inability to control internal conflict, its environmental degradation, and the great inequality of its society have increased over time. The legitimacy of its government, whether civilian or military, continues to erode, and challenges from within increase. Developmental aid to Pakistan has been used to shore up a centralized authority structure. That reinforced authority structure, a kind of bureaucratic authoritarianism, has been in place since the 1950s. The apparent contradiction between Pakistan's continued growth in the face of internal conflict and domestic terrorist activities defies traditional development logic and raises important questions concerning governance factors, institutional design, and foreign aid, which simultaneously support development while entrenching fragility.[1]

YEMEN: THE POLITICS OF PERMANENT CRISIS

In 2003, an International Crisis Group (ICG) report noted that "Yemen has made substantial progress since its unification in 1990 and civil war in 1994. A nascent democracy with the most open political system in the Arabian Peninsula, its government has shown a general commitment to developing the instruments of a modern state" (ICG 2003). It is difficult to see how such an assessment could have been made considering that the country's fragility rankings have worsened since the 1990s. Indeed, we argue that the country's poor performance can be traced to a Yemeni leadership that has proven itself adept at exploiting the "politics of permanent crisis." Yemen's fragility trap is a function of mutually reinforcing structural constraints built around a rent economy. Ali Abdullah Saleh, president of Yemen for thirty-four years, carefully constructed a patronage system that provided benefits to a select few of his clients and clan

The Fragility Trap: Yemen and Pakistan

members (Clark 2010). But that narrow support base also constrained Saleh's ability to improve the country's economy—for example, through structural adjustments and improved social services. As long as resources were available, the regime was secure and did not need to reform, though the country itself remained deeply fragile. When those narrowly distributed benefits began to diminish, so too did Saleh's hold on power (Carment and Samy 2011). Ultimately the concentration of personal power and neglect of the periphery left the field open to new challengers, including disaffected southerners, Islamist groups, and the northern Houthi movement (Institute for Economics and Peace 2016).

Even before the country transformed into a sanctuary for extremists and despite modest overall economic performance, its people remain poor. The country ranked 133 out of 169 on the Human Development Index, with a per capita GDP of about $1,000, compared to an average of about $26,000 for the other Gulf states. Yemen's GDP annual growth average of 2.6 percent is far below the regional average of 5.9 percent (Carment 2011). Literacy and life expectancy are among the lowest in the world. There is a plethora of small arms scattered among Yemen's diverse tribal peoples, making security a major challenge.

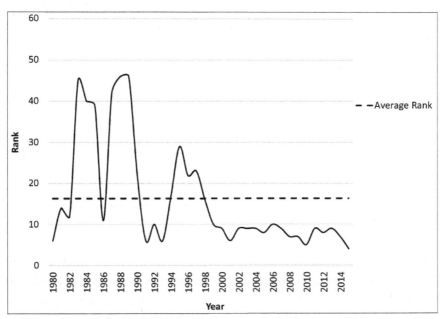

Figure 3.1 Yemen's fragility ranking, 1980–2014

Yemen has ranked in the top twenty most fragile states in most years since 1990. In examining figure 3.1, we see that the country's standing has deteriorated in the last twenty years. Prior to unification, Yemen experienced fluctuating, yet moderate, levels of fragility, generally ranking in the mid-forties each year except 1986. This increase in fragility corresponds to the South Yemen Civil War, which occurred the same year. Yemen experienced a sharp increase in fragility following unification, falling from a rank of forty-sixth in 1989 to sixth in 1990. Yemen's fragility rank remained low in the following years before increasing to twenty-ninth in 1995, marking a return to stability and growth that lasted until 1998 (Engers et al. 2002). In 1998, Yemen's fragility once again fell into the top twenty, receiving a rank of sixteenth and reaching a low of sixth by 2001. Yemen has remained among the top ten most fragile countries since then, falling to a low of fourth place in 2014 following the outbreak of civil war.

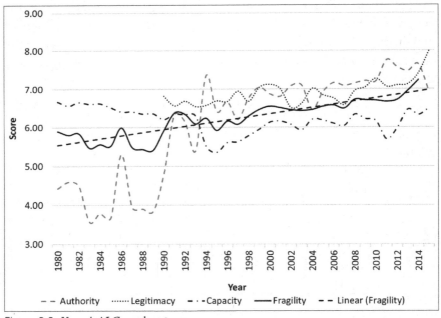

Figure 3.2 Yemen's ALC trends, 1980–2014

The ALC trend analysis in figure 3.2 shows that authority and legitimacy are the most important drivers of Yemen's fragility. Authority in particular is the most volatile cluster, varying from a low of 3.57 in 1983 to a high of 7.76 in 2011. Yemen's authority scores peaked in the postunification period

(1990–94) as well as before and during the 1994 civil war. Over the past decade, authority measures rose and fell with conflict and terrorist events, rising sharply with the increase in violence since 2010 (Almosawa and Kirkpatrick 2014; *Economist* 2015; BBC 2017). Yemen's legitimacy was relatively high over the same period, with scores remaining between 6.0 and 7.5 since data became available in 1990. Interestingly, Yemen's legitimacy scores were the poorest of the ALC variables in the postunification period, suggesting early challenges with regime support. Yemen's legitimacy scores remained relatively high throughout the 1990s, dipping slightly in 2001 corresponding to Yemen's support for the GWOT. Yemen's legitimacy scores deteriorated considerably during the 2000s, reaching a high of 7.42 in 2014. This decline corresponded with the declining legitimacy of Saleh's regime, his removal from power, and the success of the Houthis in seizing control of the government in 2015.

Adding to problems of political instability, Yemen has a very high population growth rate of 3.46 percent and an extremely large "youth bulge" of 46.4 percent of the population (Boley et al. 2017). More than 18 percent of its total labor force is unemployed, with higher rates in urban areas. Its urban population is growing at a rate double that of the total population, and city infrastructure is increasingly unable to handle that growth. Nearly half of Yemen's population lives below the poverty line with a daily income of $2.00 or less (Carment 2011). Although many natural resources are located in the south, a reduced portion of public funds from an unsympathetic government leaves southerners hindered by grinding poverty. An analysis of Yemen's budget during the Saleh period shows the regime's priority was military spending, an area dominated by Saleh's relatives. Military expenditures have been typically four times the amount spent on health care (Boley et al. 2017).

Until the precipitous drop in 2008, oil rents accounted for almost 90 percent of export earnings and around 70 percent of government revenue, making the country susceptible to internal shocks such as droughts and floods and external shocks such as oil price fluctuations. Based on current trends, oil reserves are expected to be depleted in less than fifteen years (Carment 2011). Yemen is one of the most water-scarce regions in the world, with water tables falling by about two meters a year, a rate of extraction that exceeds precipitation by about 70 percent. Without corrective action, groundwater supplies in Yemen's capital, Sanaa, are expected to be exhausted very soon and already are unsafe to drink. Some fifty thousand Somalis flee to Yemen each year, leading to the diffusion of their conflicts (Boley et al. 2017).

YEMEN'S STRUCTURAL TRANSFORMATION

History shows that Yemen's latest crisis is one of several that have plagued the country before and after reunification. For example, inconclusive border wars were fought between North Yemen and South Yemen in 1972 and 1979 (Dunbar 1992, 458). Over the next decade, cooperation remained elusive. Both the Yemen Arab Republic (YAR, or North Yemen) and the People's Democratic Republic of Yemen (PDRY, or South Yemen) wanted "unification" but under their tutelage; both states laid claim to the entirety of Yemen (ICG 2003). Furthermore, the two states had very different political systems. The PDRY was a Marxist state, nationalizing much of the economy, introducing land reform in rural areas, eroding tribal structures, and generally promoting a centralized and planned economy. The YAR by contrast was a conservative and autocratic state with a much more liberal economic system, where tribal leaders held significant power (Bertelsmann Stiftung 2006).

The fact that the two countries had distinctly different economic systems was more or less swept aside. Ministries were unified, but many tended to self-segregate, especially on social policy issues such as education and health. The upper echelons of the military were integrated, and there was some "trading" of units between north and south, but most of the troops remained divided along preunification lines (Dunbar 1992; Clark 2010).

When reunification was back on the table by the late 1980s, Yemenis in the south were openly criticizing the government for its antagonistic policy toward the north and marched in favor of unity. In the north, Saleh was personally invested in unification. He understood that he lacked a "big idea" to underpin the legitimacy of his rule and believed that achieving unification—itself a long-held idea among many Yemenis—would offer him that legitimacy. By 1989, Saleh had sufficiently consolidated power against northern tribal leaders, allowing him to pursue unification discussions. Indeed, unification was also seen as a way to further weaken tribal leaders' power (Clark 2010). The PDRY's comparative weakness, allowed the north to essentially impose many of the details of the unification agreement (EIU 2002). By early 1990, Saleh's forces, backed by tribal militias and returning mujahideen fighters from Afghanistan, seized the initiative and attacked the south. Despite calls for a cease-fire by the United Nations Security Council and other regional powers, Saleh pressed his advantage, and Aden fell on July 6, 1994, effectively ending the short war. In all, roughly fifteen hundred people had been killed and six thousand wounded in the seventy-day conflict (HRW 1994).

The 9/11 attacks had a significant impact on Yemen's political future. Saleh had opposed the stationing of troops on Yemen's soil for the purposes of liberating Kuwait as part of the Gulf War in the early 1990s, siding instead with Saddam Hussein's Iraq. This cost Yemen dearly in the international arena. Approximately 880,000 Yemeni migrant workers were expelled from various Persian Gulf countries and repatriated to Yemen in the span of a few months. The country not only lost remittance income but also had to find ways of incorporating a sudden influx of unskilled labor into the economy. It is estimated that the country's population increased by 7 percent during this period and its labor force grew by 30 percent. Saleh's initial opposition to the American-led coalition against Saddam Hussein led to Saudi Arabia and other Gulf countries expelling Yemeni migrant workers, with devastating economic consequences. For example, Yemeni migrant workers in Saudi Arabia, critical to the Yemeni economy, accounted for roughly $3 billion in remittances per year. Estimates are that between two hundred thousand and six hundred thousand were deported since 2003. Many of these countries also withdrew their aid around the same time (Colton 2010). When Saleh subsequently backed the United States in its GWOT, the realignment accorded him more international legitimacy abroad. Yet at home, the majority of Yemenis were opposed to such cooperation, and this further reduced his influence there. American intelligence activity against al-Qaeda suspects ramped up quickly, and Yemen saw mass arrests, detentions, and asset freezes. This move led to rising tensions among various tribal leaders. In December 2001, for example, an attempt by the government to arrest al-Qaeda suspects in the tribal-controlled area of Marib ended with twenty-four people killed, nineteen of whom were government soldiers (EIU 2002).

Many former fighters began attacking more moderate Muslim institutions and symbols in the south, especially targeting Sufi Muslims. The Yemeni government, eager to offset its secular left-wing political rivals in the south, tacitly supported and included radical Islamists in its governing coalition (ICG 2003). This climate allowed for the emergence and consolidation of groups such as al-Qaeda in the Arabian Peninsula (AQAP) and Ansar al-Sharia.

With American support, security forces began to gain the upper hand in the conflict with Islamist groups. Nevertheless, serious attacks increased. In October 2002, the French supertanker *Limburg* was bombed off the southeastern coast of Yemen. In December 2002, American missionaries were killed in a hospital in Jibla. In 2006, a jailbreak of senior militants in Sanaa signaled the consolidation of al-Qaeda in Yemen (later renamed al-Qaeda in the Arabian Peninsula [AQAP]). In 2007, a group of Spanish tourists were killed in a suicide bomb attack in Marib (EIU 2007). AQAP expanded its control in the southern Abyan Province, seizing the towns of Zinjbar and Jaar (Haddad and Bollier 2012).

By the time the situation had completely unraveled in 2011 and to preempt a growing crisis, the Gulf Cooperation Council (consisting of six of Yemen's Persian Gulf neighbors), with the backing of the United States, arranged a negotiated settlement in April that would see Saleh's departure and the transfer of power to the then vice president, Abd Rabbu Mansur al-Hadi. In June, Saleh was seriously wounded in a bomb attack on his presidential compound and was forced to leave for medical treatment in Saudi Arabia (*Telegraph* 2011). Following his forced departure in 2012, open fighting began between Houthi rebels on one side and, on the other, Salafi fighters and militants linked to the Islah political party and the Ahmar family.

While Saleh's formal resignation dampened reformist fervor, the security situation continued to deteriorate. In May 2012, a suicide attack killed approximately one hundred Yemeni soldiers as they were rehearsing for the National Unity Day parade. Assassinations and attacks on military leaders became commonplace: eighty-five middle- and high-ranking officers in the Yemeni military were killed in such attacks in the first half of 2013 alone. Over the same period, 115 attacks on the country's energy infrastructure were reported (Fattah 2014).

Nor did the support for the GWOT make Yemen immune to external influences. The rise in piracy off the Horn of Africa, for example, had a significant impact on Aden's economic activity. More recently, the regional rivalry between Saudi Arabia and Iran has been playing out in Yemen, with a Saudi-led coalition (backed by the United States and the United Kingdom) conducting air strikes in support of ousted president Hadi and Iranian support for the Houthis. Yemeni migrant workers were again expelled en masse from Saudi Arabia beginning in 2013, although the kingdom has relented since the conflict erupted in 2015 (HRW 2015).

Taking advantage of the deteriorating security situation, northern and southern secessionist insurgent groups have expanded their control. In particular, the Houthi rebellion, which began in 2004, has increased to the point where Houthi rebels occupied significant portions of the country. In February 2015, the Houthi advance forced President Hadi to flee the capital. The rebels quickly took control of the capital of Sanaa and the major port city of Aden. In March, a Saudi-led coalition responded to a request from Hadi for an intervention and began launching air strikes on Houthi positions (BBC 2015). The strikes failed to dislodge the rebels, although anti-Houthi forces saw some gains in Aden, and all cease-fire attempts have broken down. Over ten thousand people have died since the beginning of the air campaign, and over 80 percent of the population is now in need of humanitarian aid (BBC 2015).

YEMEN'S DRIVERS OF FRAGILITY

In turning to Yemen's drivers of fragility, we conclude that Yemen's fragility trap emanates from two main sources: undergoverned spaces and patronage politics tied to Yemen's rentier state status. Authority, legitimacy, and capacity performance are related to both in varying degrees. Politically, tribal identities have mixed with regional divisions, resulting in secessionist movements and conflicts that have plagued the country since the end of the civil war prior to unification. Islamist-inspired militant movements such as AQAP—and more recently groups linked to the Islamic State (IS)—have added to the challenge of maintaining security and stability in the country. The patron-client relationship established by Saleh after unification came under pressure as its chief sources of income, ranging from oil rents to remittances, weakened over time.

It is tempting to view the country's fragility as one of perpetual equilibrium carefully achieved through internal clientalism and external support. But that equilibrium had by 2011 started to give way to internal stresses that had built up over the previous decades. Not only was the Arab world's poorest nation challenged by mass protests, which had toppled tyrants in Egypt and Tunisia, brought civil war to Libya, and forced concessions from oil-rich despots in Bahrain and Saudi Arabia—it also became home to a resurgent al-Qaeda, a northern Shia uprising, and a revived southern secessionist movement. By 2012, Yemen had replaced Afghanistan as the most important al-Qaeda stronghold in the world (Carment 2011).

Nor is Yemen's fragility solely a result of Sunni-Shia sectarianism, although that fissure has more recently played a role. For example, the 2011 Arab Spring reenergized the Houthi movement (a Zaydi Shia movement), which led to the overthrow of the Saleh government. Abd-Rabbu Mansour al-Hadi took office as interim president in a transition led by a coalition of Arab Gulf states and backed by the United States.

Despite early optimism with the departure of Saleh and the announcement of a national dialogue to resolve tensions, the Hadi government struggled to maintain authority and summarily collapsed in 2015 when Houthi rebels seized control of the capital. Repeated air strikes by Saudi Arabia and other allies and regional and international political pressure failed to dislodge the rebels or contribute to a political solution, leaving the country in civil war in the midst of a humanitarian disaster.

Undergoverned Spaces

Yemen's authority trend line parallels the country's overall fragility line. This is largely because Saleh's government historically struggled to exert control in rural areas, especially in the south. This is not to say that the government enjoyed little influence in these areas but rather that its power projection was a function of continual negotiations, bribes, and bargaining with local authorities. Undergoverned spaces may be paramount in explaining Yemen's fragility trap, but it is important to note that they are inextricably linked with legitimacy issues. That is because Saleh's leadership ideology was one of regime survival. Saleh's legitimacy stemmed from two main factors: his ability to maintain stability and his ability to provide rewards to his clients based on rents from core industries. Over time, the inability to secure these rents undermined Saleh's legitimacy in the eyes of regional elites and the population they controlled.

For example, there were a number of cases where government soldiers were killed after entering areas without the permission of the local leadership (Phillips 2007). Undergoverned spaces are particularly evident in Yemen's worsening conflict and terrorism indicators. Despite significant government spending on its military apparatus, Saleh proved incapable of exerting influence in the hinterlands legally and institutionally (Brehony 2011).[2] This lack of power projection had specific impacts on the state's incorporation of displaced groups and minorities and ultimately their depoliticization, including the crippling of the government's ability to provide demographic and human development–related services and to enforce environmental and sound economic policies beyond the capital.

Although Saleh "won" the 1990s civil war, he was never able to fully control the south, continually confronting secessionist movements as time progressed. Though his regime deliberately sought out key Islamist figures, either in the governing coalition or the opposition coalition, many chose to remain outside his ad hoc power-sharing frameworks. In the 1990s, Yemen faced an influx of tens of thousands of former fighters from Afghanistan, many of whom formed their own groups in Yemen. AQAP may be the most prominent example of Islamist-based armed groups in Yemen, but it is not the only one.

Capacity functions as Yemen's stability ceiling. While Yemen's capacity scores are almost universally better than its fragility scores, they also move in tandem, increasing with fragility over time. The decline in capacity was inextricably linked to Saleh's inability to control territory and exert influence over the hinterland. In turn, as time progressed, the government's declining legitimacy was driven by its inability to reward concessions to regional elites over their control of the country's oil and gas sector. Lacking the ability to impose control over rural areas, the government relied on co-opting key leaders by incorporating them into the patronage system as well as buying off potential challengers in opposition (Fattah 2014).

The lesson that the Saleh regime appeared to have taken from the civil war is that too much democracy emboldens secessionism. His regime proved reluctant to open up the country politically. It curtailed and ultimately repressed many of the democratic promises made over the years. Only in the last few years of his hold on power was there any significant effort to bring peaceful regime change.[3]

Accommodation, democratization, and decentralization are often seen as solutions for moving a country away from this kind of limited-access authoritarianism. Yet there is little reason to believe "democracy" ever offered a way out for Saleh. Most of the country's major institutions were controlled by him and remained, after his departure, largely dysfunctional.

The country suffers from an underdeveloped and haphazard rule of law, uneven and inequitable economic development dividing the north and the south, an extremely corrupt civil service and judiciary, a weak educational system, poor service delivery, and a government that struggles to control excessive spending on the military (Carment 2011). Its leaders have been heavily dependent on foreign aid to finance budget deficits and development programs. Yemen's taxation system is almost nonexistent, meaning the government is accountable to few. Its weak agricultural sector, under threat due to water scarcity and a chronic inability to buy inputs such as fertilizer, puts at risk more than half of the country's economically active population that works in agriculture.

Patronage Politics

Based on patronage and clan loyalty, the political and economic structures that Saleh developed are textbook examples of a closed-access system (North et al. 2007). The incentives for Yemen's leadership to maintain the status quo were durable enough that any significant developmental reforms would require a destruction of the country's intricate system of patronage. Maintenance of this system required a delicate balancing between collaboration with the United States to ensure access to foreign aid while using the cover of antiterrorism to suppress opposition to Saleh's regime. The net result was highly centralized personal power with decentralized governance and weak institutions.

How this came to be can be traced back to the 1990 unification of "republican" North Yemen with the formerly Marxist South Yemen. The civil war that followed in 1994 ensured the domination of Saleh's northern forces and his tribe's control of the country's political institutions. Saleh then established an intricate network of patron-client relations in the north, while largely ignoring the economically weaker south. With respect to patronage, Saleh's government was heavily influenced by al-Qaeda Arabs, jihadists who fought for him in the 1994 civil war after their return from Afghanistan. Saleh also faced continued rebellion in the north from a band of very capable Shiite rebels in the Saada region on the border with Saudi Arabia.

Northerners, especially members of his tribe, dominated the most important government posts, but he did include a mixture of southerners and prominent Islamists. The opposition, while standing up to the regime on some issues, mainly existed to extract concessions within the patronage system (Phillips 2007). Such a system meant that corruption was pervasive, which further reduced the government's legitimacy.

Indeed, much of the country's economic activity, and by extension its patron client system, has been driven by two sectors: the hydrocarbon industry and the khat industry, both of which have had negative long-term impacts as their outputs decline. The country has limited known oil reserves, and rents fell precipitously starting in 2008. Since Yemen's water supply remains critically low, the water-intensive khat industry also weakened over time. Such problems could have been offset by economic diversification, but the incentive for reform was minimized by the gains for elites who benefited from the status quo (Fattah 2014). A third economic input—namely, the reduction in remittances following the expulsion of Yemeni migrant workers from Iraq in the early 1990s—made the country even more reliant on the hydrocarbon industry.

To be sure, from 1990 to 1992, authority and capacity scores improved, peaking in 1994 before beginning the trend of gradual deterioration. Both North and South Yemen were facing significant financial/economic problems before unification, and the discovery of oil deposits in the late 1980s provided an opportunity for the newly unified state to generate economic activity and for its elites to gain rents from that activity. Policies were enacted, including protections for press freedom and universal suffrage, even though both states beforehand had been one-party states. A fifty-fifty power-sharing arrangement had been agreed upon by the YAR and the PDRY, despite the former being almost four times the size of the latter in terms of population.

In this atmosphere, the 1992 elections, owing to demographic realities, reduced the south's influence in parliament. The Yemen Socialist Party (YSP) lost its 50 percent share in these elections, and Saleh seized the opportunity to nullify the previous power-sharing arrangement. This development reflected a fundamental bargaining problem faced by the two rivals agreeing to power sharing. In a limited-access system, it is difficult for elites to make concessions that would undermine their base of support. Accountability is achieved when each side has assurances their side has adequate and even favorable representation. Saleh's decision, while tactically shrewd, essentially committed his government to the path of dominating the south while simultaneously neglecting it.[4]

PAKISTAN: TRAPPED AT BIRTH

Pakistan, a country of just over two hundred million people, has struggled to establish legitimacy since its independence from former British India in 1947 (Carment, Prest, and Fritzen 2007). Pakistan has undergone three military coups (1958, 1977, and 1999) and is caught up in a series of unending conflicts over the controversial Kashmir region and the contested Federally Administered Tribal Areas (FATA) (Mazerra and Aftab 2009. Despite these challenges, Pakistan has made significant economic gains since 2000, almost quadrupling its GDP from $73 billion in 2000 to $269 billion in 2015. This growth led Pakistan to attain lower middle-income status in 2008 (World Bank 2016b). While Pakistan is predicted to continue experiencing relatively high rates of economic growth, reaching 4.5 percent and 4.8 percent over the 2016 and 2017 fiscal years (Asian Development Bank 2016), it simultaneously remains one of the most dangerous countries in the world (Institute for Economics and Peace 2016; *Economist* 2008).

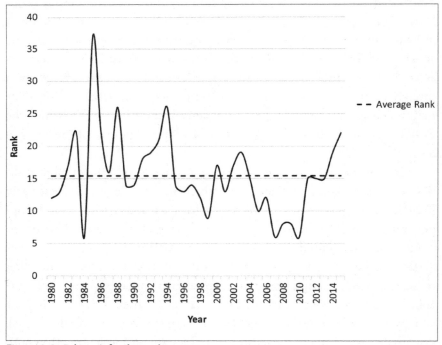

Figure 3.3 Pakistan's fragility ranking, 1980–2014

The Fragility Trap: Yemen and Pakistan

As seen in figure 3.3, several of Pakistan's most notable declines in fragility rankings are linked to regime change. For instance, in the years following President Muhammad Zia-ul-Haq's death in 1988 and the reemergence of civilian government, Pakistan fell to fourteenth in terms of global fragility. Similarly, in 1999, the year of President Pervez Musharraf's infamous coup and conflict in the Kashmir region, the state of Pakistan's fragility declined to ninth in the world. More recently, Pakistan reached a low fragility rank of sixth in both 2007 and 2010. That rank in 2007 corresponds to mass protests in response to the suspension of Chief Justice Iftikhar Muhammad Chaudhry, the Red Mosque disaster, and Musharraf's declaration of a state of emergency. In 2010, the low fragility rank corresponds to Pakistan's flood disaster and a marked rise in sectarian violence.

Since 2010, Pakistan has made modest improvements to its fragility rank, moving up to twenty-second in 2015. Despite uncertain aggregate gains, it is important to note that over the period 1980–2015, Pakistan had an average fragility rank of fifteenth, firmly in the top twenty most fragile states. Despite episodes of relative stability (and except for 2015), Pakistan has not broken out of the top twenty most fragile countries since 1994 and has been "trapped" in fragility over the past two decades. Despite high growth, Pakistan faces a range of development challenges in the areas of primary school enrollment, health expenditure, and respect for human rights. Pakistan is ranked 147th out of 188 countries on the 2016 UNDP Human Development Index. High numbers of refugees hosted further exacerbate tensions in certain areas of the country.

In reviewing Pakistan's ALC trend lines in figure 3.4 we observe consistently poor performance since 1980, with fragility scores that fluctuated between 5.6 and 6.7. Pakistan's authority score showed an initial spike in 1984 following General Zia's implementation of martial law before falling in subsequent years. From 1995 onward, however, Pakistan's authority scores increased and began to hover above 6.5, the cutoff for high fragility, with scores exceeding that in each year that followed. After authority and legitimacy peaked in 1998–99, Pakistan's legitimacy scores dipped in 2002–3, signaling a slight overall improvement but continued challenges to security and stability. This decline appears to be linked most closely to a decline in Pakistan's legitimacy score, as Musharraf launched a 2003 referendum to extend his time in power. Musharraf won the vote, receiving forty million votes out of forty-three million votes cast, increasing regime legitimacy by securing the popular vote.

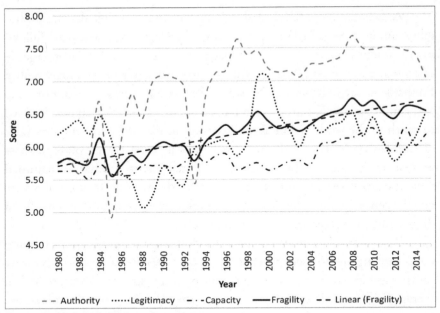

Figure 3.4 Pakistan's ALC trends, 1980–2014

In the years that followed, Pakistan's overall fragility scores further deteriorated, peaking again in 2008 and 2010. In 2008, the change in fragility scores were correlated with spikes in legitimacy and authority. This reflects political turmoil and uncertainty in the aftermath of Musharraf's political defeat as well as a declining security situation as violence escalated in the FATA region. Further, the slight spike in Pakistan's fragility score in 2010 was driven by rising capacity scores and reflected the government's response to mass flooding, where increasing scores suggested an inability to effectively respond to this disaster. The next few years saw a slight decline in overall fragility to 6.4 in 2012 before rising to 6.5 the following years. These changes closely mirror changes in Pakistan's capacity, suggesting that deterioration was driven by the poor response to natural disaster following a 7.7 magnitude earthquake, which hit Pakistan in September 2013, ongoing bombings in city centers, sectarian violence, a deterioration in service delivery, and increasing economic inequality.

PAKISTAN'S STRUCTURAL TRANSFORMATION

In an effort to explain Pakistan's pattern of fragility, we argue that at its core the challenge facing Pakistan is one of legitimacy. Pakistan's inability to manage ethnic tensions, to reduce internal conflict, to regulate environmental deprivation, and to address increasing inequality are matched by poor legitimacy rankings. Pakistan's legitimacy is closely tied to the kinds of ethnic and economic policies it pursues. Narrow policies favoring one group are ultimately less sound than broad distributive ones. In the absence of strong, secular organized parties and strong institutional structures, state-society relations become the focus for understanding Pakistan's deterioration. Ultimately it has been the state's actions that are directly responsible for the erosion of Pakistan's political system (Center for Systemic Peace 2010).

Drawing on insights from Brass (1985) and Kohli (1990) among others, we argue that the Pakistani state does not merely respond to crises produced by uneven ethnic mobilization and social change but is itself the dominating force, providing differential advantages to regions and ethnic groups. The net result is a pernicious feedback loop in which the central government's policies in the form of entitlements for majority groups encourage minority groups to organize for political action and confrontation. In turn, these challenges generate greater resistance to change from the state-center.

In examining Pakistan's main structural transformations, we highlight several crucial points in the country's development. Pakistan emerged as an independent state in August 1947 in response to calls by Muslims seeking a homeland separate from Hindu-dominated British India (Ahsan 2003). Muhammad Ali Jinnah, a former member of the Indian National Congress and leader of the All-India Muslim League, rallied Muslims to the cause of separatism around the belief of a discrete Muslim identity (Ganguly 2008). Governance challenges emerged shortly after separation as structural weaknesses of the Pakistani national movement—namely, the presence of considerable sectarian, linguistic, and religious differences across the Muslim territory—made crafting a free political order and functional state a difficult task (Ganguly 2008).

In particular, the question surrounding the role of Islam in the new state was a key challenge. Critical decisions concerning the choice of national language were used in an attempt to bind disparate sections of the country. Urdu was adopted, despite only 7 percent of the population considering it their mother tongue (Ganguly 2008).[5] Simultaneously Pakistan adopted a system of parliamentary democracy inherited from the British. Yet persistent civilian and military manipulation of democratic structures contributed to a dysfunctional system (Mazeera and Aftab 2009). Most important, Pakistan's Kashmir conflict not only shaped Pakistan's relations with India, it also contributed to the military's dominance of domestic politics (Carment 2003; Weiner 1971; Schofield 2011). For example, Pakistan's first coup attempt in 1951 was led by Maj. Gen. Akbar Khan in response to the civilian mishandling of the Kashmir issue (Shah 2008). In the years that followed, the army's belief in the incompetence of civilian government, which frequently called on the military to aid civil missions, further exacerbated civil-military tensions. In 1958, following the first national party elections that appeared to shift power to civilian politicians, the military, led by Gen. Ayub Khan, seized power (Shah 2008).

The crushing defeat of Pakistan's military at the hands of the India-supported Bangladeshi opposition in 1971 brought with it a period of relative stability as the discredited military was replaced by the democratically elected Pakistan People's Party (PPP), led by Prime Minister Zulfiqar Ali Bhutto (Shah 2008). In 1973, Bhutto introduced a new constitution and sought to "coup-proof" the government by purging potentially disloyal soldiers, creating constitutional barriers, and reducing the army's dominance over defense policy by establishing a committee for defense command (Shah 2008). In 1977, electoral deadlock gave way to Pakistan's second military period as General Zia seized power from the Bhutto government. Zia declared martial law, which was eventually rescinded in 1985.

Throughout the 1970s, Islam was used indiscriminately to garner support from the religious right. In the mid-1970s, for example, the quintessentially secular Bhutto began using Islam to build electoral support and legitimacy for the regime by banning the sale and consumption of alcohol (Mazeera and Aftab 2009). Upon gaining control in 1977, Zia created parallel Islamic courts and declared that Islamic laws would be enforced in efforts to establish the Islamic society for which Pakistan had initially been created (Ganguly 2008). In 1979, Zia introduced the Hudood Ordinance, which allowed the use of Sharia-based punishment for liquor use, theft, and adultery (Mazeera and Aftab 2009) The media was also included in Zia's Islamicization campaign, as Arabic news bulletins were introduced and female anchors were required to wear veils.

During his eleven years in power, Zia introduced the Eighth Amendment to Pakistan's constitution, giving the president the power to dismiss the National Assembly in instances where the prime minister has lost the confidence of the House or if situations prevented the government from continuing in accordance with the constitution (Marshall and Cole 2010). In 1988, Zia's death in a "mysterious" plane crash that also killed the US ambassador to Pakistan paved the way for a third democratic period.

From 1988 to 1999, civilian governments alternated between the PPP, led by Benazir Bhutto (daughter of the former prime minister), and Nawaz Sharif's Pakistani Muslim League (PML-N). Bitter rivals over the period, each attempted to use the state's authority, particularly anticorruption bodies, to undermine the political opposition (Mazeera and Aftab 2009). In the years that followed, both Bhutto and Sharif would be exiled on charges of corruption (Center for Systemic Peace 2010). While the military generally did not interfere with daily domestic politics, it continued to play an influential role in international affairs and through its influence was able to force the resignations of both elected prime ministers (Center for Systemic Peace 2010).

This period also saw an exacerbation of religious and ethnic tensions in some regions. Tensions between religious sects rose as religio-political parties sought to realign themselves following a loss in the 1993 national elections (Malik 1996). Conflict between two parties, Anjuman-i-Sipah-i-Sahaba-i-Pakistan and Tehreek-i-Nafaz-i-Fiqah-i-Ja'afria, which championed Sunni and Shia causes, respectively, escalated to sporadic violence, while other parties, including Jama'at-i-Islami and Hamiat-i-Ulama-i-Islam, "demanded a *jihad* against India and Kashmir and a more interventionist Pakistani role in the ongoing Afghan civil war" (Malik 1996, 674).

Ethnic polarization, especially in Karachi, was an ongoing problem as the Muhajir Qaumi Movement (MQM) mobilized descendants of Muslim immigrants from India in a refusal to cooperate with the civilian administration. In 1992, the military looked to impose peace in Karachi as the administration was unable to control regional ethnic disputes. Further strife erupted following the withdrawal of troops from the area in 1994.

The 1990s also witnessed increasing corruption and politicization of democratic institutions, particularly the state judiciary (Diamond 2000). The period was marked by the "personalization" of executive powers and the "politicization" of criminal prosecutions, which brought the political use of the judiciary to a new low (Diamond 2000). In the late 1990s, the justice system was used by the Sharif regime as a tool to "destroy" Bhutto's opposition party, while supposed efforts to fight terrorism resulted in the abuse of civil liberties and the creation of military courts by the ruling regime (Diamond 2000).

In early 1999, conflict again erupted in the Kashmir region after India launched air strikes against forces backed by Pakistan that had infiltrated the Indian-administered region, apparently without the full knowledge of the Pakistani government. The conflict ended after Prime Minister Sharif ordered the withdrawal of insurgents following pressure from the United States. Later that year, when an "enraged" Sharif attempted to sack General Musharraf for his handling of the Kashmir crisis, Sharif was unseated by the military, marking the beginning of Musharraf's reign (Shah 2008; Tudor 2014).

Musharraf's ascension to role of president was followed by a crackdown that reduced civil liberties, saw the arrest and torture of opposition politicians, restricted media outlets, and banned public rallies (Shah 2008). While political parties were allowed to operate during this period, their influence was curtailed by party factionalism, a lack of leadership, and intense government control (Center for Systemic Peace 2010). Musharraf used a lateral-entry policy to appoint twelve hundred military officers to senior positions within the government. The combination of silencing political opponents and restricting political liberties would eventually challenge the legitimacy of the general's regime.

In 2001, President Musharraf's decision to support the American antiterrorism campaign in Afghanistan coincided with a crackdown on Islamic-driven political actions in Pakistan (Center for Systemic Peace 2010). While radical Islamic nationalism had enjoyed the support of past governments seeking to enhance support for policies and deflect opposition to historically poor economic performance, the rise of radical parties and pressure from international efforts focused to reduce the power of Islamic groups (Center for Systemic Peace 2010).

Ethnoregional rivalries in Pakistan remained an ongoing challenge throughout this period. Political advantages enjoyed by the majority Punjabi ethnic group harbored resentment that resulted in violence, particularly from Sindhi and Baluchi minorities seeking greater autonomy and control over provincial resources (Brown et al. 2012). At the same time, sectarian violence between the Sunni majority and Shiite minority dating back to General Zia's government remained a challenge.

In 2007, opposition to Musharraf's prolonged rule pressured the government to open discussions with exiled prime minister Benazir Bhutto, a supporter of democratic rule in Pakistan. The pair are said to have reached a deal prompting her return to Pakistan. Following Bhutto's return,

Musharraf announced a successor to his role of military chief and lifted his state of emergency on December 15 after securing his place as president. Shortly afterward, Bhutto was assassinated.

In early 2008, Musharraf was defeated in legislative elections by a coalition of PPP and PML-Q forces led, respectively, by Asif Ali Zardari (the widower of Benazir Bhutto) and Nawaz Sharif. Despite renewed political hope in the aftermath of the election, which was seen as the end of "dictatorship" and a step toward new "democracy," 2008 was marked by escalating violence and political discord (Nelson 2009; Carment, Prest, and Fritzen 2007). At the same time, the new government faced escalating unrest in the FATA region and international pressure for Pakistan to increase military action against Taliban and al-Qaeda affiliates (Nelson 2009).

After facing a declining security situation that saw more than two million people displaced due to fighting between the military and Taliban forces, Pakistan's highly populated Indus River Valley was hit with the worst flooding the country had seen in eighty years (Oxfam America 2010; BBC 2016). More than seventeen hundred people were killed in the floods, and more than two thousand more were injured (Oxfam America 2010). The floods had drastic economic effects, causing an estimated $25 billion to $40 billion in damages to housing and public infrastructure and destroying 20 percent of Pakistan's cropland.

DRIVERS OF FRAGILITY

The story of Pakistan's sustained fragility is identified by three drivers that underlie continued bouts of violence, insecurity, underdevelopment, and instability. Most notably, these drivers focus on elite manipulation of ethnic and religious identities, elite capture, and bureaucratic authoritarianism.

Social Cleavages

Pakistan's ethnic, linguistic, regional, and sectarian diversity has presented a key challenge to stability in Pakistan. The problem is as old as Pakistan itself (Ganguly 2008). While Pakistani leaders sought to build a national identity capable of uniting citizens, its traumatic history has "challenged the idea of Pakistan as a unified nation-state with fixed boundaries and shared identities" (Mazeera and Aftab 2009, 16). In particular, elite manipulation of ethnic identity has contributed to several violent episodes throughout the country's history. Of Pakistan's five ethnic groups that were present at independence, Bengalis, Punjabis, Pashtuns, Sindhis, and Baluchis, four have actively contested the legitimacy of the administrative structure of the state, with one, the Bengalis, succeeding in breaking away and creating their own state, Bangladesh (Khan 2005; Carment 2003). Additionally, the continuous breakdown of political pacts between central authorities and Baluchistan elites have resulted in in sustained violence (Brown et al. 2012; Hasan 2016). The most recent breakdown and call for separation of a Baluchi state reached a phase of negotiation in 2014 (Hasan 2016), but recent violence has caused the security situation to deteriorate.

Ethnic tensions are further exacerbated by the relatively privileged position of one ethnic group, the Punjabis, who enjoy political advantages and remain relatively more prosperous than other groups (Mushtaq 2009). Notably, the Punjabis have dominated Pakistan's economy and political system as well as Pakistan's armed forces, with some estimates suggesting that 75 percent of military personnel are Punjabi (Mazeera and Aftab 2009). Such domination has led one commentator to note that "Punjab can thus be seen both as the cornerstone of the country and as a major hindrance to national integration," pitting the privileged center against the provinces (Talbot 2002, 51). Ethnic fissures coupled with the political dominance of Punjabi and Sindhi people has, at times, left minorities feeling alienated from the state, contributing to poor state legitimacy and contributing to violence (Carment 2003; Diamond 2000; Carment, Prest, and Fritzen 2007)

Coupled with the centralization of power and unrepresentative nature of Pakistani regimes, such dominance has led to backlashes against central authorities who are said to exploit provincial resources for personal gain (Haqqani 2004). Control over natural resources and the perceived dominance of the central government has been a source of tension contributing to the Baluchistan conflict (Brown et al. 2012). Pakistan's ongoing water-supply crisis has further highlighted this tension as provinces blame Punjab for appropriating the bulk of the country's water supply.

Sectarian tensions between Shia and Sunni Muslims have been called "the most destabilizing factor for the country's political, social, religious and security order" (Afzal, Iqbal, and Inayat 2012, 19). Episodes of sectarian violence are littered throughout Pakistan's history and across all provinces. Such violence has tended to follow policies of "Islamization" used by various governments to unify the state and overcome ethnolinguistic differences, such as the policies introduced by Zia in the late 1970s. More recently, external pressures, the rise of extremism, and spillover from the war in Afghanistan have exacerbated sectarian tensions and related conflict in Pakistan (Afzal, Iqbal, and Inayat 2012).

In sum, while a common Islamic identity is often called upon to create unity, violence between religious sects has "dealt an additional blow to political stability, [and] escalat[ed] the overall levels of violence, terrorism, and insecurity," reflecting a rejection "of the legitimacy of the democratic system" (Diamond 2000, 93; Haqqani 2004).

Elite Capture

While social cleavages appear to contribute to continued violence, ongoing elite dominance in Pakistan has contributed to fragility by perpetuating elite capture of both political institutions and resources. Historically, wealth and, subsequently, power have been concentrated in a small group of elites and the military—namely, from the Punjabi and, to some extent, the Sindhi ethnic groups. For instance, in the 1960s, 66 percent of industrial wealth and 87 percent of insurance and banking wealth was held by just twenty-two families (Easterly 2001). In the years that followed, growth in the manufacturing and agricultural sectors disproportionately benefited the dominant class (Malik 2012).

The power of such elites is so great that they have continually, and successfully, used political institutions to serve personal rather than public interests. Pakistan's elite have maintained political control in Pakistan since its birth. Indeed, the "patrimonial elite has been able to use its control over economic and social resources to maintain their position of authority in successive Pakistani governments" (Mazeera and Aftab 2009, 25). Once in power, officials typically use their power to advance personal interests and sustain their rule.

In particular, elites appear to have captured key institutions crucial for democracy, including the electoral process, the judiciary, and the constitution. In terms of elections, elite control appears pervasive (Carment, Prest, and Fritzen 2007). In addition to Zia's martial law, Musharraf's 2002 election, designed to enhance his legitimacy as the country's political leader, was considered "deeply flawed" by international observers due to the presence of "pre-poll rigging" by Musharraf's military (Shah 2003). While more recent elections held in 2013 have been heralded as "free and fair," some have alleged the presence of electoral fraud (Tudor 2014).

Perhaps more insidiously, the elite have sought to ensure their rule through a series of changes to Pakistan's constitution and judiciary designed to suit their specific needs (Mazeera and Aftab 2009; Carment, Prest, and Fritzen 2007). Since achieving independence in 1973, Pakistan has drafted three different constitutions, the most recent of which has been amended seventeen times in five decades. During civilian control in the 1990s, Pakistan's judiciary became increasingly corrupt. Moreover, Pakistan's judiciary does not possess strong independence and has routinely been used by the political executive to retain power. For instance, the judiciary approved each of the seventeen constitutional amendments, including a 1985 amendment that gave Zia the right to dismiss the National Assembly, in essence legitimizing the coup. Such "personalized" use of governance institutions to pursue private interests has demonstrated clear abuses of power and further reduced the legitimacy of Pakistan's political institutions.

In terms of resources, increasing inequality as a result of Pakistan's economic growth highlights the economic dominance of ruling elites (Jamal 2009). Dominance over economic resources and power has contributed to continued service-delivery deficiencies. Despite general hardship for the population, there is no urgency for elites to reform government, provide public services, or extend equitable justice as long as the system continues to serve elite interests (Kaplan 2013). For instance, there is little incentive for Pakistan's elite to revise taxation laws that block direct taxation on agricultural income typically earned by the ruling elite, placing the brunt of the taxation burden (80 percent) on the urban poor and middle class (Malik 2012).

Elite control of resources also explains Pakistan's poor development progress in spite of strong economic growth. There are limited efforts to reform because aid has historically not been sufficiently focused and selective enough. Some suggest that slow progress toward development is driven by elite desires to suppress human capital development, thereby providing a cheap source of labor. For instance, Easterly (2001) finds clear differences in educational attainment across gender and class, suggesting that such differences could be interpreted as the manifestation of elite dominance, whereby elite classes attempt to perpetuate low literacy in efforts to retain control. In 2010, the Pakistani government made education a basic right and promised to increase education spending, suggesting a desire to support human development in Pakistan. Few tangible improvements have been achieved (UNDP Pakistan 2014).

In sum, Pakistan's high legitimacy challenges are being driven by issues arising from elite capture. Poor capacity emanates from perverse incentives that allow elites to be taxed minimally while reaping the benefits of public money. Similarly, the incentive for elites to limit literacy indicate that low capacity and underdevelopment are linked to elite rule.

Bureaucratic Authoritarianism

The perpetuation of elite rule in politics actively limits democracy promotion by facilitating a bureaucratic and military culture based on patrimonial linkages, corrupt practices, and diminished judicial autonomy. All these hinder the legitimacy of Pakistani state institutions (Carment, Prest, and Fritzen 2007). Traditional political analysis believed that countries with low or minimal political culture were the most susceptible to bureaucratic authoritarianism. Huntington (1968) describes a "praetorianism." Indeed, since independence Pakistan has been witness to a cycle of "praetorianism" in which its diverse social heterogeneity and overdeveloped authority structures resulted in departicipation, power concentration, and patron-client relations (Schofield 2011). At independence, the initial solution to hinterland disengagement was to reorganize Pakistan's Muslim League along populist lines in pursuit of apparent and open democratization (Brown et al. 2012).

In reality, the provinces demonstrated increased independence as conflict with India escalated over time (Schofield 2011). Indeed, for Pakistan's elites the answer lay not in democratization but in responding to defense imperatives as India simultaneously increased its war potential. Thus, the emerging disjunction between state authority and established notions of representative government led to positions of power within nonelected, mainly bureaucratic, and military institutions rather than bases of support within society. The sum total of Pakistan's ongoing conflict with the provinces confirms this institutional imbalance and weak political identity.

Pakistan's bureaucratic authoritarianism has two main influences: instrumental, the achievement of rapid economic growth, and consummatory, a resort to Islamic appeal within a controlled electoral process. For Pakistan's elites, it was apparent that the military was crucial in finding a balance between the two. A combination of elite capture and rapid economic growth engendered widespread economic polarization that in turn created a need for political order, which the military would provide. Appeals to Islam would give structure and meaning to the military's direct involvement in public affairs. The net result was intervention of the military in domestic affairs, a process justified by economic agendas wherein the resort to Islam was a political tactic to achieve social cohesion. This interplay between civilian and military rule was exemplified in the coups and military regimes of 1958–62, 1969–71, and 1977–85 and into the 1990s.

To be sure, there were partial exceptions to this general pattern. Rizvi (1991), for example, notes that with Bhutto's victory in 1988 there was a perceived desire to limit the military's role in driving the economy. Thirty years later, similar desires would be played out under Musharraf when he rose to power. Why this break from the cycle of coups and praetorianism took place at these points in Pakistan's history relates to a number of factors. According to Cohen (1984), Pakistan has never been able to overcome its polarization between an urban population and its Western institutions and a rural population largely disengaged from the country's political economy. Similarly, others have suggested that military dominance is a reflection of deep ethnic cleavages (Horowitz 1985; Harrison 1981) and a persistent inability to properly manage them, including the absence of a working federal political order.

Initially, Islam was seen as the ideology that would help legitimize accommodation between state and society. But Pakistan's intraregional diversities proved so great that even Islam fell short of providing a complete worldview for a rural population economically and politically marginalized. Regional cultures further divided by class, caste, clan rank, and privilege divided rather than united. Similarly, those politicians like Bhutto who pursued a secular identity for Pakistan only helped undermine the legitimacy of Islam, thus further generating a tension between progressive Islam and religious leaders who saw Islam as a basis for social engineering through education and language selection.

Within this cycle of increasing and decreasing levels of fragility, processes and policies were initiated by elites to bring Pakistan out of its trap. Chief among these is the civilianization process begun in 1985 and ongoing two decades onward. If Pakistan has been for much of its history a state dominated by nonelected institutions—namely, the military and the bureaucracy—it remains evident that transformation to elected institutions is unlikely. This is partly because the justification for Pakistan's military domestic role continues to dominate, whether that is in addressing regional grievances, confronting Pakistan's precarious relations with India and Afghanistan, quelling disaffected youth and urban unrest, or confronting terrorism.

Externally, the risks that Pakistan poses have been shaped by its historical rivalry with India and influence over Afghanistan. In addition to supporting separatist movements in India, Pakistan has provided sanctuary, training, and arms to other hotbeds of conflict throughout Asia, including the mujahideen in Afghanistan during the war against Soviet occupation. US policy toward Pakistan is best exemplified by the long-term aid programs of Presidents George W. Bush and Barack Obama as a result of its support for allies in the GWOT. At the height of the war in Afghanistan, the United States was willing to turn a blind eye to Pakistan's internal problems in exchange for its support in fighting al-Qaeda. That effort coincided with a crackdown on Islamic-driven political actions in Pakistan (Center for Systemic Peace 2010).

In addition, the alliance forged by the United States and the Musharraf regime against "global terror" hindered the Pakistani government's authority over the contested FATA bordering Afghanistan and the Baluch region (Carment, Prest, and Fritzen 2007; Brown et al. 2012). Despite officially falling under Pakistani control, such regions, particularly North and South Waziristan, remain linked to Afghanistan in practice (Carment, Prest, and Fritzen 2007). The region soon became a "safe haven" for terrorist networks, a training and recruiting ground for the Afghan Taliban, and a breeding ground for indigenous militancy (Schofield 2011). From 2004 to 2007, the Pakistani government was engaged in sustained fighting in the region against al-Qaeda militants. But that proved ineffective partly because Pakistan's engagement in the GWOT proved destabilizing because it provided the rhetoric to turn jihadists directly against the Pakistani state (Center for Systemic Peace 2010; Grare 2013).

In 2011, after a ten-year hunt, Osama bin Laden was killed by US special forces. There was considerable debate whether Pakistan's Inter-Services Intelligence organization (ISI) had been knowingly sheltering bin Laden, given that he resided in the country for over nine years. Debate also focused on the legality of the killing, with Obama and Bush administrators condoning the act not as a state-sponsored assassination but as an act of self-defense. From about 2004 to 2013, the Bush and Obama administrations conducted numerous targeted killings in Pakistan of known al-Qaeda operatives. The killings, mostly using drones, resulted in considerable collateral damage, with total drone-strike casualties in excess of three thousand persons (Grubbs and Yahnke 2017). A UN special rapporteur described these attacks as war crimes. Pakistan's legal authorities declared them illegal.

In 2013, Pakistan held its first democratic transition between governments in its history. Hailed as a "watershed" moment in Pakistan's political history, the government led by Nawaz Sharif, a once-exiled prime minister and leader of the PML-N party, took power amid a backdrop of deep-seated anti-Americanism following the Western withdrawal from Afghanistan, strained civil-military relations, and a declining security situation in Baluchistan (Grare 2013). Since then Pakistan has been witness to rising instances of extremist violence, including attacks carried out by IS. Intermittent violence and terrorist acts include the Peshawar school attack in 2014 that led to the death of 150 people, many of whom were children. In 2018, a second major suicide attack in Baluchistan claimed the lives of over 120 persons in advance of National Assembly elections.

When Donald Trump became US president, he signaled personal dissatisfaction with Pakistan's perceived handling of the security situation in Afghanistan and threatened to withdraw aid. Despite poor relations between the two countries, the United States continues to be Pakistan's largest military supplier. Politically, however, many Pakistanis consider the US drone attacks and continued US interventions on Pakistani soil as violations of the country's sovereignty. Resentment toward the US has increased significantly. Against this backdrop, the decline in US influence over Pakistan coincides with America's perceived failures in Afghanistan. When Trump announced that his government would focus on a renewed security strategy in Afghanistan, the US signaled it would be engaging other regional partners who could provide air bases and logistical support, such as Uzbekistan. This shift in strategy coincides with a rise in China's influence over Pakistan, with the two countries opening up trade routes, developing joint weapon programs, and signing agreements and initiatives to attract Chinese investment. Reflecting on this transformation, a 2013 Pew study found that 81 percent of Pakistanis responded favorably to China, while only 11 percent of Pakistanis had a favorable view of the US, with a large majority supporting the withdrawal of US troops from Afghanistan (Pew Research Center 2013).

In sum, unabated tensions between the state-center and the provinces are not merely a reflection of the difficulties involved in integrating Pakistan's linguistically and culturally diverse constituent units. The problem is more complex because finances and foreign aid—heavily skewed toward military aid— are directed toward creating a political economy of defense well beyond the country's capacities (Ganguly 2008; *Economist* 2017). The elite's response tends to be the centralization of state authority and the pursuit of development policies aimed at maximizing revenues and rents rather than social welfare, a process that has nonelected institutions and elites dominating.

We now turn to comparing our two cases. In one specific way, Yemen's trajectory as a trapped state is a bit surprising. To be sure, Yemen espouses the qualities one would expect in a fragile state, but its performance also challenges them. On the one hand, Yemen has suffered civil wars, multiple armed secession movements, and the presence of major terrorist groups. A significant portion of the population remains below the poverty line, and major indicators of Human Development, environment, and demography are very poor and worsening. On the other hand, Yemen did not undergo regime change until late in Ali Abdullah Saleh's tenure as president. Though his departure moved the country fully into chaos, the subsequent multiple secessionist movements only exposed the regime's frailties after his departure.

Looking back, a pattern in Yemen's structural transformations coupled with key drivers is clearly evident. Elite decisions were taken on a tactical basis to counter perceived threats to the regime. Those decisions eventually propagated and reinforced Yemen's structural weaknesses. Those constraints resulted in reducing the freedom of action for the next decision, thus encouraging more short-term tactical maneuvers to preserve the regime and perpetuating a vicious cycle. Saleh made a series of crucial but ill-advised decisions early on after reunification that reinforced this cycle. Both he and his opponents, looking to the immediate future, saw themselves and their fifty-fifty arrangement threatened by democratic plurality and sought to outmaneuver each other, with Saleh prevailing.

Such a system served Saleh's regime well enough that it had few internal challengers; even when opposition groups cooperated, they were unable to offer a real alternative to Saleh. The problem is that the cycle of short-term decisions reinforcing structural constraints meant that while the regime was secure, the country itself remained fragile. The massively corrupt patronage regime providing benefits not to regions on the periphery but to a select few constrained Saleh's ability to diversify the country's economy and limited social services. A limited-access system, though in equilibrium, sows the seeds of its own demise. The concentration of power left the field open to new challengers, such as disaffected southerners, Islamist groups, and the northern Houthi movement.

In brief, Yemen exemplifies the inherent problem of those trapped states suffering from weakening authority. Regimes undertake particular actions for short-term gain, but those actions only reinforce legitimacy weaknesses. With reinforced structural constraints, such as the Yemeni patronage system, future decisions became "bound" and options more limited. The trap in this case is akin to a lobster trap from which there is no escape. It is hard to see how Saleh, having governed for so long by using the country's oil wealth to pay off potential opponents, could have effected systemic transformation without bringing the political economy to its knees.

Like Yemen, Pakistan has remained trapped in fragility for decades. But unlike Yemen, at its core Pakistan's fragility challenges are linked to problems of legitimacy. Systemic social fissures that pit ethnic and sectarian groups against each other form the unsteady foundation upon which Pakistan's political institutions have been erected. Inequality between ethnic groups highlights poor state legitimacy. Various calls for self-government by provincial regions seeking autonomous control over their resources clearly demonstrate a loss of confidence in the capacity of Pakistan's regimes to secure and act in their interests. In addition, continued elite capture of power and resources has contributed to the depreciation of quality in Pakistan's key governing institutions. The result is a governance system that explicitly favors elites over a public that has little trust in ruling regimes.

In examining Pakistan's experience with fragility, there appear to be two main conclusions. First, in the absence of government systems willing to invest in development and wealth redistribution, uneven growth exacerbates tensions and contributes to instability. In Pakistan, the historic concentration of wealth and power along ethnic lines in an already divided society is problematic. Unkept promises by political leaders for improvements amid continued development challenges have undermined the legitimacy of Pakistan's regimes.

Second, and perhaps more fundamentally, elite capture of the state suggests there are few incentives for ruling regimes to enact meaningful reform. Indeed, the outgoing director of the United Nations Development

Programme in Pakistan said it best when he warned that "the only way a critical change could happen in the country was when the influential, the politicians and the wealthy, would sacrifice short term, individual and family interests for the benefit of the nation" (*Express Tribune* 2016).

Chapter 4

In and Out of Fragility

Mali and Laos—Landlocked and Unstable

For our purposes, we consider countries to be "stabilized" if they have stayed out of the top forty most fragile countries for at least the past ten to fifteen years. Laos and Mali have moved into and out of fragility for over thirty-five years and therefore are neither trapped nor exited. They are both affected by environmental impacts and regional volatility and, because they are landlocked, are dependent on their immediate neighbors for economic prosperity and political stability. They are both former French colonies and aid dependent. In this chapter, we examine the two cases separately before moving to a comparison of our findings in the last section.

Mali's spectacular collapse in recent years has sparked a reexamination of its characterization as a "model of stability" in West Africa (Bergamaschi 2014). We argue that Mali has never been such a model. Mali's recent conflict is the rule rather than the exception. The picture of Mali's fragility from 1980 to the present is a country that continually exits fragility only to reenter it further down the road.

Unlike Mali, Laos (the Lao People's Democratic Republic, or Lao PDR) has never really been considered a model of stability, and it is a country of only 6.2 million people, surrounded by larger, more powerful neighbors. Though both countries have been afflicted by environmental calamity such as droughts, Laos has shown that it can recover in the face of adversity. Since the end of the Second World War, the country has struggled to maintain internal cohesion and territorial integrity. Independence from France in 1953 merely compounded Laos's structural problems as factions fought for control and the country quickly descended into civil war. The communist takeover in 1975 provided regime stability by bringing an end to years of civil war, but since then Laos's leaders have been unable to bring meaningful reform and economic growth to their people.

MALI'S FRAGILITY ROLLER COASTER

Mali, home to just under 16 million people, has struggled since independence in 1960. In addition to three coups and multiple coup attempts, there have been three major armed conflicts in the north. Despite these problems, Mali was considered at least since the mid-1990s a model of African democracy, becoming an "aid darling" in the process (Bergamaschi 2014). These assumptions were firmly undermined by the 2012 coup against President Amadou Toumani Touré in the midst of a major secessionist conflict. That conflict, which has its immediate roots in a 2006 insurgency, effectively detached Mali's three northern provinces—Gao, Kidal, and Timbuktu—from government control and led to their occupation by Islamist groups connected to al-Qaeda. This new threat prompted a major military intervention by France, followed by a UN mission that succeeded in temporarily ousting the groups and regaining partial control of the north.

Our findings shown in figure 4.1 indicate that Mali's transitions into fragility are caused by major events that undermine the government's authority over people and borders, while its brief recovery from fragility is due to the termination of those events. However, this susceptibility to crisis is not only a function of structural factors. Elite decisions and poor leadership have kept Mali from fully recovering after emerging from fragility. Each successive wave of destabilizing events pushes Mali's economic capacity to the brink, only to move the country further down the fragility scale.

Mali has been in and out of fragility at least four times with no improvement evident. In fact, a deteriorating trend is discernible over the last eight years. The four times Mali entered the top forty are consistent with

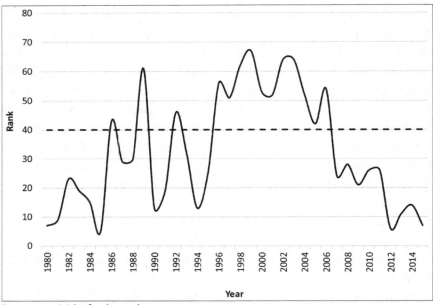

Figure 4.1 Mali's fragility ranking, 1980–2014

the historical analysis. The first entry, 1985–86, matches a period of policy upheaval combined with student demonstrations and a brief border war with Burkina Faso in 1985 and droughts in the north. The second entry, around 1990–92, correlates with the collapse of Traoré's regime, the subsequent coup, and the faltering transition to institutional hybridity. A third entry occurs around 1994, which aligns with the "restarting" of the Tuareg conflict. The final inflection starts in 2006, which matches the start of the third Tuareg rebellion and the ongoing multiparty insurgency that resulted in the 2012 coup.[1]

Mali's ALC performance as seen in figure 4.2 is indicative of how poor policy decisions produced Mali's shifts into fragility. Mali's main source of fragility is due to constant authority challenges related partly to ineffective control of territory and people. We observe spikes in authority associated with the four inflection points noted above. Deep and abiding capacity problems, most closely associated with a weak, aid-dependent, and undiversified economy, have keep Mali near the fragility cutoff over the entire period. Despite reasonable growth, poor capacity has kept Mali below the fragility cutoff, rendering the country extremely vulnerable to shocks. The inability to effect reform such as developing an efficient and

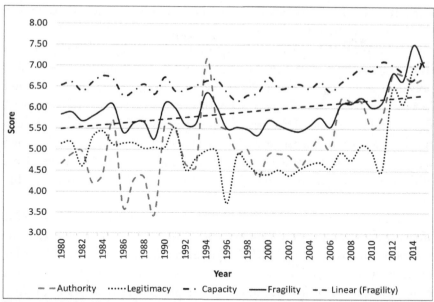

Figure 4.2 Mali's ALC trends, 1980–2014

sufficient private sector in the face of an aid-based rent-seeking economy is one of Mali's weakest points (Bergamaschi 2014). To be clear, Mali's wavering fragility is not caused directly by specific shocks such as drought, coups, or regional conflict. Mali suffers from limited carrying capacity, which pushes the country over the edge when faced with these internal and external threats. For example, we see that capacity is consistently above the general fragility trend line, which is indicative of a stability ceiling. Second, authority is generally lower than the average line but "punctures" the line during Mali's entries into fragility. This indicates that it plays a direct causal role. Finally, legitimacy is consistently lower than the trend line but is still fairly close to it.

MALI'S STRUCTURAL TRANSFORMATION

Like many West African states seeking independence from France, Mali had beginnings that were both tendentious and contrived. Gen. Charles de Gaulle's return to power in France in 1958 set the stage for the independence of most of French West Africa. On September 28, 1959, a referendum was held that gave the territories three options: stay as a part of the French

Fifth Republic, have political autonomy but remain within the French Community, or become independent.[2]

The subsequent Malian Federation achieved official independence from France on June 20, 1960, with Léopold Sédar Senghor of Senegal as president and Modibo Keïta of the Sudanese Republic as prime minister. Differences between Keïta and Senghor over issues such as relations with France and command of the armed forces quickly escalated, and the federation broke apart in August 1960 when Senegal withdrew. Keïta and his party held a congress in Bamako on September 22 and declared the independence of the Sudanese Republic, changing its name to the Republic of Mali (Imperato 1998).

Keïta, a Marxist, moved quickly after independence to model Mali after other socialist states. Mali became a one-party state with a state-run economy. His party, the US-RDA, dominated national politics. Central to its support were regional leaders and the urban elite in Bamako, the capital. Keïta also followed the trend in newly independent African states of "Africanization," which involved the rejection of influence from the West, both cultural and otherwise, which he married to his socialist program. Thus, nationalization of companies fit the aims of both Eastern Bloc–style socialism and Africanization (EIU 1998). Central to this project was his decision to withdraw Mali from the CFA franc zone (Gurtner 1999).

This decision was significant, given Mali's status as a landlocked country. Malian exports and imports had to pass through its neighbors, especially those to the south with sufficient port facilities (EIU 1998). The withdrawal and establishment of the Malian franc left Mali with an inconvertible currency that hurt the Malian economy and decimated its trade in the process.[3] In November 1968, a group of junior army officers led by Lt. Moussa Traoré overthrew the Keïta regime.[4]

Much of Traoré's first years of his twenty-three in power focused on recovering the Malian economy from the distressing lows of Keïta's rule. Although the economy initially improved, there were signs of increasing discontent focusing on protests and eventually rebellion. Student demonstrations arising from a slow economy and lack of jobs were put down forcibly by the army. By the mid-1990s, Traoré became even more repressive, crushing student protests, Tuareg disturbances in the north, and several coup attempts (EIU 1998). A key turning point occurred in March 1991 when soldiers mutinied, refusing to continue to fire on protestors after three hundred of them had been killed. At the same time that civil dissent was increasing in the late 1980s, catalyzing events unfolded leading to the Second Tuareg Rebellion. Of these, the most significant were the severe droughts that devastated northern Mali, forcing many of the nomadic peoples, especially the clan-based Tuaregs, to migrate. Many left for Algeria, Niger, and Libya, where they were exposed to more radical ideologies. Some began to plan a rebellion for Tuareg autonomy in Mali and became skilled fighters. Libyan leader Muammar el-Qaddafi actively recruited Tuareg migrants to fight for him, and they saw action in Palestine and Chad.

By the late 1980s, Tuareg migrants returning from Algeria and Niger were frequently confronted by Malian troops. Many Libyan-trained Tuaregs seized the opportunity to provoke an even larger uprising. With tensions rising in Bamako and fearing a coup, Traoré chose to keep his troops in the south and negotiated a quick settlement with the Tuareg leaders, notably the current leader of the Salafist group Ansar Dine (Defenders of the Faith), Ayad Ag Ghali (Storholt 2001).[5] That agreement resulted in more autonomy and revenue sharing in the north (Storholt 2001), but Traore's peace proved only temporary.

By the early 1990s, the country was on the brink of civil war.[6] The subsequent overthrow of Traoré in 1991 and his eventual replacement with a multiparty democracy focusing on further decentralization was a key defining event for Mali at time when the world was witnessing the so-called third wave of democratization. Such a transition was hailed as a rare success in Africa, and it shows in our analysis of the country's ALC performance. However, at the same time, the rebellion in the north by the Tuareg had pushed the country into civil war.

Traoré was deposed in 1991 by Col. Amadou Toumani Touré. For about a year, Touré served as head of state as part of a transition team paving the way for elections. In 1992, Touré handed over leadership to the country's first freely elected president, Alpha Oumar Konaré, a Malian historian and former minister of education. Touré did not run (EIU 1998). Konaré immediately confronted the Tuareg conflict. By the end of 1994, it was clear that his national government could not restore order on its own. In a fateful decision, Konaré began to order troop withdrawals from the north while simultaneously tasking civil society groups with a mandate to broker peace. While the Tuaregs lost some of their initial gains in these negotiations, including clawbacks in revenue redistribution, they still retained autonomy

(Lode 1997. Toward the end of his tenure, Konaré expanded decentralization to include almost all of Mali.

By 1996, a peace agreement for the north was finalized, and the rebel groups gathered for a ceremonial burning of their weapons in Timbuktu. Despite facing a brief political crisis in 1997 when most of the opposition boycotted presidential elections, Konaré led Mali through a relatively peaceful and stable phase until the end of his second term in 2002, when Touré was elected in his place. Under Konaré, decentralization and decision-making had shifted from local state authorities to 682 village-level communes (Hetland 2008).

Touré's subsequent election in 2002 was notable not just because of his former role in overthrowing Traoré and paving the way for democratic elections but also because he was not officially affiliated with any of Mali's political parties. Touré preferred to rule with consensus, which meant, to some, personal rule guided by a diffusion of institutional authority. To secure political support, he gave ministerial positions to most of Mali's political parties as well as to many independent candidates (EIU 2008). In terms of building personal support, this strategy appeared to work: Touré won a second term handily in the 2007 national elections and continued to rule until the March 2012 coup (EIU 2018). As a mechanism for deepening Mali's democratic institutions and increasing accountability in the north, however, it was flawed.

Despite efforts to win over political opponents and regional elites, Touré's second term was dominated by the Third Tuareg Rebellion. That started in 2006 when sixty Tuareg soldiers in the Malian army defected, seized weapons, and began attacking government convoys and remote outposts. Their leader was Ibrahim Ag Bahanga, who established links with Tuareg rebel groups participating in a simultaneous rebellion in Niger. By September 2007, Bahanga had taken at least thirty-five soldiers captive (Emerson 2011). Neither the rebels nor the government could gain the upper hand. This prompted Touré to again pursue a diplomatic solution by reaching out to moderate Tuareg leaders (Emerson 2011). With Libyan help, a cease-fire was arranged in April 2008 but soon broke down. Touré decided to launch an all-out offensive against the increasingly isolated Bahanga, and in response Bahanga and his remaining troops took temporary refuge in Libya (Emerson 2011).

The peace brought by Bahanga's retreat proved fleeting. In 2011, the onset of the Libyan Civil War coupled with decision of the North Atlantic Treaty Organization to attack Qaddafi's forces precipitated a mass exodus from Libya. Among those returning to Mali were Tuareg groups that had fled the oppressive and destitute conditions in northern Mali to find work in Libya (Shaw 2013; Belik, Grebovic, and Willows 2012). Also included were the remnants of Bahanga's forces and other Tuareg rebels who had found employment in Qaddafi's military (Pézard and Shurkin 2013).

In addition to causing widespread dislocation, the breakdown in security in Libya also allowed for significant stores of weaponry to be looted (Shaw 2013). Furthermore, pro-Qaddafi forces had distributed weapons across the country in various undisclosed storage locations, thus allowing for decentralized looting by many groups. The Tuareg migrants came back heavily armed (Ki-moon 2012).

Other actors also appeared around this time. Since the 1990s, and especially the 2000s, Islamic criminal and insurgent groups had been operating in Mali's northern provinces. Most notable among these groups was the Salafist Group for Preaching and Combat (GASP), which was formed in Algeria in the 1990s following the return of mujahideen fighters from Afghanistan. Although focused on the insurgency in Algeria, the group gradually expanded its operations across the Sahel region through the 2000s and in 2006 officially proclaimed its international focus by allying with al-Qaeda Central (AQC) and changing its name to al-Qaeda in the Islamic Maghreb (AQIM). In 2011, many of AQIM's members from black southern Mali split from the group to form the Movement for Oneness and Jihad in West Africa (MUJAO). These groups took advantage of the chaos in Libya to strengthen their firepower (Ki-moon 2012; Larémont 2011).

Initially violence was confined to isolated clashes. It soon became clear that federal forces were overwhelmed; the power balance in northern Mali had tipped decisively in favor of the Tuaregs (Shaw 2013). By January 2012, a full-scale insurgency had broken out, with the Tuareg fighters coalescing into the National Movement for the Liberation of Azawad (MNLA), a group formed in 2011 by separatist Tuareg leaders in Libya and young Tuareg urban intellectuals in Mali (Shaw 2013). Iyad Ag Ghali also joined the MNLA and attempted to become its leader. After his leadership bid failed, he formed Ansar Dine, an offshoot of the MNLA. These two Tuareg groups partnered with AQIM and MUJAO in a modus vivendi (Belik, Grebovic, and Willows 2012).

The alliance proved too powerful for Malian security forces, and they were quickly forced to retreat. Junior officers in Bamako, outraged at their quick defeat and lack of logistical support from the government, staged a coup in March 2012 to oust ATT (as Touré was called), which allowed the separatist groups to further consolidate their gains (Belik, Grebovic, and Willows 2012). Soon after their apparent victory, the MNLA were displaced by Ansar Dine and MUJAO/AQIM and forced to flee to Niger (Reuters 2012). The Islamist groups then began to press their advantage south toward the capital, which prompted a swift French military intervention to avoid a complete collapse of the Malian state. French forces went on the offensive, deploying armored and paratroop units to quickly oust the Islamist groups from the northern cities and effectively regain control of the north. The MNLA soon sided with French forces and pushed the Islamist groups out of Kidal. They signed a peace agreement with the Malian government in June 2013 to disarm and to participate in national elections (Smith 2013). In the same year, a UN peacekeeping force was deployed and took over some of the security responsibilities from departing French forces (BBC 2013).

MALI'S DRIVERS OF FRAGILITY

Mali's performance demonstrates that political and economic gains are both achievable and easily reversed. In Mali's case, we witness extreme forms of "isomorphic mimicry" in combination with elite rent seeking. Elites take on the trappings of Western institutions to generate international support while failing to incorporate and develop fundamental institutional capacity to distribute social goods. Mali's weak capacity performance is compounded by its weaknesses across the other two dimensions of authority and legitimacy. Catalyzing effects such as environmental catastrophes and regional conflict, coupled with poor decision-making, precipitate crises leading to regime upheaval and political calamity. When stressed, such as during a coup, Mali's core structural weaknesses show through and recovery is slow.

Premature Load Bearing and the North-South Divide

A core cause of Mali's fragility is the fact that the country's elites took on large structural reforms such as privatization and democratization while being deeply divided and poor. Inculcated in part by donor pressures for reform with a shallow tax base and poor policy environment, these causes denote a form of premature load bearing (Pritchett, Woolcock, and Andrews 2013). For example, 1985 witnessed two parallel challenges to Mali's leadership. Seemingly unrelated, they point to a common problem. The first was a short border war with Burkina Faso that lasted only a few days, and the second a series of student protests that occurred throughout the year. Mali's border war was relatively confined, focused mostly on natural resource claims. However, it was asserted afterward that Mali's leaders had initiated the conflict to divert attention away from political protests. In that sense, of the two challenges, the protests were the more serious because they highlight a bigger problem with Mali's donor-driven liberalization policies and the concomitant scaling back of the public sector.

Indeed, over the course of the 1980s, despite his dictatorial tendencies, Traoré increasingly aligned himself with the International Monetary Fund (IMF) and other Bretton Woods institutions in pursuit of support for contentious macroeconomic policies. In exchange for debt relief, better loan conditions, and aid, Traoré was required to reign in the public sector (Bertelsmann Stiftung 2008). These policies posed a threat to the powerful public sector, government bureaucracy, and trade unions in Bamako. From 1979 on, Traoré also cut funding to graduate students, closed upper-level schools, and instituted a requirement that all new civil servants have two years of military experience (Imperato 1989).

Traoré's cutbacks exposed Mali's structural weaknesses. On the one hand, Mali was heavily indebted at the time and in need of foreign assistance, in part simply to keep the government running and pay the army's salary. On the other hand, Mali's massive bureaucracy was putting the country into increasing debt. Throughout his rule, Traoré was dependent on outside financial assistance, mainly from France. It was France (among others) that indirectly funded Traoré's crackdowns in 1979 and 1983 because without French loans he would not have been able to pay the military. Traoré went further by limiting the urban elite's influence by privatizing state monopolies.

A series of poor decisions and events subsequently undermined Traoré's authority and control over Mali in the north and the urban south. First, droughts in the north created significant population displacements that further damaged Traoré's control there. The massive dislocation of people also worked to undermine Mali's traditional forms of Tuareg governance, further weakening Traoré's regional partners. Governance had, since independence, been "bought" by alliances with Tuareg chiefs and elites. As regional patrons, these elites, rather than investing in social services and infrastructure, acted as the local "big men" through resource-distribution networks. Traditional governance meant traditional hierarchies of groups within Tuareg society. However, many of the migrants who arrived in the 1980s were outside of this traditional hierarchy and had no reason to respect the authority of the traditional chiefs and elites. It is not surprising the Tuaregs seized upon this destabilized situation to launch a rebellion. With pressure mounting on two fronts, Traoré abandoned a reconquest of the north and sued for peace early in 1991 so that he could concentrate on economic problems in the south.

In the end, it was dissent in the urban south that overwhelmed Traoré's regime. That is because Traoré had not done much to mitigate the impact of public cutbacks. Mali's economy had not improved much since 1985, especially in terms of private-sector job creation. This closed off a "safety valve" through which to channel the excess of educated Malian elites. Further, Traoré's economic liberalization initiatives increasingly threatened those very rent-seeking elites, including bureaucrats, students, and trade unionists who supported him.

Eventually the collapse of the Soviet Union eliminated the need for Western powers to prop up ailing African dictatorships such as Traoré's. Aid from the international community was increasingly being tied to democracy promotion, something Mali had not experienced before. In Mali's case, payments to soldiers and bureaucrats alike stalled, further eroding Traoré's critical patronage base. While public dissatisfaction with economic reforms and the conflict in the north added fuel to the fire, demonstrations increased substantially in the south. Collectively the stage was set for delegitimizing the Traoré regime. His base of support dwindled, weak institutions were ill prepared for liberalization and democratic reform, and the army was discredited by its inability to manage conflict in the north.

Identity Manipulation

Under such conditions, we might expect a more resilient country to stage-manage reforms with international support guiding them each step of the way. However, a key structural feature over which international donors had little control was elite manipulation of regional identities. Thrust into Mali's north-south conflict was Konaré's newly elected government, which proved equally incapable of controlling the army, especially given the political chaos underway in the capital. His weakness ensured a "power vacuum" of undergoverned spaces would prevail in the north (Keita 1998). The north was ripe for banditry while different armed groups representing specific clan interests took advantage of the situation to enhance their own position or that of their clan relative to other groups (Benjaminsen 2008).

Over time, this power vacuum spread to the more sedentary Songhai populations who resented the "deal" made with the Tuaregs and who began mobilizing armed groups in response (Keita 1998). Their countermobilization accentuated the long-standing division between the nomadic Tuareg and Arab populations, who viewed themselves as white, and the black Malian populations of the south, such as the Songhai, the Fulani, and the Bambara (MRG 2013).[7]

Malian army units, embarrassed by repeated failures and lack of pay, began to attack Tuaregs and other nomadic peoples. These outbreaks took on an ethnic dimension, as the units essentially confronted "white" populations, whether they were Tuareg, Arab, or Moor. Eventually Songhai militias (which the army on occasion actively supported and collaborated with, most notably the militia group Ganda Koy) joined with the army (Benjaminsen 2008). While Konaré served as president, Touré was put in charge of suppressing the rebellion by force and further unified the hitherto sporadic violence by the Malian army and Ganda Koy. The escalation in turn unified many previously disjointed nomadic groups and escalated the conflict into a "white vs. black" conflict (Florquin and Pézard 2005).

The emerging rivalries that resulted from this inability to control the north are a chief cause of the Third Tuareg Rebellion. As a whole, the rebellion was largely about the pursuit of increased autonomy but underneath had more to do with interethnic relations. The Tuareg populations (along with some other nomadic groups) were, and still are, organized along clan and kinship ties.[8] Konaré's decentralization efforts, supported by Touré's crackdown, brought some stability to the north, but it also exacerbated other divisions. For various reasons, including lack of political will and significant corruption, Mali's north did not get the development investment it was promised by Konaré and Touré.[9] Much-needed development aid was subsequently canceled or squandered by corrupt officials. The only major difference under Touré was an increased but unwelcome military presence in the north (Belik, Grebovic, and Willows 2012; Cairnie and deGrasse 2016). Unfortunately, the massive upheaval caused by the Libyan Civil War in 2011 was simply too much for this weak, personalized patron-client governance system to function. In the past, Libya had acted as a safety valve for the region, allowing many of the unemployed (mostly men) to find work and remit their earnings home to sustain their families (Shaw 2013). More specifically, through his employment of Tuareg fighters, Qaddafi legitimized Tuareg political independence by offering them employment. When Qaddafi's regime crumbled, the Tuaregs, left with no employment prospects in a very hostile environment, fled to Mali (Cairnie and deGrasse 2016).

The Malian forces stationed in the region clearly saw the Tuareg migrants' return as a threat and confronted these groups. Peace was attempted, but mediation efforts failed to produce a resolution to the conflict. In fact, the conferences only encouraged further cohesion amongst the returnees as they mobilized together.[10] Touré could not stop what was happening in Libya, nor could his forces defeat the returning rebels. But his decision to keep the lower levels of the military underequipped, corrupt, and underfunded further undermined the government's ability to project its power in the north. It is perhaps not surprising that Touré wanted the military to be weak because it had initiated coups in the past, but this also ensured that the military would only be capable of dealing with low-level threats, becoming endemically corrupt in the process.

The Rent Economy under Hybridity

A third driver is the rent economy driven in large part by development assistance that lacked oversight and enforcement. While Mali has seen notable economic successes—for example, 8 percent GDP growth in 1986 and 12 percent in 1988—there were also steep losses.[11] In 1984, GDP grew by 4 percent but shrank by 11 percent in 1985. In fact, this seems to be the pattern of the Malian economy: GDP gains would be made one year followed by significant contractions the next (World Bank 2017d. These contractions and expansions were due in part to a failure to privatize the economy while simultaneously weakening the public sector. Public-sector cutbacks undercut some of the most powerful and motivated groups in Mali, students and bureaucrats, without being able to offer them anything in terms of private-sector employment.

With employment in the public sector generally unsustainable and a lack of increased employment opportunities available in the resource sector (gold, cotton, uranium), the remaining area for employment has been the general private sector (industry, service, etc.). However, Mali's structural economic conditions have constrained the development of this sector. Significant GDP growth and inflation fluctuations make investment much more risky, making small firms especially unattractive to invest in (TI 2013a).[12]

This underperformance is concomitant with an increase in international development assistance. Mali has generally been an aid-dependent country, but aid increased substantially in real terms since its attempts to transition to a hybrid form of democracy (Bergamaschi 2014). Aid doubled since 1994 (World Bank 2017h). The effects of this increase, driven in part by promises to reform economically and politically, have been staggeringly negative. That is because Mali's elite benefit from aid by "brokering" its distribution. In order to operate effectively, an internationally funded nongovernmental organization (NGO) relies on the cooperation (or at least benign neglect) of local government institutions. In Mali, this has resulted in political alliances between influential politicians cum aid brokers and key NGOs.[13]

Far from representing the interests of the people by establishing and adhering to institutional performance measures under a democratic system, Mali's politicians have made it their goal is to establish a patronage network and push for additional zones around areas over which they have more control. In comparison to elites producing policy outcomes based on a public-demand system, Mali's resource distribution system is derived from elite bargaining and strategizing about relative power gains. Groups are only co-opted into Mali's patronage system if they possess enough power to be useful, and their leaders will only get control of a local zone if they have enough power to actually control that area. The 2006 conflict in the north thus represents the deleterious effects of elite bargaining. The clans that rebelled sought additional administrative zones to be designated by the government in areas where they were dominant. These zones would then ensure their access to rents.

More generally, Mali's rent economy offers a viable option to the thin veneer of democratic reform on display to the donor community. For example, partnering with a development NGO allows local politicians an opportunity to skim funds, either directly or indirectly by influencing where the money is spent (Roy 2010). Additionally, NGOs need to engage the population. In a country where the majority of the population is illiterate, well-educated elites are hired. These elites constitute the bridge between the local and the state but operate from within the state apparatus and therefore are uncritical of it and the legitimacy that underpins it.

Thus, Mali's political control allows for two forms of resource access: development money and government money. Often, they are one and the same. Aid functions as a primary resource; instead of gaining revenue through the taxation of a productive activity, Mali's leaders encourage the cultivation of the most profitable source that provides them with "rents." Thus, as leaders of a hybrid state, Mali's are not accountable to the people but to those who pay the rent—in this case, external donors. It becomes self-evident why democratic institutions have little purpose under such an arrangement other than to provide the cloak of international legitimacy through which state and regional elites can ensure resource distribution for the people of Mali (Farah, Gandhi, and Robidoux 2019).

However, such a system has the potential to underresource key sectors of society that do not factor into the maintenance of this economic system, such as the military. Instead of centralizing power, Mali's leaders pursued a form of control akin to pyramidal segmentation in which there is a clear hierarchy of authority but only weak connections between the various groups that derive benefits from the distribution of rents. Furthermore, the rise of smuggling activity has allowed bribes to become a second source for economic growth of these groups. Those who control the smuggling routes receive payoffs from the groups who operate alongside them.[14] Indeed, the 2006 conflict and the subsequent collapse of Mali from 2012 to the present was largely about forcing the creation of separate administrative zones, in which the Ifogha clans of Mali's Kidal Region established primacy as the army stood by and watched helplessly. In fact, much of the fighting between the MNLA and the Islamist groups after the split in 2012 was around strategic border towns where the government reach relied extensively on underdeveloped patronage networks rather than direct control by its own army.

In the smuggling of cigarettes and migrant workers into Algeria and illicit consumer items and fuel (Reeve 2013), armed groups such as AQIM do not actually smuggle the goods but provide protection, or "safe passage," for traffickers. When groups vie for control, the situation is explosive. The MNLA, for example, has clashed repeatedly with other armed Tuareg groups over control of In-Khalil, the most important border crossing into Algeria. Government officials, too, benefit from control of these routes. Gao in particular is purported to be the main smuggling hub in Mali, with the active complicity of local officials (Reeve 2013).[15]

LAOS: THE BATTLEFIELD

As we show in figure 4.3, Laos has been in and out of fragility five times over the last thirty years. The entries by Laos into the top forty are consistent with the historical analysis. The first entry, from 1987 to 1989, coincided with a series of severe droughts in the country and a border war with Thailand. The second entry, in 1996, occurred amid ambushes by Hmong insurgents and severe flooding. The third, in 1998, matched the fallout from the Asian financial crisis of 1997. Then, in 2000 and 2003, a series of bombings and insurgent clashes reflecting internal party and domestic discord put the country into fragility two more times. Laos's exit from fragility from 2005 to 2009 and subsequent improvement are a result of the regime's slow but positive reforms to address security and economic stabilization.

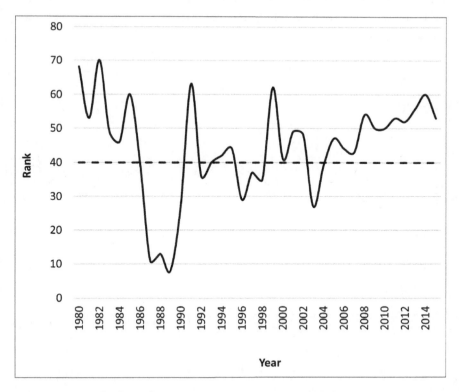

Figure 4.3 Laos's fragility ranking, 1980–2014

Laos generally hovered very close to the top forty cutoff mark. As important as the individual shifts into fragility are, they were caused by events that were not that severe. These points are illustrated in figure 4.4, showing changes in ALC over time. With the exception of a brief border conflict with Thailand, there was only a long-running but low-intensity insurgency, now dissipated with time. The Lao People's Revolutionary Party (LPRP) has been the undisputed governing party since 1975, and so there is very little political destabilization.[16] Natural disasters are important, but the most severe only caused thirty deaths; furthermore, they are a staple across the region. Yet Laos continues to struggle to generate lasting stability. Even once proximate triggers (such as a flood or a series of bombings) come to an end, Laos's advances are not unlimited. Where its neighbors improve, Laos struggles. This has been true since independence. The reasons for this are threefold: an entrenched conservative elite resistant to economic and political reform, a lucrative rent economy that benefits those entrenched elites, and a poor policy environment where contract law and property rights are weakly enforced.

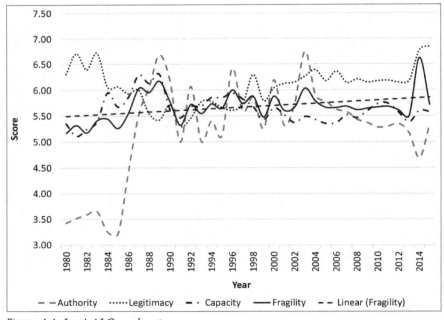

Figure 4.4 Laos's ALC trends, 1980–2014

LAOS'S STRUCTURAL TRANSFORMATION

Laos's predicament stems from its history as a colony of France. Laos was part of the larger French colony of Indochina, which included the territory of modern-day Laos, Cambodia, Vietnam, and parts of Thailand. During the Second World War, Japan negotiated access to Indochina with the French wartime Vichy regime and subsequently expanded this access, although French sovereignty was maintained in name (Savada 1995). Japan ended French administrative control, arrested all French officials, and forced the domestic Lao protectorate administration (under King Sisavang Vong) to declare Laos an independent state (Savada 1995). After the war, the French regained sufficient control of the country to set up an administration under King Sisavang Vong and granted Laos independence within the French Union. The French, however, maintained significant control over matters such as defense and foreign policy (Savada 1995).

As the French were reasserting their control in Laos, they faced increasing challenges in Vietnam, where war broke out between the French forces and Ho Chi Minh's Viet Minh toward the end of 1946. The Viet Minh linked up with anti-French resistance groups in Laos, who coalesced into the Pathet Lao, and sent thousands of agents to Laos (almost seventeen thousand by 1953) (Savada 1995). This cooperation between Vietnamese and Laotian communists would be a long-running theme throughout recent Laotian history.

Laos became fully independent on October 22, 1953, and sent a sovereign delegation to the Geneva Conference on Indochina, which ended the First Indochina War between France and the Viet Minh in July 1954 (Savada 1995). This move was both a reflection of France's impending defeat and an attempt to preempt the communist Pathet Lao forces, which were harassing the Royal Lao Government (RLG).[17]

The advent of peace negotiations between the United States and North Vietnam in 1972 provided a window for similar talks to occur in Laos.[18] An agreement was signed between the RLG and the Pathet Lao that provided for a coalition government.[19] The LPRP subsequently moved to "socialize" the country. Many large companies were nationalized into state-owned enterprises, and a policy of agricultural collectivization was imposed (Bertelsmann Stiftung 2012a). Since independence, Laos had—at least in name—functioned as a "neutral" state in the context of the Cold War. However, with the formation of Lao PDR, Laos was firmly inducted into the communist bloc. While aid from the United States was cut off, it was simply replaced with aid from the Eastern Bloc. In 1977, Lao PDR signed a twenty-five-year treaty of friendship and cooperation with Vietnam, making official the long history of cooperation between the LPRP and the Viet Minh. As part of the treaty, Vietnam retained the right to keep almost forty thousand troops in Laos, along with thousands of other civilian and political "advisers" (Stuart-Fox 1986). This effectively tied Laos to Vietnam in its internal and external relations.

While the period of 1975–80 was generally concerned with socializing the country, the early 1980s saw the end of economic socialization and a shift to a market-based economy. This shift had begun in 1979 with the decision to abandon the collectivization program; in 1978, there were over 2,800 collective farming organizations, but by 1980 they had been reduced to only 65 (St. John 2006). This opening up of the economy would form the "New Economic Mechanism" in Laos, a program designed to push Laos through a capitalist phase so that it could eventually be socialized—at least in theory. In practice, it was more likely due to a realization that centralization could not be accomplished in such a thinly populated agricultural economy with little infrastructure. If the regime were to survive, it could not destabilize the country with quick reforms (St. John 2006). Although there were some successes with the New Economic Mechanism, the results toward the end of the 1980s were rather disappointing, for two reasons. First, while reforms allowed for greater market participation by Laotians, they were not supported with proper laws and infrastructure. Contract, inheritance, and private property protection laws were not developed until the 1990s, while infrastructure such as roads remained extremely poor (EIU 2000). Second, Laos suffered severe droughts in 1987 and 1988, which cut agricultural production by one third and forced the government to import 140,000 tons of rice to feed its population. The droughts resulted in a decline in other economic activity, especially hydroelectricity generation, one of Lao PDR's main exports. Hydroelectric revenues dropped 40 percent during this time period (Savada 1995).

In 1987, a long-standing border dispute with Thailand erupted into a short border war that lasted from December 1987 to February 1988. There had been other clashes, in 1984, but these had been more serious, with

Thailand conducting bombing runs and Vietnam sending reinforcements to the Laos border (Crossette 1988). Thailand soon displaced Vietnam as Laos's most important trading partner, which is illustrated by the construction of Thai-Laos Friendship Bridge in 1994 (Dommen 1995). This is a testament to how far the two countries' relationship had come since the border conflict of 1987–88. Second, Laos and the United States normalized their relations in 1992, opening up the country to American investment and foreign aid, although American concerns about the communist regime and human rights abuses limited the amount of aid provided. This was doubly important because of the collapse of the Soviet Union, one of Laos's main foreign backers during the 1980s (Rosser 2006).

The mid-1990s posed challenges for the Laotian population in the form of natural disasters and insurgent clashes. Ambushes by ethnic-minority Hmong insurgents had occurred throughout the decade but ramped up in 1996, culminating in the killing of a French travel agent (Gurr and Birnir 2010). The agricultural industry was heavily hit by severe flooding in 1995 and 1996, the worst the country had seen since the LPRP's ascent to power in 1975. The floods impacted most of Laos's rice-producing areas, especially in the central and southern provinces, damaging or destroying tens of thousands of hectares of rice paddies and forcing the government to make emergency international appeals for aid both years (FAO 2005).

However, the main defining event of the 1990s was the Asian financial crisis. Laos had been pursuing a policy of economic liberalization and had just joined the Association of Southeast Asian Nations. Liberalization policies were beginning to have their effect in the mid-1990s with revenue increasing steadily, although the government remained dependent on foreign aid. Laos initially avoided much of the fallout of this crisis because most of its economy still focused on subsistence agriculture, with little ties to the international market. The vast majority (around 80 percent) of Laos's population is employed in the subsistence agriculture industry, one that is almost entirely composed of unskilled labor. This has limited the productivity of the industry because irrigation projects and sustainable farming (as opposed to slash-and-burn agriculture) require more skilled and better-educated labor.

When Laos's trade partners (namely, China and Thailand) were themselves impacted, they subsequently had less demand for raw materials and energy exports from Laos. These exports were the main revenue generators for the Laotian government, and the LPRP responded by trying to spend its way out of the problem through stimulus spending. Runaway inflation was underway by 1998 (Bertelsmann Stiftung 2012a) when it increased 128 percent. Laos had the third-highest inflation rate in the world in 1998.[20] By late 1998, the Laotian currency, the kip, had completely collapsed (World Bank 2017e).

The early 2000s were largely dominated by that collapse. A series of insurgent clashes and bomb attacks hit Laos in 2000 and 2003. The death of Laotian moderate leader Kaysone Phomvihane strengthened the antireformist faction within the LPRP. The economic fallout only encouraged this group to clamp down further on power. Two former Politburo members who had been expelled on corruption charges before 1996 were brought back into the government, while the finance minister and the central bank governor—both members of the "old guard" of the LPRP—were dismissed (Thayer 2000). The finance minister later was granted asylum in New Zealand.

This shed light on the divisions and internal strife within the party that was occurring as the result of the Asian financial crisis. The internal party conflict had become three-pronged, involving a "new guard" and an "old guard," northern provinces versus southern provinces, and pro-Vietnamese versus pro-Chinese factions. The military in particular took advantage of the internal chaos to further cement its position and influence over the government (Bourdet 2001).

There was increasing domestic dissent. From April to July 2000, six bomb attacks targeted shopping centers and restaurants frequented by tourists (Grammaticas 2000). The government blamed the bombings on expatriate Lao opposition groups, but little evidence was offered to support this claim. The bombings were conducted by factions either within the government or the army, resulting from internecine political struggles and business disputes between high officials (IISS 2000). In the same year, there were insurgent attacks on Laotian checkpoints along the Thailand-Laos border by Lao royalist supporters and clashes between the Hmong minority insurgents and the Laotian Army. Hmong militant groups in particular had conducted an ongoing low-level insurgency against the LPRP since it came to power in 1975. In one incident, rebels stormed and captured customs and immigration offices near the southern town of Pakse along the Thailand border, leading to five rebel deaths and twenty-six arrests (Ingram 2000).

The year 2003 witnessed another wave of bombings and insurgent clashes. The attacks were claimed by the Lao Citizens Movement for Democracy (LCMD), a loose coalition of approximately twenty groups of local militiamen, former soldiers, and anticommunists. This coalition announced in 2003 that its attacks signaled the beginning of a "revolution" in Laos to overthrow the LPRP, but none of the attacks significantly threatened the party's hold on power. Other attacks were blamed on Hmong insurgents by foreign analysts, although there has been no conclusive evidence indicating responsibility.[21] First of all, the activities of these groups have mostly been confined to their traditional areas of operation—the border with Thailand for the royalists and the north for the Hmong. Second, the bombs were placed at places either frequented by tourists and other foreigners (e.g., bars or restaurants) or directly linked to Laotian foreign relations (e.g., the Vientiane airport, the Vietnamese embassy in Vientiane). Such a selection of targets seemed designed to embarrass the government internationally by highlighting its inability to protect foreigners. This is especially important because of Laos's reliance on the international community for aid and investment.[22] Given the opaque nature of Laotian politics and government attempts to downplay the conflict and suppress information about it, the true severity of the conflict is not clear. The attacks died down toward the end of 2004, which would seem to indicate that the government had regained the upper hand in security (BBC 2011).

Throughout the 2000s, Laos continued to increase its external economic and political ties, especially with Thailand, China, and the United States. China increasingly funded infrastructure projects in Laos, including two bridges across the Mekong River and several hydroelectric dam projects. Laos's massive Nam Theun II hydroelectric dam, begun in 2005, was completed in 2010 to supply power to Thailand (Bertelsmann Stiftung 2012a). In 2010, US secretary of state Hillary Clinton visited Laos, the first such visit since 1955 and part of an increased American desire to act as a counterweight to China in Southeast Asia (BBC 2012). In advance of US secretary of state John Kerry's visit to Vientiane in 2016, a bomb blast in northern Laos killed two Chinese mining company employees (BBC 2016a).

The last half of the 2000s was marked by another internal debate within the LPRP on the extent of corruption within the party and whether it marked a serious threat to the regime's stability. Prime Minister Bouasone Bouphavanh promised to make curtailing corruption a hallmark of his term, but concrete action was limited. He also attempted to garner support among the younger members of the party and Vientiane's urban technocrats by appointing some of them to key positions. Bouphavanh resigned in 2010 in a move that was widely seen as internal party backlash against his twin attempts to displace the influence of the older members and to curb corruption by limiting mining and forestry concessions—a lucrative source of bribes and income for senior officials. His replacements, Thongsing Thammavong and Thongloun Sisoulith, have been much more cautious (Bertelsmann Stiftung 2012a).

DRIVERS OF FRAGILITY

On the surface, it appears that Laos, like Mali, falls into fragility as the result of specific shocks, such as drought and flooding, conflict, or regional economic collapse. However, Laos stays very close to the top forty. This suggests that shocks might only tip Laos into fragility, but key policy decisions related to weak reform and the rent economy have prevented the country from stabilizing over a long period. In contrast, the development of infrastructure and modified agricultural practice in the face of environmental vulnerability in addition to better control over undergoverned spaces have contributed to greater resilience over time.

Resource Management

A key driver of Laos's early fragility was the lack of capacity to properly manage both drought and flooding. Poor policy translated into weak economic growth. But its leaders adapted over time and helped make the country less vulnerable. In the early years, droughts devastated Laos's subsistence agriculture industry, and elite failure to manage drought was a function of Laos's commitment to Vietnam's economic policy. In particular, the Laotian policy of agricultural collectivization was similar to that used in Vietnam, and it was only reversed in Laos once Vietnam reversed its own policies (St. John 2006).

Collectivization exacerbated Laos's susceptibility to drought. Agricultural output, particularly in rice, declined during the collectivization years when it should have been improving (Vixathep, Onphanhdala, and Phomvixay 2013). It was not until the mid-1980s, ten years after the end of the war, that the country's agricultural production began to recover (Joiner 1987).

Collectivization was not helpful, given the country's lack of infrastructure and uneven terrain. Laos is very mountainous, with only 6 percent of its land considered arable (World Bank 2009). Land availability is an issue in the more mountainous and fragile north of the country.[23]

Agriculture is the most heavily affected by droughts and flooding.[24] Laos saw a decline in GDP growth through the drought years of 1987 and 1988. The economy shrank in 1987 by 1.4 percent and in 1988 by a further 2.0 percent.[25] Low capacity was also demonstrated when a series of floods destroyed crop yields throughout rice-producing areas of the country, combined with escalating violence and ambushes from Hmong insurgent groups in the north. While none of the insurgent groups posed an existential threat to the regime, their continued attacks highlighted the challenges in projecting Laotian government power throughout the country. The fact that they were located along the highway to Luang Prabang, one of Laos's most important tourist destinations, is indicative of the continuing power of the Hmong to challenge the government (Gurr and Birnir 2010).

Severe flooding in the central and southern parts of Laos in August 1996 further damaged agricultural output. Estimates are that almost seventy thousand hectares of rice paddies were damaged by the floods, with 25 percent to 30 percent of the paddies being completely destroyed in the provinces of Savannakhet and Champasak. An assessment mission conducted jointly by the government of Laos, the World Food Programme (WFP), and other NGOs noted that nearly all of Laos's provinces were affected by the flooding, although the damage was worst in the southern and central regions. The average Laotian family in affected areas lost half of its livestock in the floods, a significant hit to its savings mechanisms (UNDHA 1996).

What was particularly problematic about the 1996 floods was that they compounded the problem posed by severe flooding the year before (FAO 2005). Flooding is a regular occurrence along the Mekong River Basin, and the population generally understands its benefits and prepares accordingly (WFP 2006). Generally losses from one year of flooding are offset by gains the next year (with the fields yielding more because of the flooding). The second year in a row of severe flooding destroyed recovery efforts from the 1995 flooding that were underway in many parts of Laos (UNDHA 1996).

In terms of fragility data, we should, as with the droughts in 1987 and 1988, expect to see a decline in GDP growth through the flood years of 1995 and 1996. This is indeed the case, with GDP growth declining from 8 percent in 1994 to 7 percent by 1996. Further analysis shows that agricultural annual growth declined significantly through 1995 and 1996, from 8 percent in 1994 to just 2.6 percent by 1996. However, since this period we see much better growth despite ongoing flooding problems. The change is due to improved forecasting capabilities, shared Mekong watershed management, better infrastructure, and enhanced water resource policy (World Bank 2017f). This improvement is significant because the forestry industry (which is also included in agricultural data) has also shown significant growth.

From Undergoverned to Governed Spaces

Border wars and insurgency reflect an ongoing weakness in controlling territories and people and, until the mid-1990s, undermined Laotian elite claims to legitimate political authority over the country and its peoples. From 1940 to 1975, the territory of Laos was intermittently (and sometimes viciously) subjected to armed conflict, whether by domestic elements (the Pathet Lao, royalists, neutralists, the Hmong) or foreign armies (Japanese, French, Vietnamese, American). Laos's leaders have spent much of the post-1975 period trying to recover from the damage wrought by this cycle of conflict. Border conflicts posed a major challenge to state legitimacy as well, since they involve confrontations with China and Thailand, two of Laos's biggest trading partners and sources of foreign aid. Indeed, for much of its postindependence history, Laos has been a battlefield, both literally and metaphorically. After the Vietnam War, Vietnam concentrated on building up an Indochina bloc comprising itself, Laos, and later Cambodia, to act as a regional counterweight to China and Thailand. Thus, the deployment and maintenance of tens of thousands of Vietnamese troops in Laos was done to help the LPRP consolidate internal power and build legitimacy.

This, as previously mentioned, tied Laos's fate to that of Vietnam in many ways, especially economically and in foreign relations. When Vietnam invaded Cambodia in 1979 to oust the Khmer Rouge, relations were further soured with China and Thailand, which supported the Khmer Rouge. As a result, Vietnam fought a war with China and several border clashes with Thailand over the issue.[26] Laos avoided being directly brought into these conflicts, but Vietnam's presence still escalated tensions along the Laos-Thailand border. As a clientelist state, Laos was caught up in the conflicts of Vietnam. However, there were also direct conflicts between Thailand and Laos. Thailand feared that Laos could become a launching pad for insurgency, while Laos was also dealing with its own insurgency based out of Thailand. In fact, after the end of the official conflict with Thailand in 1988, Hmong resistance groups united in a loose coalition and continued the fight along the border and in the north, resulting in roughly seventy-five casualties (UCDP 2014).

In the long run, however, the drift to Thailand was inevitable, given its economic power. This connection had the greatest impact on Laotian leaders for it largely tied their political fate to economic success. Ambivalence in turn would only serve to undermine them as they struggled simultaneously to bring cohesion to a divided society. Internally the regime's goal was to decisively defeat the Hmong insurgency. Such a campaign was bound to encourage backlash, especially when coupled with the government's opium production eradication program, which threatened to significantly reduce community income among the Hmong. It should not be surprising, then, that the Hmong attack backfired under those circumstances. The longer-term cause is the LPRP's inability to successfully incorporate the Hmong, as well as other disaffected populations, into the state.

Differences in strategic objectives regarding the insurgents were largely a reflection of how the insurgents were perceived. The insurgents consist primarily of two groups: the rightists concentrated along the Thailand-Laos border, where their members fled in 1975 with ties to the Thai military, and the Hmong, who, by contrast, contain both large domestic and expatriate populations. Many Hmong fled to Thailand along with the rightists after 1975 and have continued to flee periodically since then. At the same time, about four to five hundred thousand remain in Laos. Thus, the Hmong insurgent groups are made up of both Laotian Hmong and expatriate Hmong living in Thailand, with support from Hmong groups in the United States.[27] In 2003, insurgent forces under the LCMD umbrella declared a revolution. The government in Vientiane characterized these groups as "bandits," suppressing any evidence that might identify them as a political movement, which would thus give them legitimacy (Thayer 2004).

The Laotian government historically struggled to contain and control the Hmong groups in the north, but by the end of the 1990s this changed. In 1999, the Laotian government (with heavy pressure from the United States) began a program aimed at reducing the country's opium cultivation and use. By 2006, the government claimed to have reduced both by almost 90 percent. This success constitutes a sea change in the capacity and legitimacy of

Laotian leadership because the majority of Laos's opium is cultivated in the remote northern regions of the country—especially by the Hmong people. With much more marginal land for cultivating than the south, the people in the northern provinces have generally been supported by opium production, a ready source of income.[28]

Furthermore, the mere fact that the government could conduct such an enforcement campaign in the more remote northern areas of the country itself indicates an ability to project power and influence than it had not previously enjoyed. Indeed, it appears that there was a concerted government campaign to cripple Hmong resistance; Hmong villages were often "blockaded" by Lao army troops and antipersonnel mines, and there were many documented attacks of Lao army units on Hmong civilians, including mortar strikes. Laos even called upon Vietnam to provide reinforcements to help quell the unrest (Bourdet 2001; Thayer 2004). Although there were still clashes at military outposts, there were also attacks on transportation routes and buses (Thayer 2004; Forbes and Cutler 2005).

In 2006, the Hmong insurgency collapsed with the surrender of four hundred Hmong militants, although sporadic violence continues to occur (Bertelsmann Stiftung 2012a). The longer-term problem in Laos now is what to do with the Hmong people and how to integrate them into the state. Thousands fled Laos over the course of the LPRP's rule, with most of the elite ending up in the United States. Maj. Gen. Vang Pao, the leader of the Hmong forces during the Vietnam War and figurehead of Hmong resistance since, was arrested in the United States in 2007 for allegedly plotting a coup.[29]

In 2009, the government of Thailand expelled four thousand Hmong migrants living in Thailand, including 158 registered refugees, and repatriated them back to Lao PDR, where they have not posed a significant challenge to Vientiane (Doherty 2009). In fact, most bombings were likely conducted by elements within the LPRP and the Laotian military (IISS 2000; Bourdet 2001). The response of the Laotian government seems to corroborate this. The government spent the aftermath of the bombings suppressing and confiscating any media evidence of the bombings and never announced official results of any investigations relating to them (Thayer 2004). The LPRP also never released a coherent explanation, instead variously blaming foreign opposition groups, business conflicts, and even marital problems (IISS 2000). The bombings were likely done as retribution for the political shifts that had occurred in Laos since Kaysone Phomvihane's death and that had accelerated after the Asian financial crisis. The targeting of the Vietnamese embassy in particular points to the pro-Chinese versus pro-Vietnamese dispute within the LPRP, and thus it is quite possible that the attacks were designed to "check" the government's foreign policy decisions by publicly embarrassing it (IISS 2000).

Resistance to Reform

Economic dependence has proved a double-edged sword for Laos. With a number of trading partners to work with, Laotian elites have proved adept at insinuating their own economic interests into the trade frameworks Laos has with established regional powerhouses. Though there are immense dependencies within these relationships, it has also meant that Laos has benefited from a much greater political latitude than imposed structural-adjustment programs and aid programs normally generate. In essence, Laos's exit from fragility over the last ten years can be understood from the perspective of spillover of economic success from its larger neighbors without the democratic baggage. But the country's weakness also emanates from the same source. Relatively few reform-minded elites are able to shrug off the mantle of risk-averse communist-style Politburo decision-making.

ALC changes for Laos support this observation. For example, Laos's initial shifts out of fragility around the time of the Asian financial crisis were uneven. GDP growth declined significantly from 1997 (6.9 percent) to 1998 (4.0 percent), while both foreign aid and foreign direct investment also declined (World Bank 2017g). Remittances formed an even larger component of GDP in 1998 (4.0 percent) than in 1997 (2.3 percent) (World Bank 2017i). Inflation increased from under 10 percent in 1993 to over 128 percent in 1998 (World Bank 2017e, leading to the collapse of the kip. The financial crisis was a regional development, and it would have been nearly impossible for Laos to escape its effects completely; however, much of the effects were exacerbated by bad policies.

The first main factor was the failure of reform-minded elites to take control over Laos's monetary and fiscal policy, beginning with their inability to rein in inflation. Though rampant government spending in the face of the financial crisis itself may have been a contributor (Bertelsmann Stiftung 2012a), the foundations were laid earlier. As early as 1995, the M2 (money supply) expanded significantly, bringing consumer inflation into the double digits: the inflation rate more than doubled from 1995 (13.0 percent) to 1996 (27.5 percent) and more than tripled from 1996 to 1997 (91.0 percent) (World Bank 2017e). This is especially important, given the relative poverty of the Laotian population. The poorer a country is, the more weight is given to the price of food in the consumer price basket calculations (from which inflation is calculated). So, inflation was primarily driven by food price increases, which hurt the average Laotian.

Much of the explanation for this poor performance resulted from the death of Laotian leader Kaysone Phomvihane, a reformist convert. Phomvihane was one of the original LPRP members, and thus his addition to the reformist camp had some gravitas. However, there was always another, more conservative element within the LPRP that feared that liberalization would threaten its hold on power. This faction took advantage of the death of Phomvihane to begin promoting and shuffling members of the Politburo to enhance the antireformist camp. Several key reformists were either shuffled or had their powers significantly weakened, including the president of the Committee for Planning and Cooperation (a highly powerful committee in the LPRP), the minister of finance, and the communications minister (Bourdet 1997). The economic impact of this shift is evident in the inflation data: inflation decreased substantially from 1988 (when data is first available) to 1993, but after 1993 it began rising almost exponentially.

Another important factor was the unwillingness of Lao's conservative elites to diversify their trade partners. For example, exports to Thailand and Thai investment were the primary drivers of economic growth in Laos during the 1990s. However, demand for Laotian exports decreased substantially as a result of the crisis, and investment followed suit. The Laotian government promised to diversify its trading partners, but Vietnam was much poorer than Thailand and could not offer the level of export demand and investment (EIU 2000).

A second main factor was the focus that elites had on building up Vientiane and the capital's region at the expense of the periphery, in part because of the war and insurgencies, in part because neglect of Laos's infrastructure outside of the region surrounding the capital made physical trade relations difficult to develop with China and Vietnam. While trade with China increased, much of it was illegal and hard to regulate, given the poor infrastructure.[30] Related to the lack of skilled professionals and labor, the continuing deficiencies in infrastructure are also notable and hindered further economic and social development. Much of the existing infrastructure (e.g., roads) was destroyed by successive wars and conflicts and especially by American bombing during the Vietnam War. There has been notable progress since 1975, but much of it is confined to improving links with Laos's neighbors. Logistics performance indicator scores from the World Bank tend to average around 2.00–2.50 out of 5.00, with little improvement. In fact, transport-related infrastructure actually declined from 2007 to 2010. Similarly, the quality of roads within the country also declined: 24 percent of roads were paved in 1990, while only 13.7 percent were paved in 2009 (World Bank 2017j).

Clearly one issue is that of financing. Much of the foreign infrastructure funding goes to projects designed to get Laotian resources out and Asian commodities in. The Thai-Lao Friendship Bridge across the Mekong in 1994 was primarily funded by Australia, while the Nam Theun II Dam (which primarily generates electricity for Thailand) was heavily underwritten by Thailand, France, and the World Bank. Even a planned high-speed railway is designed more to link China with Thailand than to help Laos consolidate internally. Electricity, telephone, and Internet access have all remained quite poor in Laos, with only modest improvement. Such deficiencies make it harder to develop the internal economy of the country as well as provide access to services for much of the country's rural population.

A third factor was the inability of Laotian leadership to insulate the country from shocks because of inefficient and ill-advised banking policies. Attempts to offset the financial crisis through methods such as bond sales were sporadic and inconsistent, indicating that the central bank was either unwilling or unable to intervene in the market. Laos's still-communist Politburo, while introducing economic reforms in the late 1980s and early 1990s, has not liberalized politically (St. John 2006).

The Laotian state's reliance on foreign aid for its basic financing exacerbated the effects of the crisis as well. By 1998, ODA accounted for over 20 percent of gross national income (World Bank 2017g). This was especially damaging because foreign aid was used in such crucial areas as transportation and communications, health care, and social welfare (World Bank 2017g). Thus, while the Laotian elites could not have prevented the crisis from impacting Laos, many conscious decisions taken by the party leadership made the country more vulnerable to it. Chief among these was the antireformist shift within the Politburo, which led both to increased inflation and a general inability of the country's financial institutions to mitigate the fallout.

Another double-edged sword for Laos is the benefit of political stability afforded by having a single regime for the entire period under study. That makes it unique among the cases under consideration. However, in the case of Laos, there has been a trade-off of country stability for regime stability. As a limited-access order, Laos has proven to be very slow to adopt political reforms. This resistance was especially apparent after Phomvihane's death, when opponents to further economic liberalization consolidated their power within the government, arguing that further reform would undermine the political stability of the country (St. John 2006). Politically, too, the LPRP sought to reign in what power had been devolved. Popular participation in "people's councils" at the village level was abolished, which effectively ended the democratic experiments begun in 1988.

The result of such a political economy is one that is entirely dependent on the LPRP for rent redistribution. Thus, it is understandable why the government might be fearful of independent economic oversight and management: it opens up the door for more avenues to wealth outside of support for the party (Stuart-Fox 1997). Indeed, the few sectors that did experience liberalization have been those primarily devoted to resource extraction/export, which are dominated by party or military officials. The timber industry, for example, has grown significantly since the 1990s in Laos, but it is generally controlled by the military, which benefits from the sales of concessions to logging companies or directly runs them. In fact, since the late 1980s, the military has steadily increased its influence within the antireformist camp (Bourdet 1997).

This continuing political dominance of a rent-seeking elite has resulted in what Stuart-Fox (2006) calls a "political culture of corruption," generally measured by bribes to superiors. The higher the position, the higher the bribe. It also means that the people in those positions must finance those bribes by taking advantage of their position to skim the necessary funds. Thus, organizations (and the individuals leading them) are primarily concerned with maintaining institutions that ensure access to rents. Doing nothing and waiting for a decision from superiors is often seen as the wisest course of action.

A risk-averse and conservative elite benefiting from the status quo implies uneven development. Economic reforms where rents are expected to increase, such as stronger trade or expansion of lumber exports through infrastructure development, are prioritized over political reforms that challenge access to those rents. Priority is paid to those sectors that either directly benefit government officials (e.g., timber) or foreign countries that supply the country with aid (e.g., bridges). Meanwhile, wider liberalization and infrastructure investment that benefit Laotians more broadly are resisted for fear they undermine the LPRP's grip.

Laos and Mali share structural similarities. Both states are landlocked, surrounded by regional instability, poor and aid dependent, and afflicted by environmental vulnerability. Both have neglected their hinterlands through deliberate policies of repression and lack of investment in infrastructure and political participation, and both have faced insurgencies in their hinterlands as a result. Yet we observe in them two distinct paths for countries that move into and out of fragility. As a hybrid state with pretenses to democracy, Mali sees a future that appears much bleaker than Laos's, a country that has hesitatingly taken on political reform and economic liberalization. On the one hand, Mali was never a true model of stability; it has suffered four major dips into fragility since 1980. All of these inflection points were driven mainly by challenges to authority. The lack of private-sector development and the rent economy have long kept Mali on edge by keeping capacity scores consistently high.

For countries like Mali with premature load bearing, external shocks *do* have an impact on their stability. But the actual extent of this impact is determined by the policy decisions taken by Mali's leaders. Further, aid rents distort Mali's local economies and power relationships. Instability, however, is not guaranteed: Mali has been aid-dependent for a long time but has only suffered dips into fragility four times since 1980, coinciding with poor leadership. For example, the decision to decentralize Mali's political structures would, at face value, appear to be a viable coping mechanism. But we can see now its purpose was much different than what Western policymakers associate with autonomy and institutional flexibility. Mali's decentralization was designed in part to ensure that no faction could usurp presidential authority, essentially keeping various groups less powerful than the center. It also worked to undermine the capacity and legitimacy of the military, which posed an existential threat to Mali's regimes. But decentralization also contributed to the conditions that led to the Tuareg rebellions by ensuring that Bamako had neither the capacity nor the legitimacy to project power and influence into the northern hinterland. That factions organized themselves along ethnic and religious lines is telling, considering the civilian-based structures of the nomadic Tuareg lent themselves to political orders that were at odds with the more sedentary peoples of the north and the south. It is only relatively late in Mali's weakened state that we see the rise of more militant organizations as Mali's border became a fertile place for corrupt border trafficking and terrorist organizations.

One might conclude that simply surrounding a country with economically vibrant states is sufficient to move a country out of fragility. But for Laos we have seen that its regional relations carry with it both immense risk as well as fortune. Despite being located in a region that has seen a significant increase in incomes and standards of living over the past thirty years, Laos has remained relatively stagnant.

Here we see some viable contrasts with Mali. Unlike Mali's leaders, whether authoritarian or democratically elected, the LPRP has over the course of the last thirty years demonstrated it has the ability to project its power over undergoverned spaces. The collapse of the Hmong insurgency in 2006 is a testament to this. But if there is a weakness in Laos's trajectory, it is simply that its leaders are slow to make policy decisions that could improve the lives of average citizens. Instead they concentrate on liberalizing and expanding only those sectors that they fully control, for fear that the regime could lose power. The subsequent lack of accountability limits the country's ability to capitalize on the wider regional economic boom and the resulting stability it could provide.

Second, rents must be questioned for both Laos and Mali. While Mali's leaders have raised extracting rents from aid to an art form, Laos's leaders have shown that more and better development comes when it is tied primarily to the growth of its regional trade partners, even when they themselves benefit directly from those investments. Roads and bridges across the Mekong to Thailand, a high-speed railway between Thailand and China, and electricity for Thailand from the Nam Theun II Dam are all testament to this.

Chapter 5

Fragility Exit

Bangladesh and Mozambique—A Fine Balance

Bangladesh and Mozambique have been fragile for much of their existence. Yet, unlike the other fragile states examined in this volume, both countries have managed to pull themselves out of the crucible of regional conflict, civil war, and entrenched poverty and have stabilized over time. For our purposes, a country that has exited fragility has moved out of the top forty and stayed there for at least a decade. Bangladesh qualifies because from 1980 to 2015 it gradually improved its fragility ranking, in particular its capacity ranking. Our assessments point to Bangladesh being one of the few states to have succeeded in exiting severe fragility, having left the ranks of the forty most fragile states in 1991 with the era of military rule finally coming to an end and parliamentary democracy restored.

For its part, Mozambique exited severe fragility at the end of its civil war in 1992. The primary trend for Mozambique since the mid-1990s has been improvement in its authority and capacity clusters from a ranking of the fortieth most fragile state in 1980 to less than half that severe by the middle of this decade. Moreover, the ALC trend lines for both countries have begun to stabilize and cluster together, which is a recognition of decreasing volatility. Bangladesh and Mozambique are also the youngest nations in this study, having achieved statehood in the early 1970s. Perhaps their improvement and progress, while halting and still far from perfect, are simply a reflection of how serious their political and economic situations were at independence: Bangladesh highly indebted, deeply divided, and still recovering from its vicious and destructive breakup with West Pakistan; Mozambique one of the poorest countries on the African continent following its protracted, gruesome, and equally horrific civil war.

Indeed, since their calamitous and inauspicious beginnings, both Mozambique and Bangladesh have been beset by assassinations, mass killings, internecine political infighting, and deep corruption. Yet their economic circumstances have improved significantly, despite an enduring dependence on foreign aid (Carment and Samy 2012). To be sure, both Mozambique and Bangladesh face significant structural problems that hamper their economic growth and political development, in particular Mozambique, whose economic weaknesses are beginning to reveal themselves (Jones and Tarp 2016). As hybrid democracies, both countries have substantial difficulties in managing elections without partisan violence. Mozambique has been a nominal one-party state since independence, though its constitution introduced multiparty elections in 1989. Bangladesh is a multiparty democracy but one consistently undermined by corruption, violence, and cronyism.

BANGLADESH FROM BREAKUP TO GROWTH

When Bangladesh gained independence from Pakistan in 1971, its future seemed bleak. Its economy was in shambles, its people divided, and its leadership powerless. The postindependence government led by Sheikh Mujibur Rahman soon descended into authoritarianism and military rule (Zaman 2012). Within a few decades, Bangladesh's fortunes reversed course in 1991 as repressive military rule was supplanted by a promising but dysfunctional multiparty system. Its economic performance improved over the years, moving from a low-income country to a low-middle-income one in 2016 as it grew by an average of 6 percent every year since 2004 (World Bank 2016a). In 2017, its GDP per capita exceeded Pakistan's (World Bank 2017k).

Often hailed as an economic development success, Bangladesh has progressed more than most other countries of similar economic status

(Asadullah, Savoia, and Mahmud 2014). Manufacturing, especially in the garment and textile industries, has been the engine for the country's growing economy. At the same time, a harsh environment with a high propensity for flooding and other natural disasters has rendered the country more fragile than it otherwise would be.[1]

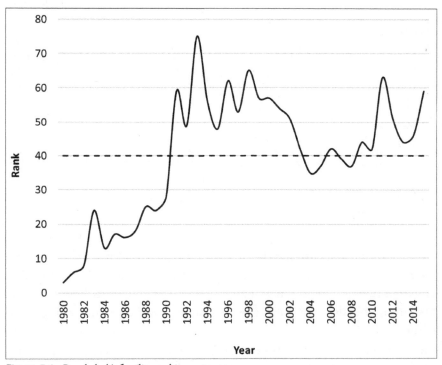

Figure 5.1 Bangladesh's fragility ranking, 1980–2014

Bangladesh's transition is reflected in the country's ranking in figure 5.1. Despite comprehensive structural weaknesses and uneven, if not ineffective, periods of poor governance, Bangladesh has gradually improved its fragility scores over the past three decades. It has only qualified as fragile twice since the 1990s (2004–5 and 2007–8). On the whole, Bangladesh's situation has improved remarkably over the course of the thirty-five-year period, given that it began as the third most fragile state in the world (EIU 2017). As figure 5.2 shows, this structural transformation is the result of an overall improvement in Bangladesh's ALC rankings. However, each of these remains high as of 2016, leaving Bangladesh potentially vulnerable to a return to fragility if adverse conditions were to emerge.

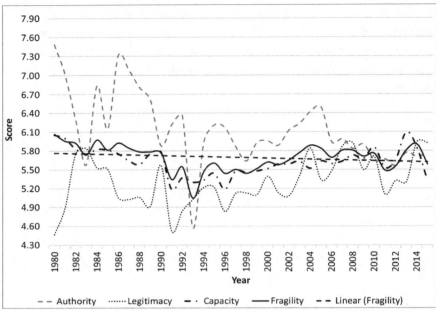

Figure 5.2 Bangladesh's ALC trends, 1980–2014

Though Bangladesh's overall fragility trend did not exhibit a large change, the convergence of authority, legitimacy, and capacity over time is worth noting. For the first half of the 1980s, authority scores fluctuated dramatically, improving, then worsening, and then improving again. Conversely, legitimacy scores worsened and then improved over the same time frame, with authority changes lagging one to three years behind. This pattern of authority following legitimacy represented a general trend for the next twenty years. From about 2000 onward, A, L, and C converge and fluctuate less, indicating the country reached a period of greater stability. Indeed, though deteriorating slightly in the last five years, capacity did not fluctuate very much over the entire thirty-year time frame, despite Bangladesh having a growing economy and absorbing a large amount of development and humanitarian aid. In essence, capacity has had an important role in guiding Bangladesh's transition out of fragility. As the economy improved, that underpinned the legitimacy of government actions. When the economy deteriorated, legitimacy was weakened as well.

BANGLADESH'S STRUCTURAL TRANSFORMATION

Our findings indicate that Bangladesh's exit from fragility followed a four-stage path in which contentious and violent political events were matched by elite efforts, civilian and military, to rebalance the political order. These four stages were themselves divided into two core phases. The first phase consisted of military rule and a halting and uneven civilianization process. The second phase, the rise of coalition parties and the co-optation of smaller parties, led to a highly personalized, combative, and dynastic two-party political rivalry (Islam 2013). In this important second phase, instead of a ratcheting up or a negative feedback loop in which instability begets greater direct military involvement, there is a ratcheting down where political parties increase their toehold on government, build coalitions, and mobilize their followers to intervene in the political space for (mostly) peaceful protest and action. In essence, Bangladesh has managed to avoid the legitimacy trap that befell Yemen and Pakistan.

It is during this second phase that we see the beginning of Bangladesh's shift from a limited-access order to an open-access order, from a hybrid political system to a system attempting to deepen its commitment to democratic and institutionalized political processes but not quite succeeding. Each stage in this transformation reflects about a six- to seven-year period with rapid fluctuations of ALC rankings in the first fifteen years diminishing over time. Even under unstable authoritarian leadership in the first phase driven primarily by several coups and assassinations, Bangladesh's forays into fragility are eventually channeled through an "elite compact" that strengthens civilian, and for the most part representative, government, while recognizing the important role of the military in bringing stability to the country. Though the military formally withdrew from politics in the late 1980s, its presence is still clearly felt in the form of paramilitary forces that have in recent years become more violent and direct in their treatment of political opponents and mass unrest (Thompson 2012).

Furthermore, despite the fact that the country has been led by women for the past twenty-five years, Muslim cultural values have served to keep women politically less engaged outside the political mainstream (Panday 2013). Since 1997, Bangladesh has had a system of reserved seats for women with direct elections to local government bodies. These changes were partly a result of supportive donor policy and directives and mechanisms created by the state (Nazneen and Tazneem 2010). Since then, female representatives have achieved a degree of political voice and social legitimacy, and to some extent even gender imbalances have improved with time as the Awami League, as well as opposition parties including a coalition of small parties making up the Bangladesh Nationalist Party (BNP), have sought to strengthen the role of women in society (Panday and Rabbani 2011, 2013; Khan and Ara 2006).

Turning to Bangladesh's inauspicious start, we can briefly consider the country's first president, Sheikh Mujibur Rahman. Inheriting a country that was weak in most respects, Mujibur immediately ran into problems of law and order, a deeply divided society, and an economy that was failing. Following a decision to scrap Bangladesh's nascent multiparty system in 1975, he was assassinated by field-grade officers looking to bring some credibility to the military, to restore law and order, and to ensure his leftist political policies would not bear fruit (Sisson and Rose 1991). It was during Mujibur's time in power that Bangladesh reached its nadir. His one-party rule with the formation of the Bangladesh Krishak Sramik Awami League was marked by widespread censorship and judiciary abuse. Corruption was widespread. Food shortages and poor distribution led to a disastrous famine (Sisson and Rose 1991; Ali 2010).

Subsequent to Mujibur's assassination, Bangladesh witnessed two periods of military rule: the first under Gen. Ziaur Rahman, the second under Hussain Mohammed Ershad. Zia was assassinated in 1981 by army officers, but, overall, Zia's tenure marked a shift toward positive change in civil-military relations. In particular, he worked to divorce Bangladesh from the policies of Mujibur by including urban elites and the military in politics (Sisson and Rose 1991). He held referendums during elections and increased the military's budget. As in Pakistan, the civilianization process did not necessarily mean a complete withdrawal of the military. Zia's success was also due to bringing stability and growth to the economy and obtaining rural support for his policies.[2] It is under Zia where we witness the emergence of competing coalitions though patron-client relations—some co-opted, such as the rural poor, and some with vested interests in controlling resource distribution, such as military and business elites.

General Ershad, who eventually replaced Zia, was not a 1971 war of independence hero like his predecessors and was initially seen only as a temporary leader without a clear plan for the country. Ultimately Ershad's success would come, like that of his predecessor, from co-opting opposition leaders and satisfying the needs of the army. But these objectives came at a cost. By 1982, Ershad had suspended the constitution and banned all political parties. In essence, Bangladesh's tentative and halting exit from fragility really began with Zia, who sought to carefully construct a more democratic society during his five years in power. It is at that point that Bangladesh's fragility path was driven by changes in its authority structures and by improvements in the economy.

Zia had been largely perceived as a more legitimate presence in politics, and Ershad's coup and his subsequent leadership were initially not well received. For example, Ershad proved adept at cracking down on threats to his regime, focusing on, at least for the first several years, wastefulness and corruption in the civilian government. These actions only served to alienate the elites previously co-opted by Zia (Ali 2010). By 1983, when Ershad officially became president of Bangladesh, he decided to take on the inefficiency of the Bangladesh bureaucracy as a way of moving the government away from Zia's more socialist-oriented approach with its emphasis on a large public sector. Ershad also sought to increase the role of Islam in society and decentralize government decision-making to combat corruption. Limited political activity was permitted by the beginning of 1983. Among those taking advantage of new openings in the political arena were the popular Awami League and the BNP. They were the two major political movements that worked to publicly expose the vagaries and weaknesses of Ershad's autocratic tendencies.

For his part, Ershad had plans to steer the country toward a multi-party democratic system and in doing so to co-opt the opposition. However, the opposition parties were unwilling to cooperate while martial law was still in effect. Ershad's initial, somewhat tentative response was to organize a referendum on his policies in 1986, winning handily amid protestations of fraud from the opposition (Ali 2010). Local elections were held, with a great deal of politically motivated violence occurring across Bangladesh. When Ershad stepped down as army chief of staff in order to run for presidential elections under the Jatiya Party banner, major opposition parties boycotted the election, organizing mass strikes and demonstrations. In response, martial law was relaxed, and parliamentary elections were held. Again, the elections were marred by violence and corruption, and the BNP boycotted the elections in protest. The Jatiya Party, supported by Ershad's government, won a majority in parliament.

At the same time, Ershad skillfully increased the political distance between the Awami League and the BNP by meeting with Awami opposition leader Sheikh Hasina, daughter of Mujibur, ensuring she would have a place in his government (Ali 2010). Her subsequent inclusion would set in motion a trajectory of political dynasties and her party's role in ensuring what amounted to a competitive one-party state rule (Suykens 2017). Sheikh Hasina not only served as opposition leader from 1986 to 1990 and from 1991 to 1995 but also as Bangladesh's prime minister from 1996 to 2001—and again from 2009 to today (Suykens 2017). To be clear, her agreement to engage in politics ensured not only her personal political longevity but also helped legitimize Bangladesh's nascent democratic institutions. In essence, by agreeing to take part in controversial elections, the Awami League's inclusion helped normalize the political process and in turn encouraged the political participation of ordinary Bangladeshis, on whom the Awami League drew for support. To be sure, the league suffered initially from a lack of cohesion and direction. It was infighting among its coalition leaders that allowed Ershad to consolidate his power, thereby preventing any chance of a coherent opposition movement challenging the Jatiya Party.

Indeed, such was Ershad's power that he was able to withstand domestic and international scrutiny. For example, during the 1986 election both opposition leaders and foreign media alleged voting irregularities, including a far lower number of votes cast than were actually reported. Corresponding to Ershad's heavy-handedness, and perhaps due to his perceived steady hand at the tiller and lack of coherent opposition, his regime was able to withstand these pressures. Eventually, however, in reaction to Ershad's policies, designed to further entrench the military within the civilian government, the five major parties became even more united. Collectively their leaders promulgated numerous strikes, including a fifty-four-hour general strike that paralyzed cities and towns across the nation and resulted in eleven deaths, seven hundred injuries, and many jailed (Bertelsmann Stiftung 2016.

If the first period up to 1986 constituted the most unstable period in Bangladesh's history, then 1987–99 constitutes a second inflection point of slow and deliberate civilianization and constant challenges to regime stability. For example, massive flooding destroyed property and crops in 1987 and 1988, coupled with increasing political protests. To crack down on protests,

Ershad declared a state of emergency, arrested leaders of the opposition, tightened security, and placed restrictions on public gatherings. In order to again legitimize his rule, another parliamentary election was held in 1988, with the Jatiya Party again winning a majority because of boycotts by the major opposition parties. Only 10 percent to 15 percent of eligible voters participated (Ali 2010).

Outwardly, it appeared that the opposition campaigns of civil disobedience could not dislodge Ershad from power (Ali 2010). While he remained generally disliked, Ershad did take practical steps to improve the country's economic situation (Khasru 2010). He privatized hundreds of formerly nationalized industrial assets and banks, set up a board of investment to attract foreign direct investment, and oversaw construction of massive investments in the country's infrastructure, including roads, bridges, railways, and power grids. He also helped create a new elite class of entrepreneurs and investors by promoting such activities and by offering tax breaks and other incentives to those willing to participate. Indeed, many of these policies are linked to Bangladesh's improved capacity scores, as seen from the mid-1980s well into the 1990s. By 1991, Ershad was forced to resign due to an unprecedented popular movement against his regime. He was subsequently imprisoned on charges of corruption (Ali 2010).

During this period of political instability, Khaleda Zia, widow of Zia ur Rahman and a member of the BNP, was elected prime minister by a narrow margin in 1991. She subsequently made the decision to shift executive power to her office. When she took office in 1991, Zia was the first woman in the country's history and second in the Muslim world (after Benazir Bhutto) to head a democratic government as prime minister (Smillie and Hailey 2001). Soon after Zia became prime minister, Cyclone Marian killed about 140,000 people and left millions homeless throughout the country. The young, inexperienced government did not deal well with the disaster, and confidence in its ability to deal with future significant crises was brought into question. Taking advantage of Zia's inexperience, Sheikh Hasina, then leader of the official opposition, claimed that Bangladesh's democracy had become a "dictatorship of the Prime Minister," a phrase that Zia would use against Hasina some fifteen years later (Ruud and Islam 2016). Indeed, opposition parties often walked out or boycotted parliament, and the disputes between the "two ladies" became increasingly bitter and personal as the two women vied for public attention in the political area (Barry 2015). A 1994 by-election culminated in even more unrest due to the opposition's frustration with what it saw as a lack of political inclusion. The result was an increase in the country's instability driven largely by party-organized violence (Ruud and Islam 2016; HRW 2017).

The period 1996–2004 saw Khaleda Zia elected once more. As was the case in previous elections, the losing opposition viewed the outcome as illegitimate, and shortly thereafter the government was forced to conduct new elections (Thompson 2012). By this time, Zia's economic record was relatively solid, with GDP growing at an average rate of 4.5 percent, reducing poverty levels to 36 percent from the 43 percent before she came to power (Ahmed 2010). In the runoff, the Awami League won with support from Ershad's Jatiya Party. Sheikh Hasina became prime minister. On the political front, she attempted to govern by consensus, in that upper executives within her coalition drew on members from different political parties (Ruud and Islam 2016). The economy continued to grow at an average of 4.5 percent over the decade.

The BNP opposition, which was more leftist than the Awami coalition, had a number of grievances, complaining that opposition members were harassed by government forces. Moreover, Hasina's administrative performance was far from exemplary, with unrestrained macroeconomic spending, a lack of transparency in the stock exchange markets, and a lack of competition in key industries such as telecommunications, power, and transportation. Finally, promises to improve decentralized governance and its institutions were not met (Ahmed 2010, 2017; Khan 2016).

Over time, these cumulative economic failures led the BNP to boycott parliament, initiating similar strategies of civil disobedience as was seen during the Ershad period. Political protests and general strikes would become more commonplace over the next fifteen years as each party, dissatisfied with the electoral outcome, would mobilize its supporters in response. In 2001, the Awami League government stepped down to permit a caretaker government to supervise parliamentary elections, while celebrating the government's completion of its "five year mandate."[3]

Despite its progress over the years, Bangladesh was labeled the most corrupt country in the world from 1997 to 2001 (Kabeer, Mahmud, and Castro 2012). This designation further assisted the BNP in its bid for power. In the end, the BNP won more than two-thirds of parliamentary seats and presided over a relatively stable government for the next five years, with the Bangladeshi economy growing at unprecedented rates after wide-scale economic policy reforms further liberalized the country. Over this period, legitimacy, authority, and capacity all began to converge, indicating that Bangladesh had begun to stabilize for the most part. Some of the still relevant problems include a lack of genuine political will and support for local governance reforms and a capture of the local political space by central actors (Alam and Tiecher 2012).

The last stage of Bangladesh's political and economic trajectory stretches from 2005 to the present day. While economic growth continued unabated over the 2000s, population pressures served up new challenges to quality-of-life indicators (Mahmud, Ahmed and Mahaj 2008). Bangladesh is one of the most densely populated countries in the world, and this affects per capita resource availability for services such as health care, education, sanitation, and more. This issue accounts for the upward trend in fragility scores in the late 2000s. Another factor is Islamic extremism, which has played an ever-increasing role in Bangladeshi society. In August 2005, more than 350 small explosives were set off across the country, aimed at administrative buildings and courthouses. A banned right-wing Islamic extremist group took responsibility for the attacks and demanded that the civilian court system be replaced with sharia law. This attack weakened the legitimacy of the government, even though many members and leaders of the group were arrested and prosecuted, with six top-level leaders executed for their roles in the bombings.

In the political realm, elections were slated for 2007, but controversy over the choice of a caretaker government led to increased political violence across the country, and the military, led by the caretaker government, eventually took over security (Moniruzzaman 2009a). The BNP and the Awami League were again at odds with one another, with the Zia-versus-Hasina battle capturing more followers than ever before. Indeed, it took threats from OECD donors and India, who noted that if elections were held unfairly or held up by the military, the new government would not be recognized as legitimate and would thus lose the lucrative foreign aid and peacekeeping contracts on which the military depended (Alam and Tiecher 2012).

Elections were finally held in late 2008, with the Awami League capturing more than 250 of 300 seats in parliament and Sheikh Hasina being sworn in as prime minister again. Economically the country remained functional despite a slow recovery from the global financial crisis of 2008.

Subsequent elections such as the one in 2014 witnessed an intense rivalry between the two parties, and personalization of politics resulted in unprecedented paralysis (Moniruzzaman 2009b).[4] In January 2015, the then opposition leader Khaleda Zia began a campaign of political strikes and transportation blockades to force Sheikh Hasina to call new national elections. Hundreds of people were killed in fire-bombings, and opposition leaders were thrown into jail (Barry 2015). A World Bank report released that year showed that Bangladesh's economy lost $2.2 billion, or around 1 percent of GDP, as a result of the sixty-two days of political unrest.[5]

To summarize, Bangladesh's structural transformations are most closely associated with its economic growth amid intense elite infighting. But such rapid growth has come at an immense cost. The country's leaders have institutionalized mechanisms and tools of dynasticism as its democracy has failed to consolidate. As Ruud and Islam (2016) argue, networks of political activists, enforcers, businessmen, and bureaucrats are all crucial to the success of these dynasties.[6] But, as Ahmed (2010) has convincingly shown, these networks also conspire to block political development as corruption, cronyism, and rent seeking move in lock step with economic growth (see also Paul 2010). The military has been the final arbiter in Bangladesh's politics. Where reforms took place, they proved unsuccessful in dislodging old party politics characterized by, among other things, "over-concentration of power in the party chief, inter-party rivalry and suspicion, lack of mutual trust, dynastic domination of party leadership, and lack of democratic orientation of parties" (Ahmed 2010, 23).

BANGLADESH'S DRIVERS OF FRAGILITY

Bangladesh's process of democratization should not be conflated with equivalent improvements in governance (Moniruzzaman 2009a). As Alam and Tiecher (2012) argue, there remain significant problems related to an inadequate capacity of local government institutions combined with a lack of continuity in policy and practices and a low degree of popular participation. Nor should it be assumed Bangladesh's exit from fragility is complete. As we have seen, the country has transitioned from an unstable authoritarian state to an unconsolidated and almost equally unstable hybrid democracy (Ahmed 2006; Ahmed 2010). But the military's shadow looms large. Indeed, there have been a few attempted coups since the transition to democracy, most notably in 2007, when the military installed a caretaker government that was removed from power after elections the following year (Alamgir 2009).

Corruption and Rent Seeking

We argue that Bangladesh's enduring corruption and poor human development indicators demonstrate relatively weak institutionalization of policies and poor output legitimacy. Corruption has been a particularly significant issue in Bangladesh due to patron-client relations throughout government at both the national and grassroots levels (Knox 2009). But this corruption has proven to be a double-edged sword. On the one hand, corruption is part of the country's political and economic fabric. Elites from political parties generate rents that are then distributed among their followers, thereby helping legitimize the electoral process by encouraging large voter turnouts. On the other hand, it means democratic outcomes will always be openly and violently contested because the stakes are so high. To ensure the instability inherent in this system does not escalate, the military acts as guarantor, occasionally stepping in when civil unrest threatens the economy.[7] Both major parties take extreme actions during elections, such as arresting opponents, in order to secure electoral victories, harming the overall legitimacy of the government as a result (Riaz 2014).

Economic growth is affected. Rana and Wahid (2017) note that growth rates decline in particularly turbulent years, such as when elections take place. Thus, as Paul (2010) argues, despite general improvements in political and economic development, Bangladesh's political stability has been undermined in part by endemic corruption within the government. While corruption does not foster growth, it greases the wheels of commerce in Bangladesh's regulation-heavy systems that would otherwise impede businesses (Paul 2010). Most Bangladeshi corruption has largely taken the form of patron-client relations, which is related to social stratification in rural regions of Bangladesh (Islam 2013). The effects of this are plainly apparent at the local level of politics, with prominent individuals being offered leadership positions so that their contacts and authority can win votes, with various economic benefits being offered in exchange (Islam 2013).[8] But this elite bargaining carries a cost and is ultimately unsustainable. At the national level, there is less money available for the government to spend on education, which already receives less as a share of GDP than other states with similar income levels (Kabeer, Mahmud, and Castro 2012; Asadullah, Savoia, and Mahmud 2014). Grassroots-level corruption, meanwhile, has negatively impacted Bangladesh's horizontal equality due to bribes becoming necessary to obtain critical services, such as health care and education (Knox 2009). Furthermore, corruption has led to various political appointments, including the judiciary, to reward supporters and target opponents, with rule of law being undermined as a result (Riaz 2014). In sum, government functions, such as law enforcement and the provision of health care and education, are compromised by patronage, with bribery having become a necessity (Knox 2009; Asadullah, Savoia, and Mahmud 2014). Public expenditure on government services also remains low relative to countries with a similar socioeconomic performance as the misappropriation of funds is common (Knox 2009).[9]

Redistributed Resources

As we argue above, Bangladesh's exit from fragility has occurred in spite of uneven governance and corruption (Asadullah, Savoia, and Mahmud 2014). Despite the political chaos that has unfolded over the last fifteen years, Bangladesh has transitioned to a manufacturing economy, maintaining an average growth rate of 6 percent per year for the past decade (Rana and Wahid 2017; World Bank 2016a). At the same time, poverty has been substantially reduced, going from 70 percent in the 1970s to 32 percent in 2010 (Khandker, Baqui Kahlily, and Samad 2016; Rana and Wahid 2017). So, in examining the potential drivers that account for Bangladesh's exit from fragility, we see that manufacturing would certainly be paramount, as would international and domestic development initiatives. In particular, the widespread use of microfinance institutions to fund small household enterprises has helped the country overcome some of its structural weaknesses, most notably poor output legitimacy.

More significant, microfinance has helped strengthen the social contract by giving voice to some of Bangladesh's rural poor. While not fundamental to Bangladesh's economic development, its compensatory effects are instructive for a fragile state with poor output legitimacy and a disengaged and partly disenfranchised rural population. For decades, microfinance institutions have allowed poor households to access credit when it would otherwise not be possible, enabling them to lift themselves out of poverty by starting their own small enterprises. Originally, institutions such as the Grameen Bank and the Bangladesh Rural Advancement Committee (BRAC) were meant to disburse credit and mobilize savings but have grown since the 1990s to create employment (Khandker, Baqui Kahlily, and Samad 2016).

The loans disbursed by these institutions have had mostly positive effects on household welfare in a few selected areas. For example, households that are members of microfinance institutions tend to have higher incomes and school enrollment rates than others (Khandker, Baqui Kahlily, and Samad 2016).[10] The increasing role of credit-funded microenterprises may also contribute to reductions in poverty, as the number of rural households considered to be extremely poor declined from 80 percent in the 1970s to approximately 33 percent by 2005, with those that possess microenterprises having substantially lower rates of both moderate and extreme poverty than those without (Khandker and Koolwal 2010; Khandker, Baqui Kahlily, and Samad 2016).

While microfinance has helped reduce poverty in Bangladesh, it has not proven entirely effective in compensating for weak state service delivery. Microcredit works best where conditions such as education and infrastructure are already in place and supported. In particular, the benefits of microfinance are higher for households with members who have completed school and are skilled with oral math (Khandker, Baqui Kahlily, and Samad 2016). Furthermore, many of those who qualify as extremely poor are unable to take advantage of microfinance institutions. The extremely poor in Bangladesh often fail to meet even minimal qualifications and are unable to escape poverty as a result (Chemin 2008; Khandker, Baqui Kahlily, and Samad 2016). Large households similarly appear to gain little benefit from microfinance (Chemin 2008). For example, the lack of infrastructure in rural regions has proven problematic, as the gains from microfinance for rural enterprises appear to be largely limited to those based in villages with electricity and paved roads (Khandker, Baqui Khalily, and Samad 2016).[11]

State-Society Relations

Civil society, particularly NGOs, are often praised for playing a significant role in Bangladesh's development (Bdnews24.com 2017). NGOs also compensate somewhat for Bangladesh's poor governance, especially at the local level (Smillie and Hailey 2001). More diffuse and unfocused than the small-credit scheme, NGOs have nevertheless been instrumental in a variety of ways, ranging from combating poverty in rural areas to advocating for governance reforms in rural areas. The effectiveness of these organizations has changed over the years, however. Over time, changes in Bangladeshi politics have sharply reduced the ability of these organizations to push for further democratic reform, though they remain important in combating poverty. Civil society organizations in Bangladesh originally worked to foster not only social development but democratic governance as well. These organizations largely emerged following Bangladesh's secession from Pakistan in the 1970s, as they were necessary for building the capacity of the newly formed state (Parnini 2006).[12]

During the years of military rule, these organizations were strong proponents of democratic freedoms and have been credited by some as playing an important role in both limiting authoritarian rule and encouraging a return to democracy (Parnini 2006). Since the early 1990s, however, the effectiveness of civil society organizations in promoting democracy has markedly declined, in part as a result of governance issues becoming increasingly complex but also due to the consequences of increased politicization (Parnini 2006). On the one hand, they have been more successful in working toward development goals in rural regions, where they have essentially superseded the government in providing services (Kabeer, Mahmud, and Castro 2012; Tasnim 2012). These roles are divided along a continuum, with one extreme being those that specialize in microfinance, such as the Grameen Bank, and the other being those that focus exclusively on service provision, such as Samata (Kabeer, Mahmud, and Castro 2012). On the other hand, these organizations have been largely ineffective in influencing government policy due to the presence of clientelism in Bangladeshi politics, which encourages NGOs to become more partisan in nature.

Patron-client relations have always been present in Bangladeshi politics, and policy implementation is difficult at the national or local level without elite support (Parnini 2006). To augment NGO activity, the government has pursued a reform agenda, as evident in the Local Government Reform Act of 1997 (Union Parishad). However, these decentralized local governance structures are not as effective as they could be in ensuring development, participation, transparency and accountability, and an equal distribution of services (Panday and Rabbani 2011). That is because the party that forms the government typically attempts to assert control over legislation and other aspects of governance, while the opposition party often refuses to contribute to parliament. This has led to NGOs becoming increasingly partisan, both in perception and in reality, as both of the major parties co-opt key institutions to maintain their power. NGOs must often involuntarily comply with party political agendas in order to receive funding (Parnini 2006; Tasnim 2012). More governance-oriented NGOs have been subject to political harassment and a lack of support from other organizations, further limiting their ability to encourage reform (Kabeer, Mahmud, and Castro 2012).

As a result, most civil society organizations have avoided making forays into issues relating to politics in order to avoid jeopardizing themselves, but it also means their direct influence on governance has become more limited with time. Where they have been most successful in achieving development goals is poverty reduction. Most of these, such as the Grameen Bank noted above, were not originally founded with these issues as their primary goal, instead focusing on promoting democratic habits; the onset of military rule in the 1980s, however, pushed NGOs to focus on service delivery instead (Kabeer, Mahmud, and Castro 2012). It is here where NGOs have been credited with significantly reducing poverty in rural areas, where people would otherwise be forced to take out high-interest loans from moneylending elites (Smillie and Hailey 2001; Tasnim 2012). At the same time, numerous organizations have been providing social services in rural areas, such as education, to the point of essentially replacing the state (Parnini 2006). The emphasis on microfinance has been argued by some as coming at the expense of broader service provision. As expenditures on microfinance rose during the 1990s other NGOs reduced their own (Kabeer, Mahmud, and Castro 2012).[13]

MOZAMBIQUE: ON THE BRINK

Mozambique exited severe fragility at the end of the civil war in 1992. The primary overall trend since then has been improvement as seen in figure 5.3. Moreover, authority, legitimacy, and capacity have begun to stabilize and cluster together at this lower level of fragility.[14] The in-depth cluster-based analysis in figure 5.3 below serves to further deconstruct the dimensions of fragility that have allowed Mozambique to so drastically improve its overall situation.

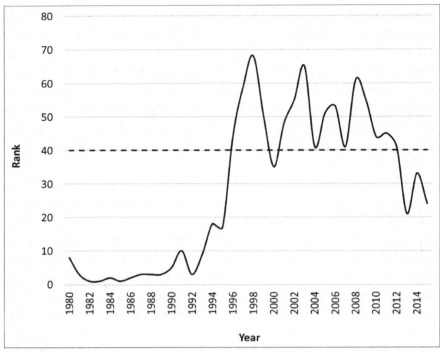

Figure 5.3 Mozambique's fragility ranking, 1980–2014

Mozambique's irregular exit from fragility was witness to three inflection points. For our purposes, the period under study began in the midst of the civil war at the onset of the thirty-five-year window through which we track fragility processes. The first inflection point occurred between 1977 and 1991 with the signing of a peace agreement. The second inflection point occurred between 1992 and 1994 with international oversight to enforce the peace agreement. The final inflection point occurred between 1995 and 2016 where Mozambique slowly becomes less fragile and the government remains in power through two more sets of elections. In the last five years, we see a deterioration in Mozambique's ranking. This is a reflection of the country's increasing debt load, increasing internal challenges to one-party rule, and a decline in export earnings (Jones and Tarp 2016). At the same time, the country has become victim to the same decline in growth that has beset other commodity-producing countries in Africa. Higher consumer spending and increased investment in energy, transportation, and resources have not sufficiently offset these declines.

Fragility Exit: Bangladesh and Mozambique

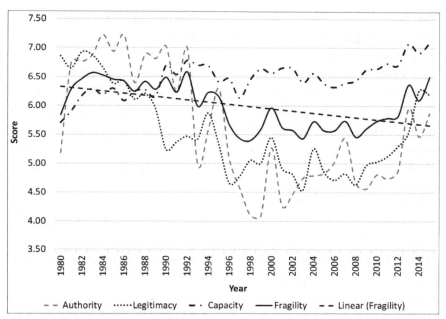

Figure 5.4 Mozambique's ALC trends, 1980–2014

Figure 5.4 shows the overall ALC sequencing profile for Mozambique. Legitimacy rankings improve ahead of authority and capacity performance. Through the period of the civil war from 1980 to 1989, legitimacy scores slowly improved and from 1989 to 1990 saw their largest overall improvement. Following improvements in legitimacy were comparable improvements in authority scores. Authority scores remained high for approximately three years after the major improvement in legitimacy was seen, and thereafter a similar improvement was seen in authority, from 1992 to 1993. This pattern indicates that it is possible that improvements in legitimacy were correlated with, if not driving, subsequent improvements in authority.

MOZAMBIQUE'S STRUCTURAL TRANSFORMATION

Of all the fragile states examined in this book, Mozambique is the only one where the period examined began during a civil war, which was a struggle between the ruling Marxist Frente de Libertação de Moçambique (Frelimo) forces and the anticommunist forces of the Resistência Nacional Moçambicana (Renamo).[15] In order to identify key significant structural changes in Mozambique from 1980s onward, we focus first on the consequences and impact of the war, then on the subsequent efforts to rebuild the country.[16]

From 1980 to 1983, Renamo, with the support of South Africa, built up its ranks and established a presence in each of Mozambique's provinces (Hanlon 1984).[17] Due to Frelimo's support for the African National Congress (ANC), South Africa supplied the rebel group Renamo with weapons, communications equipment, and training. Portugal also provided equipment and counterinsurgency training. In turn, neighboring allies of the Mozambique government, including Tanzania, Zambia, and Zimbabwe, provided military support to the government in Maputo.

Renamo, with over ten thousand troops, sporadically attacked infrastructure and military targets within Mozambique (Hanlon 1984)., Because of the escalating violence and worry about Renamo's intentions, Frelimo began to mobilize and train local progovernment militias, attacking Renamo's headquarters and causing the rebels to scatter and escape across the border to South Africa in 1982 (Hall 1990). Their initial defeat, along with pressure from South Africa's apartheid leaders, resulted in Renamo starting a more aggressive expansionist strategy with the aim of taking control of Mozambique by direct attacks on urban centers (Minter 1989). By 1982, Renamo forces were directly engaged in attacking larger population centers. Widespread atrocities ensued.[18] In response, the Frelimo leader and president of Mozambique, Samora Machel, armed villagers and appointed provincial military commanders to oversee these newly created militias.[19]

President Machel took a strong personal interest in the war and was heavily involved in the planning of the 1982 offensive, in which up to fifteen thousand troops participated (Alden 2001). Renamo saw the intentions of the government forces, however, and was able to avoid a large-scale direct confrontation through careful maneuvering.[20] Renamo pushed southward into Maputo Province, home of the capital city. This alarmed the government, and high-level diplomatic meetings were convened in which Mozambique pleaded with South Africa to discontinue its support for the rebels. South African forces both supplied and fought alongside Renamo militants, greatly increasing their capacity to destabilize the country. An agreement was made to bring peace to Mozambique, and in return the Mozambican government agreed to lessen its support for the ANC, the main political rival of the South African government. Frelimo forces successfully repelled the attacks in Maputo Province after several months of fighting (Manning 2002).[21]

On the diplomatic front, Machel's government sought support from the five permanent members of the United Nations Security Council for assistance in fighting Renamo. While the countries provided support such as uniforms, boots, cargo/personnel vehicles, and other nonlethal equipment, they would not provide assault rifles. All five members condemned the South African policy of supporting Renamo (Hume 1994).

In response, Renamo representatives from around the world met in West Germany under protection of the German intelligence services. Representatives of France and the United States also joined the meeting. Buoyed by the results, Renamo leader Orlando Cristina began to push back against what he saw as South African domination of the party. Shortly afterward, Cristina was shot dead in his Pretoria home at night despite tight security surrounding him (Fauvet 1984).[22] Renamo's military campaigns did not cease after its leader's death. Instead, negotiations between Mozambique and South Africa continued to develop, eventually resulting in the March 1984 Nkomati Accord, which was also known as the Agreement on Non-Aggression and Good Neighbourliness between the Government of the People's Republic of Mozambique and the Republic of South Africa.[23]

The war nonetheless continued unabated from 1984 onward, with neither side gaining a strong advantage over the other. Stalemate ensued.[24] On October 19, 1986, President Machel's plane crashed, killing Machel. Claims that the South African government was involved became commonplace, despite a lack of conclusive evidence (Munslow 1988). Mozambican foreign minister Joaquim Chissano assumed the role of president and pushed for a stronger relationship with the West along with increased economic liberalization. He also refused a negotiated end to the war, instead directing government forces to conduct a strong counteroffensive against the Renamo rebels.[25]

In April 1990, Chissano addressed Mozambican dissidents in Portugal, inviting them back to Mozambique to participate in the debate on a new constitution. Representatives of Renamo saw this as a positive sign, and leaders of Frelimo and Renamo finally met for direct peace talks in Rome in 1990, bringing an end to the seventeen-year civil war in 1992 with the Rome General Peace Accords. Chissano "promised no prosecutions or punishments" and promised Renamo fighters 50 percent of the positions in the

Mozambican army (Vines 2013). The Renamo rebels later established their own political party.

Economically, Chissano chose a dual strategy to bringing stability to Mozambique. He would work with the World Bank in order to prevent the mass starvation that was looming. With guidance from the IMF, Chissano launched an economic recovery program in 1987, in an effort to bring the economy back to levels not seen since 1981 (Alden 2001). The program included a reworking of the trade system to better favor agricultural producers, a restructuring of the taxation system, a major devaluation of the national currency, a decrease in public spending, and increased wages for workers. Despite this ambitious program, very little progress had been made by 1990. Inflation soared, agricultural production rose a mere 6.3 percent, and the economy itself grew only 4 percent per year on average (Alden 2001).[26]

Along with the military, foreign policy, and economic reforms, Chissano's government also introduced political reforms allowing party members to engage in private business; the separation of legislative, executive, and judicial powers; the establishment of presidential elections and a limit on terms; establishment of freedom of the press and habeas corpus; and, finally, multiparty elections (Alden 2001; Ottaway 1988). All of these actions served to improve the legitimacy of the government and signaled exceptional foresight on Chissano's part.

Formal intervention by the international community ended after Frelimo won the 1994 elections, and the economy opened up to international investors. The economy could have gone into another period of turmoil due to rising a food prices and high unemployment. However, Chissano was able to keep inflation under control (Alden 2001). Overall, this period was relatively successful: the economy grew at double digits (Alden 2001).

To achieve these results, Chissano continued to focus on expanding the market-based nature of the economy. However, this was difficult, given the high level of destruction of both human capital and infrastructure (De Sousa 2002). Revitalization of Maputo as an economic hub was vital to these goals. In addition, attracting foreign investment and at the same time sustaining flows of foreign aid acted as the other two pillars of Maputo's economic strategy. This meant that Frelimo's elite were in the best position to secure the material benefits of liberalization for themselves, leaving little room for the common person to share in the new growth (Hanlon and Mosse 2010). Exports and foreign investment were key areas of growth for the new economy. Agricultural and fishery exports grew relatively well over this period, although most of this growth was achieved in the urban areas as opposed to the countryside, which was still suffering due to poor infrastructure development.

The World Bank and IMF policies pushing for liberalization and privatization of key rural industries such as cashew exports were unsympathetic to the invested populations and served to highlight the fragile relationship between rural and city dwellers. By 1998, over 850 state-owned assets had been sold off to private companies, with foreign investment in such acquisitions sitting at 50 percent (Alden 2001). Chissano's government embraced these reforms despite the potential political consequences. Spikes in legitimacy and authority leading to the spike in fragility scores in the late 1990s and early 2000s can be partly attributed to political protests and unrest. The 1999 elections saw an increase in political partisanship, with each side demonizing the other and blaming it for the country's ills. (Dinerman 2006). The results of the election were close, with Frelimo winning a second narrow victory over Renamo. Rioting by Renamo supporters claiming the election was rigged led to upward of forty deaths and contributed to worsening peace and security indicator rankings for that year (BBC 2018).[27]

Throughout the 2000s, the country's economy continued to grow at an average rate of about 8 percent per year. By 2004, the rate of absolute poverty had dropped to 54 percent, down from 69 percent in 1997 (OECD 2013). However, poverty, health, and education indicators remained stubbornly high. State capacity and services remained weak due to low taxation and a small tax base, human capital and law enforcement (marked by a weak judiciary and legislature) (OECD 2013). The government was and still is dependent on foreign aid, with an average of $1 billion per year.[28]

While the country moved away from being extremely fragile and is unlikely to see another civil war, urban development is not being fully realized by the rural population (Hanlon and Mosse 2010; Hanlon 2004). With only limited pressure on the government to reform, the likelihood of change is low. The development of a vibrant independent civil society in Mozambique has been slow to pick up, as the political and societal culture remains orchestrated from above (Addison 2003). There are few effective linkages across community-based groups, citizens, and government bodies (Hanlon and Mosse 2010).

An entrenched elite is equally problematic. For example, when Chissano stepped down in accordance with the term limits set out in the constitution and Frelimo candidate Armando Guebuza won the election with 64 percent of the popular vote, the results were contested by Renamo and its supporters. In 2009, another national election was held, with Frelimo again winning control of parliament. This trend is likely to continue, with Frelimo continuing to hold on to power indefinitely (EIU 2013). The party is deeply rooted in all aspects of urban Mozambican society, and its patronage networks are imposing (Hanlon and Mosse 2010; Hanlon 2004). It is extremely difficult for the opposition parties to access any further financial support for political activities. The exclusion of the majority of the rural population from the political realm continues undiminished.

DRIVERS OF FRAGILITY

The challenge for any state looking to transition out of fragility is to find a path for elite bargaining and power sharing while opening up the political process to ensure these same leaders are accountable and the resources they control are effectively distributed. In a postwar society, that challenge is amplified by the need to find a balance between reconciliation and power sharing and the divisive nature of election campaigns that democratization inevitably brings (Manning 2002; De Sousa 2002). Such balancing is rarely possible without a minimum of security guarantees for opposition parties under the watchful eye of international actors.

Balancing Domestic and International Legitimacy

It is clear that Mozambique's main turning point from fragility was the Rome General Peace Accords signed in 1992. That agreement was a key driver precisely because it occurred in an international environment conducive to a reduction in fragility, not just because its provisions included an opportunity for the rebels to become a political entity and join the army. The United Nations, an important player in drafting the agreement, was also responsible for the implementation of most of its key provisions. Although Chissano and his party had technically already voted in a new constitution based on the principles of multiparty democracy, the government itself had no experience implementing such a wide-sweeping policy after the war. Thus, a Supervisory and Monitoring Commission was established by the UN to oversee the implementation of the peace agreement, and it comprised representatives from both parties as well as the United States, the United Kingdom, France, Italy, and Portugal. Even with UN support there were a number of roadblocks, but in 1994 the UN mission was able to successfully uphold its mandate by holding the first democratic elections in the history of the country. In addition, the United Nations Operation in Mozambique (ONUMOZ) from December 1992 to December 1994 was responsible for monitoring the cease-fire and the withdrawal of foreign forces and promoting demilitarization of the sixty-three thousand government and twenty thousand Renamo troops (Alden 1995; Dunne 2006).

A new national army consisting of equal numbers of soldiers from each side was promised, but in reality this was difficult to achieve because the financial incentives for demobilization were greater than those for remaining under arms (Alden 2001). Regardless of some of the roadblocks faced by the UN mission, a coordinated effort for implementing democracy, demilitarization, a new police force, a new framework for disbursing humanitarian assistance, and the return of hundreds of thousands of refugees was implemented (Alden 2001). These staggering tasks were seen as victories by the international community, and, in return, the leadership of the ONUMOZ, Renamo and Frelimo demonstrated an unprecedented willingness to work together. For its part, the government of Mozambique gained international support for ending the war, bolstered by the government's willingness to liberalize the economy according to Western-recommended structural adjustment programs (De Sousa 2002). This increasing participation in international organizations also helped strengthen Frelimo's international standing.

Two clear incentives for international cooperation were the promise of economic assistance and demining. In the former case, subsequent economic reforms and liberalization policies contributed to Mozambique's overall growth and prosperity. In the latter case, demining freed up vast amounts of agricultural land. Another incentive was the promise of political longevity for both Frelimo and Renamo. Simply put, both became part of a political process that was formalized and institutionalized with international oversight.[29] Taking its fight to the political arena meant that Frelimo was obliged to make its economic and social policies more accountable. To be sure, some of its policies were aimed at undercutting the programs proposed by Renamo by moving away from the communist foundations of the state.

Overall, these transformations were very much a function of the confluence of a set of larger, and ultimately unique processes that occurred at the end of the Cold War. In that sense, Frelimo's efforts to build up international legitimacy after the protracted civil conflict must be seen in light of its leaders' pragmatic decisions to move from socialist policies to liberalization, the diminished influence of both South Africa and the Soviet Union in Mozambique's internal affairs, a robust UN, and an international and concerted commitment to bring many of the Cold War–legacy conflicts to an end. Moreover, exceptional changes in the international arena meant that negotiations would get critical support from a wide range of outside parties.[30]

None of these conditions are easily replicated and therefore in our opinion do not present themselves as crucial ways in which future fragile states will transition out of fragility. Further, international legitimacy might help explain Mozambique's exit from fragility, but it cannot fully explain why the transition has lasted so long. Domestic legitimacy is perhaps the more crucial element here, and this is where Frelimo performed poorly at first but gained strength over time. At the outset of the conflict, there were no major challengers to Frelimo, therefore the party was well positioned to take full control of the country and shape it as it so desired with only limited accountability. The 1992 Rome General accords marked the turning point for Mozambique because the agreement ushered in the potential for greater accountability and the possibility that economic gains would be more broadly distributed. In turn, understanding that the organization either adapt or perish, Renamo's leader, Afonso Dhlakama, moved from a guerrilla army to a political party.

The dependence of both warring parties on foreign aid, military and financial, meant that the international withdrawal, or the threat of withdrawal, of such aid acted as a major catalyst to future elite bargaining and cooperation.[31] Frelimo's leaders hinged their support for these concessions on the belief that they would both reduce the appeal of Renamo as a viable political choice once it became a legitimate political party and at the same time would force Renamo to the bargaining table by taking away its principal political leverage— namely, the threat of force (Alden 2001).

Although promises were made that liberalization would lead to economic growth and improved outcomes for the people of Mozambique, in reality economic and development outcomes were not significantly affected by a transition to multiparty democracy (Jones and Tarp 2016). Nor were these outcomes more widely distributed across society. Rather, the chief effect of this political opening up was to consolidate Frelimo's political control by creating the perception of its legitimacy as one of several participants in a functional democracy (Dinerman 2006). Political maneuvering has seen Renamo participate (and lose) in every election since.

This kind of political bargaining is important, considering where both groups started. During the war, Frelimo's leaders became habituated to the use of terrorism and violence. It was, after all, an insurgent group interested in toppling both Rhodesia and South Africa. But Frelimo would, over the course of the conflict, also use such tactics against its own people, a key factor in alienating the government from a disengaged and rural population. In retrospect, had the government focused on its domestic economic policies by providing services to its populace rather than getting involved in regional struggles, Renamo would not have come together as a cohesive force for change in Mozambique. Hence, the civil war was in many ways self-inflicted.[32] Once Renamo was established, it was impossible to turn back the tide. Rural Mozambicans grew increasingly opposed to the heavy-handed and occasionally violent policies implemented by Frelimo and were more willing to cooperate with or even join Renamo in its fight against the government. Crucial missteps on behalf of the Frelimo leaders included publicly committing themselves to agricultural reform while not implementing it, not addressing grievances between southerners and northerners, persecuting religious communities, and promoting state-sponsored violence against political enemies (Cahen 1993).

Machel as a major supporter of communist ideals stood, in the eyes of some, as a roadblock to progress. He met resistance both within the party as well as outside of it. The lack of awareness exhibited by Machel at this time regarding the limited enthusiasm for his party's radicalism was a key factor in the intensification and duration of the civil war. If Machel had recognized the growing discontent earlier and addressed some of the aforementioned grievances among the Mozambique people, Renamo guerrillas would not have had the freedom to move about the countryside and enjoy other forms of support from the populace. It was only in the early 1990s, with international and domestic pressure building after Machel's death and a vocal opposition, that Frelimo instituted pragmatic policies focused on more inclusive economic growth.

Rent Seeking and Isomorphic Mimicry

The 1980s witnessed a series of bad economic policies that worked to alienate the rural population from the government. The government pursued a set pricing policy that gave farmers an incentive to sell their products on the black market. Government resettlement programs, intended to ease resource scarcity, essentially took the form of forced relocation projects, alienating the rural population. An unwillingness to import all but those goods deemed essential by government bureaucrats led to the demise of rural trade markets. The lack of foreign currency limited imports of raw materials and other industrial necessities, leading to a cash-strapped resource sector (Alden, 2001).

Following Machel's death, Mozambique's economic polices became increasingly dominated by the World Bank in the late 1980s and, from the 1990s onward, by the IMF. The latter imposed tight restrictions on social program spending, even capping foreign aid (Hanlon 2004). In 1995, with Mozambique being an "aid darling," the IMF lifted the cap on aid disbursements to the country, and the World Bank regained its influence (Hanlon and Mosse 2010). During this period of neoliberal economic policy, many multinationals made inroads into Maputo and beyond. South Africa became Mozambique's main trading partner, accounting for 30 percent of exports. The economy grew from diversified exports, including aluminum, coal, bulk electricity, lumber, cotton, prawns, cashews, sugar, and citrus. According to the African Development Bank, Mozambique achieved an economic growth rate averaging 7.5 percent over ten years since 1998; political and macroeconomic stability became the hallmarks of this time period (Phiri 2012; African Development Bank 2008). Investments in sectors such as services, industry, and mineral resources, buttressed by strong donor support, substantial policy reform, and pro-poor government expenditure, also contributed to growth (World Bank 2007).

Unfortunately, the country's newer industries, such as mining, natural gas, and manufacturing, have produced limited benefits for the average Mozambican, particularly in rural areas. Moreover, Frelimo party elites have become adept at rent seeking, with many becoming extremely rich over the 1990s and early 2000s as agents or brokers for international investors and through bribes and widespread corruption (Stasavage 1999; Hanlon 2004). Mozambique's elites, especially those who are members of Frelimo, perpetuate a delicate balance: they participate actively in a political system that appears to be democratic, while at the same time they are able to keep their hands in the coffers of donors, multinational companies, private businesses, and government agencies. Frelimo's political and economic dominance has meant that Renamo has been unable to seriously compete on the electoral stage, creating a positive feedback loop whereby corruption fuels political success and the votes that matter can easily be bought.

In comparison to other countries examined in previous chapters, the exit from fragility of both Mozambique and Bangladesh is more clear-cut, if not remarkable. These two countries illustrate that while long-term stability is not easily achieved, it is possible, given the right mix of decisions, support from the international community, and reasonably independent political institutions. The key driver shaping improvement in both countries has been exceptional export-driven economic growth. At the same time, enhanced state-society relations have proven to be both stabilizing and destabilizing. For Bangladesh, rapid economic growth empowered a large number of citizens while at the same time left their political voices increasingly unheard. To be clear, Bangladesh's economic growth has been the foundation on which the country's political and social development is built. As goes the economy, so goes the political fortunes of its ruling elite.

Mozambique's trajectory is less certain than Bangladesh's. After more than twenty years following a peace agreement, remarkable economic growth, coupled with stubbornly high levels of poverty, show that Mozambique remains a conundrum. On the one hand, its exit from fragility is far from guaranteed. On the other, the country has demonstrated extraordinary resilience considering where it stood just three decades ago. For Mozambique, political and economic interdependencies were most evident in its formative years after the war. Where catalyzing negative effects had the potential to shift the country downward, political leadership moved both countries in a more positive direction. When stressed, as in a time of political upheaval, Mozambique revealed a modest ability to recuperate.

To be sure, both aid and extractive industry rents have aggravated Mozambique's fragility by undermining regime legitimacy and effectiveness due to poor distribution (Ottaway 2003a). Maputo's growth is not matched by equivalent gains in the hinterland (Stasavage 1999). Perez and Le Billon (2013) argue that Mozambique's continued low development is a function of a low tax burden on elites, which in turn puts minimal pressure on these elites to provide social spending for all Mozambicans. The absence of accountability is key.

Output legitimacy hangs in the balance. For example, the country's supply of food is at risk, leading to alarming numbers of people lacking permanent food security. Forty-four percent of children under five are chronically malnourished, and at some point during the year at least a quarter of the population suffers from acute food insecurity (Phiri 2012). Mozambique is the third most at-risk country from weather hazards in Africa, with droughts, flooding, and other climate-change-induced, high-temperature weather patterns acting as a destabilizing force (WFP 2011). These statistics illustrate some of the consequences of the lack of spending on social welfare and infrastructure, which occurs in tandem with increasing corruption and cronyism (TI 2013b). If the political leaders of Mozambique are able to recognize ahead of time that their continued rent-seeking behavior will eventually lead to massive discontent within the general population, a pulling-out of donor countries from aid arrangements, and a risky economic climate for investors, then they may be able to stave off some of these risks.

It is here that Bangladesh provides lessons for Mozambique. For example, Bangladesh's ultrapoor, who constitute the poorest 17.6 percent of the population, are supported by various initiatives, including a program to drive down that number even further. Similarly, the Grameen Bank provides credit to small and medium-sized enterprises (SMEs), further strengthening capacity among the rural poor. Bangladesh represents the virtue of investing in human capital.

We have yet to see either country fully institutionalize democratic processes. While outcome legitimacy in the form of improved service delivery and human development has improved through a growing economy, process legitimacy remains in shambles. Both countries' elites have not yet realized the benefits of respecting the results of an election. To counter these fundamental constraints on interelite cooperation, resilience comes in the form of strong patron-client relations, which helps mobilize a wide swath of interests from the urban elite to the marginalized rural poor. For Mozambique, there is a strong urban-rural split, which serves as a brake on effective distribution of resources. In Bangladesh, there is some evidence of deepening social capital capacity that is mostly related to the involvement of NGOs and civil society networks. In this instance, rather than generating political departicipation, the general populace is actively engaged along party lines and across economic lines.

In essence, the key structural transformation for Bangladesh was the removal of overt military control in domestic crisis management and its replacement with political mobilization opportunities that would be channeled through party contestation and political reforms. So, despite crises being partly a function of elite political machinations and rivalries, there are specific factors and processes that have helped Bangladesh progress. Key among them is the conscious decision to incorporate civil society within the political process, thereby broadening the political arena for the inclusion of new political parties and the pursuit of high-growth export-driven manufacturing and production that would mobilize a work force in overpopulated urban centers. To be sure, both countries are heavily dependent on export production, with attendant and extremely high levels of corruption and rent-seeking proclivities always visible. Low taxation rates are indicative of this. While rent seeking remains a fundamental feature of Mozambique's political economy, it became central to Bangladesh's political economy more recently after its export economy began to take off.[33]

Chapter 6

Explaining the Fragility Trap and What to Do about It

In this book, we asked why some states successfully exit fragility while others do not. We were particularly interested in those states that have been trapped in fragility for long periods of time. While there has been a lot of attention paid to fragile states generally and to the causes and consequences of fragility, there is comparatively less research on countries trapped in fragility. Indeed, there is a lack of theorizing about the so-called fragility trap and the combination of factors that can help us understand why some countries fail to see sustained progress over time. In answering these questions, our research objective was to determine what if any features these states have in common and to compare changes in those features over time with states that have successfully exited. The purpose of this concluding chapter is to briefly summarize the findings from each chapter and then draw on these insights for a discussion of the book's theoretical and policy implications.

We found scant evidence in support of the idea that exits from fragility are a unidirectional occurrence associated with a postconflict peace process, economic development, or democratization. Our research shows that fragile states move both forward and backward in terms of their political and economic development, even when examined over the long run. Further, our research has shown that causal explanations focusing only on economic development, for example, or political development are unsuitable. Rarely do states end up where they are because of only one main factor. Some states are stuck despite copious amounts of aid because of problems related to reform failures, aid fungibility and distortions, and even overaiding, while others engage in isomorphic mimicry emulating open institutions while immunizing themselves from external influence.

In the introduction we argued that existing research on fragility traps was relatively meager because of underdeveloped causal explanations of the trap, relying instead mostly on inference and correlational analysis derived from structural indicators. Much of the research we noted was driven by monocausal explanations that tended to emphasize poverty, conflict, or governance and in a few cases some combination thereof. It is not clear how this combination of factors is linked to create situations where countries are unable to move out of fragility. Our case studies in chapters 3 through 5 provide more nuance to the evolution of states, using CIFP's methodology—namely, the ALC framework and various clusters of performance.

Few are the studies that focus on the policy implications of the trap. For example, an early study we cited was Chauvet and Collier's 2008 assessment of fragility persistence, which found the average duration of a failing state is a prolonged period of five decades because external financing for resource exports and aid tend to embolden and support rent-seeking elites and retard reforms. Andrimihaja, Cinyabuguma, and Devarajan in their 2011 World Bank study cited a combination of weak property rights enforcement, corruption, insecurity, and violence, which conspire to create a low-growth equilibrium. But what neither of these studies clarify is how these factors work together to create the trap.

On the one hand we have elites who are resistant to change, and on the other their resistance is reflected in damaging and self-interested behavior such as corruption and political violence. With a focus on symptoms rather than causes, policies are rarely successful, because they do not get to the core of the fragility trap problem. International and domestic incentives—whether political or economic—for leaders of trapped states to embrace reforms that affect their personal interests are often too weak. Indeed, policies intended to induce reform are not only misplaced but also often counterproductive.

For example, there is an extensive literature on conditionality associated with aid programs reinforcing our point that aid conditionality fails more often than not (Collier 1997).

To elaborate on this point, we argued in chapter 1 that causal explanations focusing on one factor such as economic development or political development by themselves are insufficient. In many conventional interpretations, fragility is usually associated with poor policy environments, aid-absorption problems, conflict, and poverty (Naudé, Santos-Paulino, and McGillivray 2011). In conducting our literature review and analysis, we found that even among these core assumptions, empirical validation varies. Some trapped states experience large-scale violence, while others do not. Moreover, within a given state, conflict intensity is not constant. Nor are economic underdevelopment and weak institutions solely responsible for explaining why states are trapped. Overall, it is hard to find a singular explanation for why countries are stuck in a fragility trap.

To lend credence to these observations, we focused on testing four different traps that we thought would be the basis for a more refined model. We came to this conclusion by examining four traps prevalent in the literature. The first was the poverty trap, in which the poor are unable to save and accumulate enough capital per person for investment and as a consequence remain trapped in poverty. We found that the poverty trap is not empirically true for all fragile states, nor is it true among the trapped states. In examining the conflict trap, it was argued that once countries fall into civil wars, the risk that conflicts will happen again increases significantly. Our evaluation of this linkage found only a minor correlation with the fragility trap. In our evaluation of the capability trap, which relates primarily to problems of service delivery and government effectiveness, we found the causal mechanism to be unclear, since isomorphic mimicry is informed by a combination of behaviors, including rent-seeking behavior, elite capture, and hybrid politics. Nevertheless, empirically there was strong evidence that trapped states do indeed suffer from a capability trap.

Finally, we evaluated the legitimacy trap, finding a strong linkage between legitimacy and fragility persistence. In sum, we showed that capability, legitimacy, and conflict to some extent were most related to the fragility trap. For subsequent application to our case studies, we associated the capability and conflict trap explanations with CIFP's authority cluster and legitimacy with CIFP's legitimacy cluster.

Though this initial testing did not differentiate between process and output legitimacy, it highlighted the importance of identifying potentials for reversal and backsliding among fragile states. It also highlighted the structural problems of trapped states—namely, that improvements in capacity do not guarantee that countries will be able to escape the fragility trap, especially when corresponding improvements are not happening to authority and legitimacy. Capacity becomes important once countries are able to exit the fragility trap.

In the second part of chapter 1, we broadened the scope of the analysis by considering two other types of countries: those that have moved into and out of fragility and those that have exited fragility over several years. Our objective was to find out whether the factors that lead countries to be trapped are unique to these countries or whether they are also found among these two types of countries identified. For example, one might expect that the sequence of changes observed in a trapped country would work in reverse for a country that successfully exits fragility. Thus, and to ensure comparability with the analysis for trapped countries, we tested the relevance of the four traps for countries moving into and out of fragility and countries that exit it. While we were expecting the capability trap to be more significant for countries that exit fragility—thus "mirroring" what was observed for the trapped countries—it is, in fact, the ability of countries to avoid conflicts (improving authority) and hence build legitimacy that seems to matter the most for exited countries. In other words, exited states are not the mirror image of those that are trapped.

In the case of countries that have moved into and out of fragility, the conflict trap is significant. Fragility scores did not improve permanently even as governments of these countries became more capable because they were unable to exercise control over their people and territories (i.e., exercise authority). It would be tempting to think that conflict is a major factor; it was, however, neither perpetually intense nor constant in their case. We argue that conflict matters not in and of itself but because of other factors such as endogenous shocks or when the state exhibits low carrying capacity. Overall, the findings from chapter 1, and the introduction, indicate that legitimacy and authority are important factors behind the evolution of states, while capacity is less important.

In chapter 2, we argued that policies focused purely on structure will be misplaced if leaders of trapped states have limited willingness to reform.

We emphasized the importance of state-society relations, specifically the role of legitimacy in underpinning the behavior of political, social, and economic elites, in the formation of undergoverned spaces and a coercive state apparatus, rent-seeking behavior, and elite capture, and in building a less resilient society overall. These assumptions were premised on claims regarding interactions between the superordinate elements of state authority, capacity, and legitimacy and not just economic development and democracy. For a state that has exited fragility, positive changes in authority that address societal well-being not only provide valuable guidance for government policy—they also reduce barriers to commerce and economic development (measures of capacity) such as restrictions on citizen movement and assembly (measures of legitimacy). Responsiveness also induces governments to produce policies addressing popular concerns that are not growth-focused, such as wealth distribution and social programming, and that by extension increase state legitimacy.

Efforts in factoring legitimacy into an explanation of the fragility trap, and why countries get out of it temporarily or permanently, were applied to our six case studies in chapters 3 through 5. We found the evidence from our six cases generally supported the large-sample findings, though not always. Specifically, we saw similarities and differences when we compared the average results for groups of countries according to different typologies (chapter 1) with those of individual cases extracted from these typologies (chapters 3 through 5). For example, in regard to conflict, we found that it was present in all six cases, though none was trapped by it. In brief, while all six cases experienced low-intensity conflict during the thirty-five-year window, the two states that exited fragility did so after major civil wars and humanitarian crises (Bangladesh and Mozambique). Of the four remaining, two have had much less intense conflict and experienced it only sporadically (Pakistan and Laos), while just two (Yemen and Mali) have fallen back into major conflict, though they have been deeply fragile for some time. To suggest, then, that conflict is a key determinant of fragility is misplaced.

Furthermore, in the case of the trapped countries examined in chapter 3—Yemen and Pakistan—we found that legitimacy was the most significant factor that led these countries to be trapped. Nor was regime stability a dominant factor across cases. For example, three of the six cases—Bangladesh, Pakistan, and Mali—experienced multiple coups, while two—Yemen and Mozambique—experienced at least one coup or coup attempt. This point was reinforced, for example, in our examination of the case of Bangladesh (chapter 5). As we argued, significant improvements in capacity during the second stage, rather than authority and legitimacy, allowed the country to exit fragility.

If we break down the conflict analysis by type, we see that the two countries that successfully exited—Bangladesh and Mozambique—emerged from large-scale civil war that cost millions of lives and destroyed their economies. But their transitions proved successful insofar as political and economic processes emerged that were sustainable and reasonably legitimate. In Mozambique's case, legitimacy was a clear driver of the country's exit from fragility, followed by authority and capacity. In contrast, our two "in" and "out" states, Mali and Laos, experienced sporadic conflicts, but these were regionally driven, low-intensity insurgencies that drained the capacity of the state to project authority and build legitimacy. Challenges to authority in the case of Mali and weak capacity despite strong control over territory in the case of Laos prevented both countries from exiting fragility permanently.

Finally, our trapped states have long-running low-intensity conflicts. Only in Yemen's case might we conclude that unresolved conflict has contributed to its trapped status. In fact, both legitimacy and authority challenges have prevented the country from getting out of the fragility trap. While Yemen failed to overcome its long-standing and deep north-south divide, Pakistan has not yet collapsed under intense internal pressure despite, and perhaps because of, the military's dominance in political affairs. But that dominance comes with the cost of deteriorating state legitimacy and limited political freedoms. In relation to democratization, we also found some inconsistencies. Overall, three of the six cases have been or are de facto one-party states over the thirty-five-year period (Mozambique, Yemen, and Laos), whereas the other three are hybrid or civilianized bureaucratic authoritarian states (Mali, Bangladesh, and Pakistan). The lack of a clearly discernible pattern here suggests that a focus on weak democratic institutions alone is misplaced.

Finally, in regard to growth, we note that six of six have seen economic growth during the thirty-five-year period—6 to 8 percent in some periods for all of the countries under examination—implying that capacity is always improving. Further, four of the six have sustained that growth over the last ten years or so (Pakistan, Mozambique, Bangladesh, and Mali). This finding is consistent with our observation that capacity is not a determinant of the fragility trap.

While we did not examine other trapped states such as Afghanistan, the Democratic Republic of the Congo, or Somalia in more detail, we argue that the findings in this book could be generalized to these countries. For example, they face the same challenges to authority and legitimacy that came out of the in-depth analyses of Pakistan and Yemen (chapter 3). All of these countries do not have full control of their territories and peoples, they are characterized by ungoverned spaces, they cannot always provide core public goods to their citizens (despite receiving significant amounts of international assistance), and neither can they guarantee a secure environment for their citizens. The governing regimes of these countries cannot command public loyalty and are unable of building domestic support for their legislative agendas. For example, in a quarterly report to the US Congress, the Special Inspector General for Afghanistan Reconstruction reported that only about 57.2 percent of the country's territory was under Afghan government control or influence in November 2016 (SIGAR 2017). Afghanistan remains one of the most corrupt countries in the world, and successive governments have failed to build trust between leaders and citizens.

We can also compare specific patterns in relation to country type in terms of ALC interactions, key drivers of changes, and elite commitments to reform. Our overall conclusion is that trapped states are most prone to lethal and pernicious feedback loops. In general terms, strengthening authority structures without appropriate resource distribution goes hand in hand with declining legitimacy. Capacity is skewed to maintaining control over the distribution of resources and rents in favor of entrenched and often unelected elites. Fissures based on ethnic cleavages, elite capture, and rent-seeking behavior are met with coercive measures to maintain stability but come at the costs of further declines in legitimacy.

Lethal feedback loops occur when regime survival is tied to a declining rent economy, leading to reduced capacity and control over territory and ultimately collapse. Undergoverned spaces increase over time as patron-client politics and resources weaken simultaneously. Under these conditions, elites express only a minimal commitment to reform. This is because the centralization of state authority and the pursuit of development policies aimed at maximizing revenues and rents, rather than social welfare, produce a process that has nonelected institutions and elites dominating. There is only a limited opportunity for elites to pursue reforms.

Let us turn to why we think this is the case, first empirically and then in theoretical terms. In looking at our specific trapped-state cases in chapter 3, we see that once Pakistan experienced internal legitimacy challenges, there was an effort to reinforce oppressive authority structures, no matter how weak they were, as a bulwark against further decline. Such an emphasis, exemplified in the United States' long-term aid program for Pakistan (as a result of its support for allies in the GWOT), led to a potential distortion in both the selection of aid recipients and the type of aid provided. A large amount of aid, including billions of dollars in US military aid, has been given to Pakistan regardless of the legitimacy of the regime in power. The results are deeply unpopular and contribute to the persistence over the years of nearly illegitimate regimes dependent on external aid that can be unstable over the long term.

The negative reinforcement of Pakistan's authority structures is achieved through an institutional system, political structure, and popular media in Pakistan that collectively reinforce the identity of state-centric nationalism. The Pakistani state is not so much a subordinate to dominant ethnic groups as a partner with them. This partnership is reinforced when the state is challenged by regional minority groups, itself a response generated by assimilative pressures, policies on immigration, economic competition, and more recently political threats of secession. Simply put, the sequencing of Pakistan's increasing fragility begins with a weakness in legitimacy structures, which rather than being adaptively modified in a positive way are negatively reinforced, with the consequence of increasing instability over the short run.

Yemen's fragility trap is a function of mutually reinforcing structural constraints built around the rent economy. A carefully constructed patronage system provided benefits to a select few clients, but it also constrained Ali Abdullah Saleh's ability to improve his country's economy—for example, through structural adjustment and improved social services. As long as resources were available, the regime was secure and did not need to reform, though the country itself remained deeply fragile. When those narrowly distributed benefits began to diminish, so, too, did Saleh's hold on power. Yemen exemplifies the inherent problem of those states suffering from weakening authority over time. With heavily reliance on the rent economy driving the Yemeni patronage system, future decisions became "bound," and options more limited.

In examining the experiences of Pakistan and Yemen, we draw two implications. First, in the absence of governance systems willing to invest in equitable development and wealth redistribution, uneven growth exacerbates tensions and contributes to stagnation and fragility persistence. Trapped states with a high concentration of wealth and power along ethnic lines have two possible futures: a more coercive state or a collapsed state. It is hard to see how Saleh, having governed for so long by using the country's oil wealth to pay off potential opponents, could have effected systemic transformation without undermining his own political fortunes. We call this a lethal feedback loop because the eventual outcome for a trapped state like this is ruin. Legitimacy is thus a key challenge in both the Pakistan and Yemen cases.

In turning to our "in and out" countries in chapter 4, we see that limited capacity for both acted as a stability ceiling. For Mali, its fall into fragility coincided with structural adjustment and a neglect of the north. When faced with managing political and economic challenges, decentralization and weak borders resulted. For Laos, regional dependencies and a weak policy environment shaped its capacity to project authority along its borders and to achieve sustainable growth. Both countries exhibited only a low commitment to reform. Mali has attained limited private-sector development while local elites act as brokers in the aid economy. Laos's elites concentrate on liberalizing and expanding only those sectors that they fully control, suggesting a long process of slow political and economic development.

Laos's performance shows that regime stability does not guarantee country stability. Nor does being landlocked, resource dependent, and divided by conflict guarantee permanent fragility. Laos has the potential to permanently exit from fragility should its entrenched elites accept reformist measures. Here we see some viable contrasts with Mali. Laos is different from Mali in that it has had the same regime for the entire period under study. And unlike Mali's regime, vacillating between authoritarian and democratically elected governments, the LPRP has over the course of the last thirty-five years demonstrated it has the ability to project its power over undergoverned spaces. The rent economy is also slightly different in each case. While Mali's leaders have raised extracting aid rents to an art form, Laos's leaders have shown that more and better income comes when it is tied primarily to the growth of its regional trading partners.

Thus, for countries that move into and out of fragility, there are two different paths. One is the possibility of regression and succumbing eventually to lethal feedback loops. The other is stable exit. The likelihood of a stable exit assumes that reformists within government eventually succeed in resource distribution. Conversely, a lethal feedback loop awaits those countries with poor economic performance, coupled with an economy based on aid dependence. Under such conditions, a focus on security issues at the expense of stronger state-society relations undermines further economic growth.

In our examination in chapter 5 of those states that have exited, we see that even moderate commitments to reform made a big difference. Bangladesh realized a respectable level of civilianization of its military leaders and a nascent if not partly dysfunctional multiparty political organization. The leaders of Mozambique's Frelimo showed flexibility and pragmatism in the aftermath of protracted war. Instead of focusing on revenge, they focused on economic growth. For Bangladesh, the country's strong improvement in capacity fueled by rapid economic growth was reinforced by powerful, deep-rooted patron-client relations, resilience in the face of adversity, and a strong civil society presence. Mozambique, in contrast, though its economic growth is strong, is run by a rent-seeking political party that appears unwilling to relinquish control.

Both countries exited from fragility through two stages: first, by overcoming the adversities of war as well as meeting the challenges of natural and man-made disasters (flooding in the case of Bangladesh, land mines in the case of Mozambique) and, second, by focusing on economic growth with significant reforms implemented with support from the international community. During the first phase, we see decreasing volatility in both legitimacy and authority and only later in the second phase improvements in capacity based on export growth and more diversified economies.

Both aid and extractive industry rents have aggravated Mozambique's fragility by undermining regime legitimacy and effectiveness due to poor resource distribution. Maputo's growth is not matched by equivalent gains in the hinterland. The absence of accountability is key here. We agree with Perez and Le Billon (2013) that Mozambique will ultimately fall back into fragility because elites are not accountable and wealth needs to be more efficiently redistributed.

Politically, as hybrid democracies both countries have substantial difficulties in managing political transitions without violence and political unrest. Mozambique introduced multiparty elections in 1989, though Frelimo has ruled ever since. Bangladesh is a multiparty democracy but one consistently undermined by cronyism, corruption, and dynasticism. To be fair, much of Bangladesh's and Mozambique's corruption might be reinvested in their respective economies, creating a kind of virtuous, if inefficient, feedback loop. But other virtuous feedback loops are present, including investments in human capital projects, to some degree gender empowerment (in the case of Bangladesh), and spontaneous forms of privatization. These all serve to indirectly improve legitimacy and authority by reducing social unrest and improving legitimacy outputs.

IMPLICATIONS FOR THEORY

Our implications relate to those countries that have exited as well as those that are trapped. Exiting, while never guaranteed, must come in two stages. A first stage consists of improving state-society relations (i.e., legitimacy), achieved in part by political incorporation and a widening of political participation under modest growth. The second stage sees the rise of further political consolidation under further economic growth and distribution of wealth. This two-phase exit from fragility is necessary because fragile states are most susceptible to crises at the earliest formative stages. Each successive wave of destabilizing events must correspond with improvements in legitimacy and capacity to help move the country out of danger.

Conversely, if stability is achieved through coercive and repressive acts, legitimacy will deteriorate, leading to countereffortrs to rebalance the delicate equilibrium. Legitimacy in this instance pertains not only to institutional performance but also to outputs such as improved service delivery and human development as well as an active civil society. Strong patron-client relations that mobilize a wide swath of interests from the urban elite to the marginalized rural poor can be beneficial if there is a perception of shared political participation and distributed growth. To be sure, rapid economic growth has the potential to empower a large number of citizens while at the same time leaving their political voices unheard and their needs unsatisfied. A balance is needed.

Conversely, a trapped state, such as Yemen, that lacks sufficient resources to retain supporters is more likely to become vulnerable to challenges that destabilize it. Disengagement of the local population occurs when elites benefit from the perpetuation of undergoverned spaces and seek out rents autonomously. This disengagement can set in a cycle of violence on the periphery, a decline in state capacity, and limited success in reclaiming territory, resulting in a weakened state.

For states like Pakistan, whose coercive capacity is undiminished, a key driver of the trap is not the inherent weakness of its institutions (which can be concealed) but deeply politicized patron-client relationships driven by unelected (and therefore unaccountable) rent- seeking elites. Even when stabilized by a civilianized military regime, such patron-client systems come at the cost of creating deeper inequalities of exchange and structures of legitimized and routinized coercive dependency. Such personal and unaccountable rule ultimately undermines the institutional coherence required for a viable democratic society because rule is ultimately arbitrary.

The inherent difficulty of a fragile state attempting to exit the trap under either of these conditions is straightforward. Leaders are able to survive with a small but powerful support base by tying private prosperity to their own prosperity. Even though the state is the primary instrument of power and may even indeed possess overwhelming coercive capacity, its leaders lack the autonomy to effect concessions for reform. Since a necessary ingredient for implementing reform is public support for such policies, elites that are unaccountable to the large population (in which the possibility of overturning the government is always present) have little incentive to pursue change. Legitimacy is weakened even further when elites are forced to expend greater resources on coercive means in order to ensure they are obeyed.

In brief, states remain trapped or fall back into fragility when they fail to provide public goods that benefit large parts of the population, even in the face of improved capacity. Situations where there is a decline in the provision of public goods are often followed by decreasing voluntary compliance, which can in turn reduce government effectiveness further. The risk that nontrapped states face is a closure of the political system even when growth is achieved. Interdependence between local and national elites is crucial as it determines whether a state will remain in equilibrium or destabilize further. That is because the government of a trapped state that lacks sufficient resources to retain its supporters is likely to lose its narrow power base at the local and regional level, thus becoming vulnerable to political challenges. Disengagement sets in a cycle of violence on the periphery, a decline in state capacity, and further suppression.

Institutional processes may be, as Andrews, Pritchett, and Woolcock (2017) argue, only superficially indicative of a functional state, while in others they are effective in inducing positive development. Further, their hybridity is a strategy to endure pressures for political reform. Such states provide social groups with a degree of freedom, which allows them to pursue a "divide and rule" strategy whereby control is maintained by playing groups against each other.

POLICY IMPLICATIONS

In terms of policy insights, we have two recommendations. First, because states stuck in a fragility trap lack legitimacy does not mean we should just look at legitimacy unidimensionally. Since legitimacy processes are important, societal consent and participation in systems of governance (local, regional, and global) and effective leadership must be examined. We also need to consider indigenous forms of political and economic organization with the recognition that partial liberalization, as seen in Mali, Bangladesh, and Mozambique, is a strategy not for democratization but to sustain control politically and economically.

Second, since output legitimacy matters, we need to examine all of its dimensions, not just service delivery. Key areas to focus on are territories that are typically undergoverned and where group cohesion is low with respect to the treatment of minorities and women. We should also examine public perceptions as expressed in surveys in response to unfair and inequitable distribution of resources for public welfare. Finally, we should reexamine Chauvet and Collier's (2008) insights on how aid can and cannot buy reform. While traditional or ex ante conditionality has failed to achieve intended outcomes (Collier 1997), selectivity or ex post conditionality (where donors target countries with good policies and governance indicators) is a problem for fragile states because they almost by definition do not have a favorable environment where aid can be used effectively. This is why understanding the evolution of various characteristics of stateness, as we do in this book, is important. If, as we have found, legitimacy is a key component of why states are stuck in fragility or not, development policies should concentrate on building inclusive relations between governments of fragile states and their citizens. Aid could thus be targeted to specific programs or projects that allow governments to deliver services that address the needs of citizens in a fair and transparent manner. Due consideration should be given to the circumstances in which aid distortions contribute to increasing fragility and the disruptive effects that occur as the aid industry evolves (Kharas and Rogerson 2012). Growth-based aid models may be an inefficient use of resources even if well intentioned.

The relationship between democracy and fragility is also worth considering. Countries with highly functional democratic processes are indeed stable but then so are deeply entrenched repressive regimes. Therein lies the problem because the most unstable countries are those with moderate levels of democratic performance. This presents a challenge to efforts to move repressive regimes toward more open and participatory forms of governance. In autocratic countries, some democratic opening correlates with higher economic growth. With this in mind, the answer to whether democracy stimulates economic growth or vice versa depends on the context.

For trapped states, the two are not nearly as interdependent as the literature would indicate. This finding is intuitively plausible and consistent with our two-stage theory of exiting fragility. But it is also consistent with our findings about trapped states where capacity had little effect on fragility persistence. Democratic participation may superficially provide direction for government policy. However, truly responsive democratic governments are more likely to produce policies addressing popular concerns that are not growth-focused, such as regional wealth distribution and social programming focusing on minority interests. This is not to say that democracy is a bad thing—only that it should not be treated as a "magic bullet" that will solve all of a fragile state's problems. Concentrating on accountability, transparency, and predictable rules governing economic interaction is more likely to produce greater wealth and increased distribution.

The complexity and range of contexts surrounding fragile states highlights the importance of examining how, and whether, members of the international community can contribute to strengthening stability by promoting countries that remain stuck in fragility traps. We argue that the capacity for donors to contribute to economic liberalization or wealth distribution consolidation is related to when their interventions are initiated in the transformation process. Those countries with an inability to provide security and services necessitate donor interventions designed to foster trust in public authority and enhance legitimacy, while efforts to provide assistance to disadvantaged populations may enhance legitimacy as well as capacity.

Unfortunately, as Grävingholt, Ziaja, and Kreibaum (2012) note, while donors appear to acknowledge the need to evaluate such trade-offs, they do not rank or organize these and other conflicting objectives in a sequential manner. In some cases, this results in donors paying little attention to competing objectives, such as security issues in development assistance that donors face when engaging in democracy promotion (Grävingholt, Ziaja, and Kreibaum 2012; Grimm and Leininger 2012). The risk is that donors will ignore competing objectives, using a "wait and see" approach to identify challenges as they arise rather than seeking to integrate conflicting objectives into their strategies at the outset.

Moving beyond the question of how such programs are initiated, the capacity for development assistance to improve legitimacy is mixed. Research has shown that aid can weaken governance quality in recipients by reducing the incentives for democratic accountability (Bräutigam and Knack 2004) and by facilitating rent-seeking behavior (Djankov, Montalvo, and Reynal-Querol 2008). Moreover, Wright (2009) suggests aid has a perverse effect in cases where political leaders expect to remain in power following democratic transitions or it helps dictators cling to power, discouraging transformation.

However, the question is not only whether donors can spark change through aid and other programming, but also what types of programs are needed to enact change in partially liberalized regimes. As we have shown in this volume, trapped states that have already demonstrated a superficial commitment to open political, economic, and social systems while their unelected elites retain power make them impervious to the incremental programming typically used to encourage accountable and elected government.

Notes

Introduction: State Fragility in a Time of Turmoil

1. While complex and multifaceted interventions are likely to be necessary in transitional regimes, Grimm and Leininger (2012, 408) recommend that donors "acknowledge the relevance of conflicting objectives and consider how intrinsic and extrinsic conflicts could develop as a part of their strategy building."

2. This follows the seminal contribution by Burnside and Dollar (2000) that shows that aid works in a good policy environment and is not effective on its own. Despite criticisms (e.g., by Easterly [2003]), the idea that aid works only in a good policy environment continues to receive broad support within the donor community.

3. According to the World Bank's recent classification of countries based on income levels, there are now thirty-one low-income countries in the world. This number will continue to decline over time, but countries can reach middle-income status and remain fragile. These so-called middle-income failed or fragile countries (MIFFs) are discussed later in this chapter.

4. For example, using data from the 2016 Human Development Report, we find, as expected, that per capita income is positively related with life expectancy across countries and is statistically significant at the 1 percent level. Further, almost 40 percent of the variation in life expectancy around the world is explained by per capita gross national income alone.

5. China, followed by India, is an excellent example of how sustained economic growth led to dramatic reductions in poverty. On the other hand, sub-Saharan Africa is still recovering from its poor growth record in the 1980s and part of the 1990s, and absolute poverty remains fairly high across that region.

6. More restrictive classifications use the MDGs or combine these with a governance index. For example, the OECD uses a fragility index to identify countries that lack political commitment and insufficient capacity to develop and implement development policies.

7. Now called the Fragile States Index, the FSI ranks states according to a complex array of indicators and events associated with shifting stakeholder agendas. Almost exclusively, those states that rank high on the list are those experiencing, emerging from, or entering into large-scale conflict. Such research tools, explanations, and assumptions are legitimate, of course, if the underlying need is to develop policy on armed conflict, but they do not enhance our understanding of the causes of fragility. Nor do they help us develop more effective policies on fragility properly understood.

8. Conditional convergence suggests that countries or regions with similar characteristics will converge to similar per capita income levels.

9. Bleany and Dimico (2011) argue and provide evidence that onset and continuation of war should not be analyzed separately but rather together because similar factors would contribute to each. With this in mind, Hegre et al. (2011) find that the risk of conflict in a country that has an onset is more than doubled for the next forty years. They find that the conflict trap is very serious for low-income countries, while the risk of a recurrence of conflict, though real, is less in middle-income countries. In addition, the risk of conflict in a country's neighborhood also increases substantially. In another "experiment," it is seen that conflict resolution (say, through a peace agreement that holds) can decrease the chances of a resurgence by twenty percentage points for more than a decade.

10. The duration of conflict will also depend on the structure of the economy. Since natural resource exports tend to be more resilient as a result of significant rents that they generate and their independence from other sectors and because economic policy and institutions deteriorate and take time to recover, countries often find themselves even more dependent on primary commodities, which increases the risks of more conflict. This is related to the "natural resource curse" or "natural resource trap"—namely, that resource-rich countries do not grow more rapidly than those that are not resource-rich. Resources may either finance or increase the incentives for conflict, negatively affect governance, and increase the vulnerability of countries to conflicts (Le Billon 2001).

11. Due to the ongoing civil war, Yemen is currently classified in the low-income category, although for the period under study it had reached middle-income status only to fall back into low-income status.

Chapter 1: A Typology of Countries, with a Focus on the Fragility Trap

1. For example, both the Fund for Peace and the World Bank now use the term "fragile states" instead of "failed states" or "low-income countries under stress." For a critical discussion of the terms "fragility" and "fragile states," see the special issue of *Third World Quarterly*, "Fragile States: A Political Concept," volume 35, issue 2, published in 2014.

2. It should be noted that since the collapse of President Blaise Compaoré's government in 2014, the situation in the country has deteriorated significantly.

3. In fact, the CIFP data goes back to 1960, but there are not enough indicators to calculate composite indices prior to 1980. In order to calculate composite indices, a threshold of at least 20 percent of the indicators used must be met.

4. The World Bank defines fragile situations as having either (a) a harmonized average CPIA country rating of 3.2 or less or (b) the presence of a UN and/or regional peacekeeping or peace-building mission during the past three years. The harmonized score is an average of the World Bank's CPIA and the respective regional development bank's CPIA score. The terminology used by the bank has also changed from "low-income countries under stress" to "fragile states" and now "fragile situations."

5. In terms of concrete examples, the poor may be unable to save and accumulate enough capital per person for investment and thus remain trapped in poverty. Or they may face nutritional deficiencies that reduce their productivity and wages and again remain trapped in poverty.

6. In addition to the conflict and natural resource traps, Collier (2007) mentions two other traps that cause countries to be stuck in poverty: the trap of being landlocked with bad neighbors and a poor-governance trap.

7. The Mozambican civil war lasted from 1977 to 1992. After a long period of post-conflict peace, there have been renewed tensions and clashes between the Mozambican national resistance, Renamo, and the government since 2013. However, the country has been able to avoid another civil war thus far. El Salvador is another interesting case because its civil war lasted from 1979 to 1992. Even if the country has not experienced another civil war, violence has continued, and El Salvador has had one of the highest homicide rates in the world as a result of gang violence.

8. There are a few other countries that could be considered trapped or borderline trapped, such as Côte d'Ivoire, Eritrea, Haiti, Niger, and Sierra Leone. However, they were not included because of our strict selection criteria.

9. All countries listed as advanced economies by the International Monetary Fund are excluded from the analysis because they are not what we would consider fragile countries.

10. We cannot consider poverty data in table 1.5 because it is available only for a few specific years.

11. The data are available as of the mid-1990s but are only available on a yearly basis since the early 2000s.

Chapter 2: Elites and the Trap

1. In the economic domain, elites influence the capacity and strength of the state to withstand shocks, use aid effectively, and promote sustainable and equitable growth.

2. Similarly, Bhaumik, Gang, and Yun (2005) explore the issue of gender equity in fragile states. They argue that female-headed households are more vulnerable to adverse economic shocks. The authors compare the per capita consumption levels of male- and female-headed Serbian and Albanian households in Kosovo, holding constant a number of other factors that can affect per capita income and expenditure, to understand the extent to which the gender and ethnicity of the head of a household impacts a family's living standards within a fragile state. While both factors appear to be relevant in determining the household's well-being, ethnicity appears to play a slightly larger contributing role in Kosovo.

3. Of particular concern are states that experience economic growth while remaining deeply fragile and undemocratic (see Przeworski and Limongi 1997; Przeworski et al. 2000). For example, according to Przeworski and Limongi, economic development is important for the sustainability of democratic regimes, whereas partially liberalized regimes that fail to enhance development tend to be more fragile and unstable than countries with higher levels of economic growth.

4. In the long term, structural factors, including income levels and inequality (Przeworski and Limongi 1997; Boix and Stokes 2003; Acemoglu, Johnson, and Robinson 2001), social control (Migdal 1988, 2001), ethnic and religious tensions (Horowitz 1985; 1993), and state capacity (Levitsky and Murillo 2009) are widely considered important preconditions for democratization (Pop-Eleches and Robertson 2015).

5. Participation can be manipulated, voluntary, or habitual (Apter 1968). In the political domain, it can be understood as both symbolic and material involvement.

6. Similarly, in examining public opinion data from various countries in Africa, Bratton (2007) found that while people are attached to the idea of democracy, they have little knowledge of its specific institutional components.

7. Parkinson (2003), drawing on Apter's (1968) distinction between instrumental and consummatory legitimacy, noted that instrumental legitimacy reduces the transaction costs of ensuring compliance because it enables the government to obtain popular consent through means other than appealing to the self-interest of its citizens. Democratic representation is especially useful for obtaining this legitimacy since it allows people to feel that they have influence over government decisions.

8. Although Börzel and Risse (2016) dispute the idea that ineffective institutions undermine legitimacy and state stability, arguing that trust in the government can allow it to rule with legitimacy even with dysfunctional state institutions. The OECD's (2010) report on state legitimacy in fragile situations notes that some indigenous sources of legitimacy, such as religious or traditional beliefs, can limit a government's ability to implement certain policies, such as those aimed at reforming reproductive health practices.

9. Rent seeking is especially prominent in postcolonial African states, where state structures established by colonial powers were taken over by elites that focused on enriching themselves and their supporters over maintaining public services, making the government appear illegitimate to the majority of the population and ensuring that state institutions were not sufficiently equipped to deal with adverse situations (Omeje 2008).

10. We are indebted to Mark Haichin for these and other insights in this chapter.

Chapter 3: The Fragility Trap

1. Cluster-based profiles for each of the six case studies covered in chapters, 4, 5, and 6 can be accessed at https://carleton.ca/cifp/failed-fragile-states/.

2. While Yemen's legal system is based on the "sole source" of sharia, the reality is a mixture of Islamic, conservative, and liberal economic policies.

3. Where there was an identifiable opposition to Saleh, it proved reluctant to push for too many reforms, implicitly understanding that repression and coercion would be imposed (Carment 2011).

4. Once Saleh was ousted from power, it was another three years before Yemen's conflict reached the point of actually threatening the Hadi regime. What explains the final collapse of the regime, and specifically why did it take a relatively long time? In the midst of the unrest, oil infrastructure, critical to the Yemeni economy, was a favorite target of opposition groups. There is even evidence that the government's preoccupation with preventing sabotage may have had the opposite effect by encouraging attacks so that groups were rewarded for "stopping" them.

5. The adoption of Urdu would later cause linguistic agitation with Bengali-speaking East Pakistan.

Chapter 4: In and Out of Fragility

1. A French-led military intervention in 2013 pushed the coalition of Tuareg and Islamist insurgents back, but the Malian state has no meaningful presence in the north. See Cairnie and deGrasse (2016).

2. De Gaulle also allowed for the territories to organize and federate if they chose, which the Sudanese Republic (modern-day Mali) and Senegal did, forming the Malian Federation.

3. From 1970 to 1993, it is estimated that over 23 percent of Mali's trade was within the CFA franc zone, the highest rate of any of the CFA franc zone countries. See Gurtner (1999, 44).

4. Although Traoré had initially promised to transfer power to a civilian authority and pave the way for democratic elections, he reneged and solidified the one-party-state apparatus begun by his predecessor. Traoré, unopposed, won all elections handily afterward (MRG 2015).

5. Ansar Dine is suspected of having ties to al-Qaeda in the Islamic Maghreb.

6. In March 1991, Lt. Col. Amadou Toumani Touré led a military coup that deposed and arrested Traoré.

7. The Bambara are Mali's largest ethnic group and have dominated Malian politics since independence.

8. Certain kin groups are more prominent due to supposed religious ties (some claim direct descent from the Prophet Muhammad), historical ethnic status (as nobles or vassals), or raw political power in their arrangements with the state. To improve their fortunes, a kin group can either attempt to bolster its religious credentials or its political power in relation to other clans (Pézard and Shurkin 2013). The Third Tuareg Rebellion was thus, in the beginning, more about inter-Tuareg relations than about north-south relations.

9. The development industry was the major source of rents. Whoever controlled local development offices became the local development broker, which further allowed powerful groups to solidify their positions.

10. The poorly trained and equipped Malian forces were no match for the well-armed and experienced fighters returning from Libya.

11. In particular, the Malian government reclaimed the majority of its shares in EDM, the company that provides electricity and water, even though it was the flagship of privatization efforts (Bertelsmann Stiftung 2008).

12. Foreign investment generally is confined to the more stable resource-extraction sectors. This makes it hard for ordinary Malians to gain access to capital. Furthermore, corruption hinders private-sector development. As previously mentioned, bribing officials adds costs to the transportation of any good, and the widespread smuggling industry means certain goods that escape tariffs are priced artificially lower than they should be, which further destroys domestic incentives for competition. In fact, the corruption is so prevalent that Transparency International lists Mali as one of the worst countries to start a business (Bertelesmann Stiftung 2012a).

13. Such an alliance is considered an integral part of a political career in Mali.

14. Cocaine in particular is smuggled from South America into West African states such as Nigeria and Guinea-Bissau and then transported to Europe by air or by land through Saharan states such as Western Sahara, Mauritania, and Mali. Smuggling activity increased significantly toward the mid-2000s as other drug-smuggling routes were shut down by interdiction activities in the Caribbean, and the drug markets simultaneously grew in Europe. Wing (2013) writes that there appears to be significant central government collusion in this system, which is why Touré never openly tried to stop the insurgent groups in the north. The military would have been an impediment (Reeve 2013).

15. We are indebted to Scott Shaw for his seminal contribution to our analysis.

16. For example, given the history of disparate and generally small-scale individual land holdings in Laos, collectivization under the LPRP was implemented because of ideological conviction and the fact that its neighbor Vietnam was pursuing a similar policy, not because of geographic necessity. It was abandoned in 1979, indicating that the regime understood that to stay in power would require pragmatic policy shifts (Kerkvliet 2009).

17. With the resumption of hostilities shortly afterward, the Viet Minh joined the side of the Pathet Lao and conducted attacks all along the Laos-Vietnam border. Delegates of the Pathet Lao political wing, Lao Patriotic Front (LPF), were arrested in Vientiane. This set the stage for a three-way civil war between the Pathet Lao under the LPF, the neutralists under Kong Le and Souvanna Phouma, and the rightists under Phoumi Nosavan (Savada 1995).

18. As the United States was increasingly drawn into the Vietnam War, it ramped up its support of Phoumi and the Royal Lao Army. The Viet Minh, in turn also increased its support of the Pathet Lao. Lacking an outside backer, the neutralists were gradually displaced by the Pathet Lao and the rightists and were essentially absorbed by each side. The Viet Minh also used the Pathet Lao–controlled areas to construct the Ho Chi Minh Trail to aid their war effort against the United States and South Vietnam. The United States tried to disrupt this supply line with an unprecedented bombing campaign, but this campaign failed to cripple either the Viet Minh or the Pathet Lao. It did, however, further destabilize Laos by killing or displacing significant numbers of Laotians, leaving a legacy of unexploded ordnances that continue to maim and kill Laotians today (IRIN 2010).

19. An essential component of the peace process was the withdrawal of all foreign troops sixty days following the formation of the coalition government, the Provisional Government of National Union (PGNU).

20. Calculated from CIFP data.

21. Given the opaque nature of Laotian politics and government attempts to downplay the conflict and suppress information about it, the true severity of the conflict is not clear. The attacks died down toward the end of 2004, which would seem to indicate that the government had regained the upper hand (Bertelsmann Stiftung 2012a).

22. We are grateful to Scott Shaw for this insight and for his detailed background research on Laos that informed this analysis.

23. Droughts are a normal feature of the climate in the region, and the historical response in Laos is for the affected populations to simply move to better land. The country was generally sparsely populated enough to accommodate such seminomadic tendencies. However, population growth since the end of the Vietnam War and government restrictions on in-country travel has limited the availability of better land (Roder 1997).

24. Furthermore, the agricultural sector itself experienced negative growth in 1987 (−1.9 percent) and 1988 (−4.2 percent) from a height of over 5 percent in 1986 and over 11 percent in 1985. Full details: World Bank 2017a.

25. Full details: World Bank 2017c.

26. How China and Thailand, two of Laos's largest trading partners outside the Soviet Bloc, approached Laos was directly influenced by their policies on Vietnam. Given the Soviet support for Vietnam's regional ambitions, the same could also be said for Chinese sentiments toward the Soviet Union itself.

27. In 2003, Hmong militants numbered around three thousand and were divided into roughly six groups. See Thayer (2004).

28. The eradication program seriously impacted the household incomes of people in those provinces because their cash crop substitutes were much more variable—both in yield and in pricing. In fact, cultivation has increased by 55 percent since 2005 as the government has lowered its efforts, signaling the importance of the crop to the communities. See Fawthrop (2011).

29. The charges were later dropped, and he died in 2011, dealing a significant blow to the Hmong opposition in exile (BBC 2011). Most of the remaining Hmongs fled to Thailand, where they claimed refugee status.

30. Since 2000, China has taken an increased interest in developing ties with Laos, with many state visits being conducted by the two countries and increasing Chinese investment.

Chapter 5: Fragility Exit

1. To be sure, diaspora remittances have been hugely important in offsetting the consequences of repeated flooding and have supplanted foreign aid as the largest financial flow. We argue that diaspora activities are important and that their externalities affect other areas of state fragility in positive ways. However, remittances in particular tend to be countercyclical and as such are not the primary solution for solving fragility (Carment and Calleja 2017).

2. This is most amply demonstrated from the period just before Zia's death to 1986. This was time of both rapid change and consolidation and improvement in Bangladesh's fragility scores. When Zia (as he was popularly known) was assassinated during a military coup, we see these scores deteriorate and fall even further when Ershad dissolved all vestiges of the former government.

3. In the run-up to the subsequent election, political violence continued, and former US president Jimmy Carter facilitated an agreement between the BNP and the Awami League that, regardless of the election results, would be respected by both parties.

4. This rivalry was compounded by problems that resulted from the 2013 collapse of the Rana Plaza garment factory on the outskirts of Dhaka, which claimed more than eleven hundred lives.

5. We are indebted to Joe Landry for his insights on and analysis of these case studies.

6. Followers depend on the leaders' ability to embody a vital but informal trust. Political dynasticism is thus more a coincidental than a strategic outcome. See Ruud and Islam (2016).

7. The competition between both political parties has grown to the point that each has become more concerned with obtaining more power for itself than anything else (Zaman 2012). Even the rule of law has been impacted by these efforts, as judges are often used to undermine the opposition and parties often take advantage of the others boycotting to unilaterally pass legislation (Islam 2013; Riaz 2014). The Office of the Prime Minister asserted absolute control over cabinet ministers, much as previous military leaders had, with the prime minister typically taking multiple portfolios (Islam 2013).

8. Political stability in Bangladesh has also been undermined by the efforts of both parties and their leaders to accrue as much power as they can at the expense of the other,

which has recently begun to escalate to outright repression. Both Khaleda Zia, leader of the BNP, and Sheikh Hasina, the current prime minister and leader of the Awami League, have been noted to have worked toward empowering their offices throughout the past quarter-century (Islam 2013). This has led to the leadership of Bangladeshi political parties essentially becoming hereditary as well as total power over the party being given to a single person (Islam 2013).

9. As a result, Bangladesh has often scored poorly on measures of corruption, with Transparency International giving it an average score of 1.83 out of 10.00 from 2003 to 2001 (Riaz 2014). Mozambique has not performed significantly better (TI 2013b).

10. Small credit has allowed rural households to gain sufficient capital to start their own small enterprises, typically referred to as microenterprises (Khandker, Baqui Kahlily, and Samad 2016). These enterprises, which can be broadly divided between rural farm and nonfarm enterprises, are seen as being in a virtuous cycle, with growth in one encouraging it in the other group (Gautam and Faruqee 2016; Khandker, Baqui Kahlily, and Samad 2016). Cause and effect are not always clear here because it is the educated with access to infrastructure who are mostly likely to qualify for credit.

11. Authors such as Matthieu Chemin (2008) have questioned previous studies that promote the benefits of microfinance, noting that they often assume random placement of institutions rather than their being deliberately placed in certain villages.

12. Local NGOs and international organizations such as the World Bank and IMF have also played a key role in pushing for neoliberal reforms in Bangladesh's economy, leading to greater market liberalization that has helped fuel its economic growth (Parnini 2006).

13. Others have noted that many of these benefits do not extend to the extreme poor, who often fail to meet even the reduced collateral requirements of microfinance institutions and are located in difficult-to-access regions of Bangladesh (Parnini 2006; Kabeer, Mahmud, and Castro 2012).

14. The 2013 Failed States Index produced by the Fund for Peace currently placed Mozambique tied for fifty-ninth worst country (Messner et al. 2013). Its five-year improvement trend made Mozambique the fifteenth-most-improved country from 2008 to 2013 (Messner et al. 2013).

15. Frelimo was the unified front of Mozambique's liberation movement, created through the merger of three smaller organizations, MANU, UDENAMU, and UNAMU (Chan et al. 1998). The Frelimo alliance began to cause problems for the Portuguese authorities in the early 1970s when Frelimo began to attack strongholds of the settlers and major infrastructure developments such as the Zambezi River hydroelectric project (Birmingham 1992). The Lusaka Accord, signed in 1974, gave Frelimo status as the transitional government, and it assumed full power on June 25, 1975 (Chan et al. 1998).

16. The conflict, which would eventually claim an estimated one million lives with five million people displaced, started shortly after independence in 1975 and ended in 1992, with the country's first multiparty elections taking place in 1994. In 2013, after more than twenty years of peace, the military arm of Renamo resurged, resulting so far in dozens of deaths.

17. The group was trained and advised in Rhodesia, with the initial set of recruits being made up of native Mozambicans, resistant Portuguese settlers, Frelimo dissidents, traditional chiefs, and former members of the colonial army (Vines 1992).

18. Records of atrocities show that both Renamo and Frelimo engaged in mass killing, rape, and mutilation of noncombatants but that the practice was more common among Renamo's soldiers.

19. These tactics were partly adopted by Renamo due to their previous effectiveness in the struggle against the Portuguese authorities.

20. The Mozambican government successfully persuaded the then US secretary of state George Shultz that Renamo was deserving of the harshest criticism. Malawi also supported the government in its efforts to thwart the group, in particular because of the economic damage caused by attacks on primary transportation corridors between the two countries.

21. We are indebted to Joe Landry for his deep analysis of and comments on the Mozambique case study.

22. An agreement between South Africa and Mozambique (official name: Agreement on Non-aggression and Good Neighborliness between Mozambique and South Africa) outlined that both countries would cease and desist in aiding third parties in one another's territory. This agreement infuriated the leadership of Renamo, and attacks became more frequent, averaging 165 a month from March to May 1984 (Robinson 2003). Renamo succeeded in nearly isolating Maputo, with attacks occurring just fifteen kilometers outside of the city.

23. Although Renamo was making inroads, they were running very low on supplies without South Africa's constant support (Chan et al. 1998). In 1984, a cease-fire was agreed to, and an agreement was drafted, but at the last minute Renamo abruptly pulled out of the talks.

24. For example, Renamo was pushed to the brink by government forces when its main headquarters in the Gorongosa Mountains was captured in August 1985 (Alden 2001).

25. Renamo secretary-general Evo Fernandes was assassinated in Portugal in 1988 (Robinson 2003).

26. In order to combat this, the government proposed a threefold strategy: (1) solicit humanitarian and development aid via international channels, (2) call on international financial organizations and bilateral donors to reschedule or relive debts, and (3) petition neighboring countries (Tanzania, Zimbabwe, and Malawi) for military assistance to defend state interests. In addition to this multipronged approach, the revival of negotiations for cooperation with South Africa, including military and economic partnerships, acted as the key component of Chissano's strategy for rehabilitating the country.

27. International election observers argued that voting irregularities were minor and would not have affected the overall outcome of the election. Frelimo maintained power as much as possible, with talks on the possibility of granting governorships to Renamo candidates in areas where their party won the election falling through at the last minute. In 1999, Renamo still saw a majority of its financial support coming from international sources such as the European Union and other bilateral donors (Ottaway 2003b).

28. In 2006, the World Bank—in an attempt to ease some of the financial and development burdens the country was facing—canceled most of Mozambique's debt under a plan promoted by the Group of Eight nations (BBC 2013; IMF 2013).

29. On October 4, 1992, the Rome General Peace Accords, negotiated by the Community of Sant'Egidio with the support of the United Nations, were signed in Rome by

President Chissano and Renamo leader Afonso Dhlakama. They formally took effect on October 15, 1992. A UN peacekeeping force (ONUMOZ) of seventy-five hundred then arrived in Mozambique and oversaw a two-year transition to democracy. Twenty-four hundred international observers also entered the country to supervise the elections held on October 27–28, 1994.

30. Policies implemented at this time included placing restrictions on religious activities, forbidding labor strikes, and nationalizing particular sectors of the economy (O'Meara 1991). Essentially, Frelimo followed the Soviet model by implementing socialist economic programs, especially for agricultural activities. At the same time, the government promoted the expansion of the industrial sector.

31. For example, when Marxist-Leninist doctrine was part of the Frelimo platform (Manning 2002), a large exodus of international financial capital ensued (Boyce and Ndikumana 2001).

32. For example, because of land mines, less than 50 percent of the commercially cultivated land that had been utilized during the colonial period was actually being used under Frelimo, despite massive investments (Abrahamsson and Nilsson 1995).

33. More recently, Bangladesh's leaders have engaged in a partisan and contentious policy of restorative justice (in violation of International Court of Justice directives), targeting and, in some cases, condemning to death leaders of the Razakars, collaborators with West Pakistan who engaged in war crimes during the Liberation War of 1971. In one such case, the leader of a radical student wing and head of the al-Badr Brigade was found responsible and executed for the killing of scores of the country's top secular intellectuals (*Hindu* 2016). But these recent revenge-driven machinations appear to be more a political diversion focused in some cases on targeting Islamists who supported West Pakistan during the war. Given that Bangladesh has seen spectacular crises of legitimacy and deep divisions between secular Muslims and more radical strains, these executions are a troubling indicator. That is because in recent years the country's secular leadership has been accused and found guilty of ongoing corruption and embezzlement of aid funds, which only strengthens Saudi Salafist funding for madrassas and Islamic charities. Indeed, Bangladesh is witnessing a growth in an underclass of poor, working-class young men shifting to a more puritan and confrontational strain of Islam.

References

Abrahamsson, H., and A. Nilsson. 1995. *Mozambique the Troubled Transition: From Socialist Construction to Free Market Capitalism*. London: Zed Books.

Abulof, U. 2017. "'Can't Buy Me Legitimacy': The Elusive Stability of Mideast Rentier Regimes." *Journal of International Relations and Development* 20 (1): 55–79.

Acemoglu, D., S. Johnson, and J. Robinson. 2001. "The Colonial Origins of Comparative Development: An Empirical Investigation." *American Economic Review* 91 (5): 1369–1401.

Addison, T. 2003. *From Conflict to Recovery in Africa*. Oxford: Oxford University Press.

African Capacity Building Foundation. 2015. *Africa Capacity Report 2015: Capacity Imperatives for Domestic Resource Mobilization in Africa*. Harare: African Capacity Building Foundation.

African Development Bank. 2008. *African Development Bank Group and Mozambique: Building Together a Better Africa*. Maputo: African Development Bank.

Afzal, S., H. Iqbal, and M. Inayat. 2012. "Sectarianism and Its Implications for Pakistan's Security: Policy Recommendations Using Exploratory Study." *Journal of Humanities and Social Sciences* 4 (4): 19–26.

Ahmed, N. 2010. "Party Politics under a Non-party Caretaker Government in Bangladesh: The Fakhruddin Interregnum." *Commonwealth and Comparative Politics* 48 (1): 23–47.

———. 2017. *Inclusive Governance in South Asia: Parliament, Judiciary and Civil Service*. London: Palgrave Macmillan.

Ahmed, S. 2006. "The Political Economy of Development Experience in Bangladesh." In *Growth and Poverty: The Development Experience in Bangladesh*, edited by S. Ahmed and W. Mahmud, 93–145. Dhaka: University Press for the World Bank.:

Ahsan, A. 2003. "Pakistan since Independence: An Historical Analysis." *Muslim World* 93 (3–4): 351–71.

Ake, C. 2000. *The Feasibility of Democracy in Africa*. Dakar: Codesria.

Alam, Q., and J. Teicher. 2012. "The State of Governance in Bangladesh: The Capture of State Institutions." *South Asia: Journal of South Asian Studies* 35 (4): 858–84.

Alamgir, J. 2009. "Bangladesh's Fresh Start." *Journal of Democracy* 20 (3): 41–55.

Alden, C. 1995. "Swords into Ploughshares? The United Nations and Demilitarization in Mozambique." *International Peacekeeping* 2 (2): 175–93.

———. 2001. *Mozambique and the Construction of the New African State: From Negotiations to Nation Building*. London: Palgrave Macmillan.

Ali, S. M. 2010. *Understanding Bangladesh*. New York: Columbia University Press.

Almosawa, S., and D. D. Kirkpatrick. 2014. "Yemen Rebels Gain Concessions from Government after Assault on Capital." *New York Times*, September 21, 2014. https://www.nytimes.com/2014/09/22/world/middleeast/yemens-prime-minister-resigns-amid-chaos-and-another-cease-fire.html?_r=0.

Andrews, M., L. Pritchett, and M. Woolcock. 2017. *Building State Capability: Evidence, Analysis, Action.* Oxford: Oxford University Press.

Andrimihaja, N. A., M. M. Cinyabuguma, and S. Devarajan. 2011. "Avoiding the Fragility Trap in Africa." World Bank Policy Research Working Paper Series.

Apter, D. 1968. "Why Political Systems Change." *Government and Opposition* 3:411–27.

Asadullah, M. N., A. Savoia, and W. Mahmud. 2014. "Paths to Development: Is There a Bangladesh Surprise?" *World Development* 62:138–54.

Asian Development Bank. 2016. Pakistan: Economy. Asian Development Bank. https://www.adb.org/data/statistics.

Asongu, S. A., and O. Kodila-Tedika. 2013. "State Fragility, Rent Seeking and Lobbying: Evidence from African Data." Working Paper no. 13/019. African Governance and Development Institute.

Azariadis, C. 1996. "The Economics of Poverty Traps Part One: Complete Markets." *Journal of Economic Growth* 1 (4): 449–86.

Azariadis, C., and J. Stachurski. 2005. "Poverty Traps." *Handbook of Economic Growth* 1:295–384.

Azarya, V., and N. Chazan. 1987. "Disengagement from the State in Africa: Reflections on the Experience of Ghana and Guinea." *Comparative Studies in Society and History* 29 (1): 106–31.

Babbitt, E. F., I. Johnstone, and D. Mazurana. 2016. *Building Legitimacy in Conflict-Affected and Fragile States.* Institute for Human Security Policy Brief no. 1(1). Medford, MA: Fletcher School of Law and Diplomacy.

Badie, B., D. Berg-Schlosser, and L. Morlino. 2011a. "Legitimacy." In Badie, Berg-Schlosser, and Morlino, *International Encyclopedia of Political Science,* 1415–25.

———. 2011b. "Political Science." In Badie, Berg-Schlosser, and Morlino, *International Encyclopedia of Political Science,* 2013–14.

———, eds. 2011c. *International Encyclopedia of Political Science.* Thousand Oaks, CA: SAGE Publications.

Bakrania, S., and B. Lucas. 2009. "The Impact of the Financial Crisis on Conflict and State Fragility in Sub-Saharan Africa." Governance and Social Development Resource Centre, University of Birmingham, Birmingham, UK. http://epapers.bham.ac.uk/643/.

Baliamoune-Lutz, M. 2009. "Institutions, Trade, and Social Cohesion in Fragile States: Implications for Policy Conditionality and Aid Allocation." *Journal of Policy Modeling* 31:877–90.

Baliamoune-Lutz, M. N., and M. McGillivray. 2008. "State Fragility: Concept and Measurement." Working Paper Series no. RP2008/44. United Nations University World Institute for Development Economic Research.

Barakat, S., M. Evans, and S. A. Zyck. 2012. "Karzai's Curse: Legitimacy as Stability in Afghanistan and Other Post-Conflict Environments." *Policy Studies* 33 (5): 439–54.

Barry, E. 2015. "Turmoil between Political Leaders Has Harmed Bangladesh's People." *New York Times,* April 12, 2015. https://www.nytimes.com/2015/04/13/world/asia/the-many-casualties-of-the-battle-of-the-two-ladies-in-bangladesh.html.

References

BBC. 2002. "India-Pakistan: Troubled Relations." BBC News. http://news.bbc.co.uk/hi/english/static/in_depth/south_asia/2002/india_pakistan/timeline/default.stm.

———. 2011. "Laos General and Hmong Leader Vang Pao Dies in Exile." BBC News, January 7, 2011. https://www.bbc.com/news/world-asia-pacific-12133710.

———. 2012. "US Secretary of State Hillary Clinton on Historic Laos Visit." BBC News, July 11, 2012. https://www.bbc.com/news/world-asia-18792282.

———. 2013. "Mali Unrest: Kidal's Deadly Race Riots." BBC News, July 19, 2013. http://www.bbc.co.uk/news/world-africa-23379122.

———. 2015. "Yemen Crisis: Fighting Breaks New UN Ceasefire." BBC News, July 11, 2015. http://www.bbc.com/news/world-middle-east-33491472.

———. 2016a. "Laos 'Bomb Attack' Kills Two Chinese." BBC News, January 25, 2016. https://www.bbc.com/news/world-asia-35397767.

———. 2016b. "Pakistan Profile: Timeline." BBC News, March 29, 2016. http://www.bbc.com/news/world-south-asia-12966786.

———. 2017. "Yemen Crisis: Who Is Fighting Whom?" BBC News, March 28, 2017. http://www.bbc.com/news/world-middle-east-29319423.

———. 2018. "Mozambique Profile: Timeline." BBC News, July 30, 2018. https://www.bbc.com/news/world-africa-13890720

Bdnews24.com. 2017. "Credit for Development Goes to Government besides NGOs, Kailash Satyarthi Tells PM Hasina." Bdnews24.com. http://bdnews24.com/bangladesh/2017/04/04/perception-of-ngos-role-in-development-changed-in-bangladesh-kailash-satyarthi-tells-pm-hasina.

Belik, A., N. Grebovic, and J. Willows. 2012. "Friction along the Sahelian Fault Line: Azawad amd Ethnic Conflict in Northern Mali." CIFP Project, Ottawa. October 31, 2012. https://reliefweb.int/report/mali/friction-along-sahelian-fault-line-azawad-and-ethnic-conflict-northern-mali.

Benjaminsen, T. A. 2008. "Does Supply-Induced Scarcity Drive Violent Conflicts in the African Sahel? The Case of the Tuareg Rebellion in Northern Mali." *Journal of Peace Research* 45 (6): 819–36.

Bergamaschi, I. 2014. "The Fall of a Donor Darling: The Role of Aid in Mali's Crisis." *Journal of Modern African Studies* 52 (3): 347–78.

Bermeo, N. 2016. "On Democratic Backsliding." *Journal of Democracy* 27 (1): 5–19.

Bertelsmann Stiftung. 2006. *BTI 2006: Yemen Country Report*. Gütersloh, Ger.: Bertelsmann Stiftung. https://www.bti-project.org/fileadmin/files/BTI/Downloads/Reports/2006/pdf/BTI_2006_Yemen.pdf.

———. 2008. *BTI 2008: Mali Country Report*. Gütersloh, Ger.: Bertelsmann Stiftung. https://www.bti-project.org/en/reports/country-reports/detail/itc/mli/ity/2008/itr/wca/.

———. 2012a. *BTI 2012: Laos Country Report*. Gütersloh, Ger.: Bertelsmann Stiftung. https://www.bti-project.org/fileadmin/files/BTI/Downloads/Reports/2012/pdf/BTI_2012_Laos.pdf.

———. 2012b. *BTI 2012: Mali Country Report*. Gütersloh, Ger.: Bertelsmann Stiftung. https://www.bti-project.org/fileadmin/files/BTI/Downloads/Reports/2012/pdf/BTI_2012_Mali.pdf.

———. 2016. *BTI 2016: Bangladesh Country Report.* Gutersloh, Ger.: Bertelsmann Stiftung. https://www.bti-project.org/fileadmin/files/BTI/Downloads/Reports/2016/pdf/BTI_2016_Bangladesh.pdf.

Bertocchi, G., and A. Guerzoni. 2012. "Growth, History or Institutions: What Explains State Fragility in Sub-Saharan Africa?" *Journal of Peace Research* 49 (6): 769–83.

Besley, T., and T. Persson. 2011. *Pillars of Prosperity: The Political Economics of Development Clusters.* Princeton, NJ: Princeton University Press.

Bhaumik, S. K., I. Gang, and Myeong-Su Yun. 2011. "Gender and Ethnicity in Fragile States: The Case of Post-Conflict Kosovo." In Naudé, Santos-Paulino, and McGillivray, *Fragile States*, 133–50.

Birmingham, D. 1992. *Frontline Nationalism in Angola and Mozambique.* Trenton, NJ: Africa World Press.

Blair, D., R. Neumann, and E. Olson. 2014. "Fixing Fragile States." *National Interest* 133:1–12. http://nationalinterest.org/feature/fixing-fragile-states-11125.

Bleaney, M., and A. Dimico. 2011. "How Different Are the Correlates of Onset and Continuation of Civil Wars?" *Journal of Peace Research* 48 (2): 145–55.

Boege, V., A. Brown, and K. P. Clements. 2009. "Hybrid Political Orders, Not Fragile States." *Peace Review: A Journal of Social Justice* 21 (1): 13–21.

Boix, C., and S. C. Stokes. 2003. "Endogenous Democratization." *World Politics* 55 (4): 517–49.

Boley, J., K. Evans, S. Grassie, and S. Romeih. 2017. "A Conflict Overlooked: Yemen in Crisis." https://reliefweb.int/sites/reliefweb.int/files/resources/1540_0.pdf.

Boone, J. 2014. "Protestors March on Pakistan Parliament 'Red Zone.'" *Guardian*, August 19, 2014. https://www.theguardian.com/world/2014/aug/19/protesters-march-pakistan-parliament-imran-khan.

Börzel, T. A., and T. Risse. 2016. "Dysfunctional State Institutions, Trust, and Governance in Areas of Limited Statehood." *Regulation and Governance* 10 (2): 149–60.

Bourdet, Y. 1997. "Laos in 1996: Please Don't Rush." *Asian Survey* 37 (1): 72–78.

———. 2001. "Laos in 2000: The Economics of Political Immobilism." *Asian Survey* 41 (1): 164–70.

Boyce, J. K., and L. Ndikumana. 2001. "Is Africa a Net Creditor? New Estimates of Capital Flight from Severely Indebted Sub-Saharan African Countries, 1970–96." *Journal of Development Studies* 38 (2): 27–56.

Brass, P. 1985. *Ethnic Groups and the State.* London: Croom Helm.

Bratton, M. 2007. "Institutionalizing Democracy in Africa: Formal or Informal?" *Journal of Democracy* 18 (3): 96–110.

Bräutigam, D., O. Fjeldstad, and M. Moore, eds. 2008. *Taxation and State Building in Developing Countries.* Cambridge: Cambridge University Press.

Bräutigam, D., and S. Knack. 2004. "Foreign Aid, Institutions and Governance in Sub-Saharan Africa." *Economic Development and Cultural Change* 52 (2): 255–85.

Brehony, N. 2011. *Yemen Divided: The Story of a Failed State in South Arabia.* New York: I. B. Tauris.

Bremmer, I. 2006. *The J Curve: A New Way to Understand Why Nations Rise and Fall.* New York: Simon & Schuster.

References

Briguglio, L., G. Cordina, N. Farrugia, and S. Vella. 2009. "Economic Vulnerability and Resilience: Concepts and Measurements." *Oxford Development Studies* 37 (3): 229–47. https://econpapers.repec.org/article/tafoxdevs/v_3a37_3ay_3a2009_3ai_3a3_3ap_3a229-247.htm.

Brinkerhoff, D. 2007. "Capacity Development in Fragile States." European Centre for Development Policy Management Discussion Paper no. 58D. Maastricht, Neth.: European Centre for Development Policy. http://ecdpm.org/wp-content/uploads/2013/11/DP-58D-Capacity-Development-in-Fragile-States-2007.pdf.

———. 2010. "Developing Capacity in Fragile States." *Public Administration and Development* 30:66–78.

———. 2014. "State Fragility and Failure as Wicked Problems: Beyond Naming and Taming." *Third World Quarterly* 35 (20): 333–44.

Brown, M., M. Dawod, A. Irantalab, and M. Naqi. 2012. "Balochistan Case Study." CIFP Conflict Report 2012. Carleton University, Ottawa. https://carleton.ca/cifp/2012/balochistan-conflict-report-2012/.

Brumberg, D. 2005. "Liberalization versus Democracy." In *Uncharted Journey: Promoting Democracy in the Middle East*, edited by T. Carothers and M. Ottaway, 15–36. Washington, DC: Carnegie Endowment for International Peace.

Brunnschweiler, C. N., and E. H. Bulte. 2009. "Natural Resources and Violent Conflict: Resource Abundance, Dependence, and the Onset of Civil Wars." *Oxford Economic Papers* 61 (4): 651–74.

Bueno de Mesquita, B., and A. Smith. 2012. *The Dictators Handbook*. New York: PublicAffairs.

Bueno de Mesquita, B., A. Smith, R. Siverson, and J. Morrow. 2003. *The Logic of Political Survival*. Cambridge, MA: MIT Press.

Burnside, C., and D. Dollar. 2000. "Aid, Policies and Growth." *American Economic Review* 90 (4): 847–68.

Buterbaugh, K. N., C. Calin, and T. Marchant-Shapiro. 2017. "Predicting Revolt: Fragility Indexes and the Level of Violence and Instability in the Arab Spring." *Terrorism and Political Violence* 29 (3): 483–508.

Buur, L., S. Jensen, and F. Stepputat. 2007. *The Security-Development Nexus: The Security-Development Nexus Expressions of Sovereignty and Securitization in Southern Africa*. Pretoria: Human Sciences Research Council Press.

Cahen, M. 1993. "Check on Socialism in Mozambique: What Check? What Socialism?" *Review of African Political Economy* 20 (57): 46–59.

Cairnie, A., and P. deGrasse. 2016. "Mali Policy Paper." CIFP Fragile States Research Project. Carleton University, Ottawa. https://carleton.ca/cifp/2017/mali-fragile-state-analysis-and-policy-options/.

Call, C. T. 2008. "The Fallacy of the Failed State." *Third World Quarterly* 29 (8): 1491–507.

———. 2011. "Beyond the Failed State: Toward Conceptual Alternatives." *European Journal of International Relations* 17 (2): 303–26.

Carment, D. 2003. "Secessionist and Ethnic Conflict in South and South East Asia: A Comparative Perspective." In *Ethnic Conflict and Secessionism in South and Southeast Asia: Causes, Dynamics, Solutions*, edited by R. Ganguly and I. Macduff, 23–58. New Delhi: SAGE Publications.

———. 2011. *The New Terrorism: Understanding Yemen*. Calgary, AB: Canadian Defence and Foreign Affairs Institute. https://d3n8a8pro7vhmx.cloudfront.net/cdfai/pages/42/attachments/original/1413673977/The_New_Terrorism_Understanding_Yemen.pdf?1413673977.

Carment, D., and R. Calleja. 2017. "Diasporas and Fragile States: Beyond Remittances Assessing the Theoretical and Policy Linkages." *Journal of Ethnic and Migration Studies* 44 (8): 1270–88.

Carment, D., J. Landry, Y. Samy, and S. Shaw. 2015. "Towards a Theory of Fragile State Transitions: Evidence from Yemen, Bangladesh and Laos." *Third World Quarterly* 36 (7): 1316–32.

Carment, D., S. Prest, and A. Fritzen. 2007. "Pakistan. Democracy and Governance Report." Ottawa: Country Indicators for Foreign Policy Project. https://carleton.ca/cifp/2009/cifp-governance-and-democracy-processes-pakistan-2008-2/.

Carment, D., S. Prest, and Y. Samy. 2008. "State Fragility and Implications for Aid Allocation: An Empirical Analysis." *Conflict Management and Peace Science* 25 (4): 349–73.

———. 2010. *Security, Development and the Fragile State: Bridging the Gap between Theory and Policy*. London: Routledge.

Carment, D., and Y. Samy. 2011. "The Social Underpinnings of the Current Unrest in North Africa and the Middle East." CDFAI Policy Update. https://d3n8a8pro7vhmx.cloudfront.net/cdfai/pages/43/attachments/original/1413676893/Social_Underpinnings_of_Unrest.pdf?1413676893.

———. 2012. "Assessing State Fragility: A Country Indicators for Foreign Policy Report." Ottawa. https://carleton.ca/cifp/recent-reports/.

Carothers, T. 2002. "The End of the Transition Paradigm." *Journal of Democracy* 13 (1): 5–21.

———. 2007. The 'Sequencing' Fallacy. *Journal of Democracy* 18 (1): 12–27.

Chan, S., M. Venâncio, C. Alden, and S. Barnes. 1998. *War and Peace in Mozambique*. New York: St. Martin's.

Chauvet, L., and P. Collier. 2008. "What Are the Preconditions for Turnarounds in Failing States?" *Conflict Management and Peace Science* 25 (4): 335–48.

Chemin, M. 2008. "The Benefits and Costs of Microfinance: Evidence from Bangladesh." *Journal of Development Studies* 44 (4): 463–84.

CIA (Central Intelligence Agency). 2013. "Mozambique." World Factbook. https://www.cia.gov/library/publications/resources/the-world-factbook/.

Cilliers, J., and T. D. Sisk. 2013. *Assessing Long-Term State Fragility in Africa: Prospects for 26 'More Fragile' Countries*. Institute for Security Studies (ISS) Monograph no. 188. Pretoria: ISS.

Clardie, J. 2011. "The Impact of Military Spending on the Likelihood of Democratic Transition Failure: Testing Two Competing Theories." *Armed Forces and Society* 37 (1): 163–79.

Clark, V. 2010. *Yemen: Dancing on the Heads of Snakes*. New Haven, CT: Yale University Press.

Coggins, B. 2014. "Fragile Is the New Failure." Political Violence at a Glance. June 27, 2014. http://politicalviolenceataglance.org/2014/06/27/fragile-is-the-new-failure/.

Cohen, S. P. 1984. *The Pakistan Army*. Berkeley: University of California Press.

Collier, P. 1997. "The Failure of Conditionality." In *Perspectives on Aid and Development*, edited by C. Gwin and J. Nelson, 51–77. Washington, DC: Overseas Development Council.

———. 2007. *The Bottom Billion: Why the Poorest Countries Are Failing and What Can Be Done about It.* Oxford: Oxford University Press.
Collier, P., V. L. Elliott, H. Hegre, A. Hoeffler, M. Reynal-Querol, and N. Sambanis. 2003. *Breaking the Conflict Trap: Civil War and Development Policy.* Washington, DC: World Bank Publications.
Colton, N. A. 2010. "Yemen: A Collapsed Economy." *Middle East Journal* 64 (3): 410–26.
Copans, J. 1991. "No Shortcuts to Democracy: The Long March towards Modernity." *Review of African Political Economy* 18 (50): 92–101.
Crossette, B. 1988. "Thai-Laos Clashes on Border Grow." *New York Times*, January 7, 1988. http://www.nytimes.com/1988/01/07/world/thai-laos-clashes-on-border-grow.html.
David, P. A. 1994. "Why Are Institutions the 'Carriers of History'? Path Dependence and the Evolution of Conventions, Organizations and Institutions." *Structural Change and Economic Dynamics* 5 (2): 205–20.
Debiel, T., R. Glassner, C. Schetter, and U. Terlinden. 2009. "Local State-Building in Afghanistan and Somaliland." *Peace Review: A Journal of Social Justice* 21:38–44.
Deckard, N. D., and Z. Pieri. 2017. "The Implications of Endemic Corruption for State Legitimacy in Developing Nations: An Empirical Exploration of the Nigerian Case." *International Journal of Politics, Culture, and Society* 30 (4): 369–84.
De Sousa, C. 2002. "Rebuilding Rural Livelihoods and Social Capital in Mozambique." In Addison, *From Conflict to Recovery in Africa*, 51–72.
Diamond, L. 1999. *Developing Democracy: Toward Consolidation.* Baltimore: Johns Hopkins University Press.
———. 2002. "Thinking about Hybrid Regimes." *Journal of Democracy* 13 (2): 25–31.
———. 2015. "Facing Up to the Democratic Recession." *Journal of Democracy* 26 (1): 141–55.
Diamond, L., J. J. Linz, and S. M. Lipset. 1989. *Democracy in Developing Countries: Latin America.* Boulder, CO: Lynne Rienner.
Diamond, L. J. 2000. "Is Pakistan the (Reverse) Wave of the Future?" *Journal of Democracy* 11 (3): 91–106.
Di John, J. 2010. "The Concept, Causes and Consequences of Failed States: A Critical Review of the Literature and Agenda for Research with Specific Reference to Sub-Saharan Africa." *European Journal of Development Research* 22 (1): 10–30.
Dinerman, A. 2006. *Revolution, Counter-Revolution and Revisionism in Postcolonial Africa: The Case of Mozambique, 1975–1994.* Abingdon, UK: Routledge.
Dizolele, M. P., and P. K. Kambale. 2012. "The DRC's Crumbling Legitimacy." *Journal of Democracy* 23 (3): 109–20.
Djankov, S., J. G. Montalvo, and M. Reynal-Querol. 2008. "The Curse of Aid." *Journal of Economic Growth* 13 (3): 169–94.
Doherty, B. 2009. "Thailand Begins Deportation of More than 4,000 Hmong Asylum Seekers." *Guardian*, December 28, 2009. http://www.theguardian.com/world/2009/dec/28/thailand-deportation-hmong-laos.
Dollar, D., T. Kleineberg, and A. Kraay. 2016. "Growth Still Is Good for the Poor." *European Economic Review* 81:68–85.
Dollar, D., and A. Kraay. 2002. "Growth Is Good for the Poor." *Journal of Economic Growth* 7:195–225.

Dommen, A. J. 1995. "Laos in 1994: Among Generals, among Friends." *Asian Survey* 35 (1): 84–91.

Doorenspleet, R. 2005. *Democratic Transitions: Exploring the Structural Sources of the Fourth Wave*. Boulder, CO: Lynne Rienner.

Duffield, M. 2005. "Getting Savages to Fight Barbarians: Development, Security and the Colonial Present." *Conflict, Security and Development* 5 (2): 141–59.

Dunbar, C. 1992. "The Unification of Yemen: Process, Politics, and Prospects." *Middle East Journal* 46 (3): 456–76.

Dunne, P. 2006. "After the Slaughter: Reconstructing Mozambique and Rwanda." *Economics of Peace and Security Journal* 1 (2): 39–46.

Easterly, W. 2001. "The Political Economy of Growth without Development: A Case Study of Pakistan." Paper for the Analytical Narratives of Growth Project, Kennedy School of Government, Harvard University. http://citeseerx.ist.psu.edu/viewdoc/download?doi=10.1.1.543.6905&rep=rep1&type=pdf.

———. 2003. "Can Foreign Aid Buy Growth?" *Journal of Economic Perspectives* 17 (3): 23–48.

———. 2006. "Planners versus Searchers in Foreign Aid." *Asian Development Review* 23 (2): 1–35.

Economist. 2008. "Pakistan: The World's Most Dangerous Place." January 3, 2008. http://www.economist.com/node/10430237.

———. 2015. "The Economist Explains: What Is Going on in Yemen?" March 30, 2015. https://www.economist.com/blogs/economist-explains/2015/03/economist-explains-24.

———. 2017. "The Pushmi-Pullyu: What Makes Pakistan So Unfathomable." July 22, 2017. https://www.economist.com/news/special-report/21725103-politicians-pull-one-direction-army-other-what-makes-pakistan-so.

Eisenhardt, K. M. 1989. "Building Theories from Case Study Research." *Academy of Management Review* 14 (4): 532–50.

EIU (Economist Intelligence Unit). 1998. Country Profile: Côte d'Ivoire and Mali, 1996–1997. Economist Intelligence Unit. http://www.eiu.com/FileHandler.ashx?issue_id=1882916588&mode=pdf.

———. 2000. Country Profile: Cambodia and Laos, 1999–2000. Economist Intelligence Unit. http://www.eiu.com/FileHandler.ashx?issue_id=313377831&mode=pdf.

———. 2002. Country Profile: Yemen, 2002. Economist Intelligence Unit. http://www.eiu.com/FileHandler.ashx?issue_id=1335686333&mode=pdf.

———. 2007. Country Profile: Yemen, 2007. Economist Intelligence Unit. http://www.eiu.com/FileHandler.ashx?issue_id=1182516503&mode=pdf.

———. 2008. Country Profile: Mali, 2008. Economist Intelligence Unit. http://www.eiu.com/FileHandler.ashx?issue_id=533414038&mode=pdf.

———. 2013. Country Profile: Mozambique, 2013. Economist Intelligence Unit ViewsWire. http://www.eiu.com/index.asp?layout=VWcountryVW3&country_id=380000038.

———. 2017. Country Profile: Bangladesh, 2017. Economist Intelligence Unit, October 16, 2017. http://country.eiu.com/bangladesh.

———. 2018. Country Profile: Mali, 2018. Economist Intelligence Unit. http://country.eiu.com/mali.

Emerson, S. A. 2011. "Desert Insurgency: Lessons from the Third Tuareg Rebellion." *Small Wars and Insurgencies* 22 (4): 669–87.

Engers, K., S. Williams, N. Choueiri, Y. Sobolev, and J. Walliser. 2002. "Yemen in the 1990s: From Unification to Economic Reform." IMF Occasional Paper no. 208. Washington, DC: International Monetary Fund. http://www.imf.org/external/pubs/nft/op/208/.

European Commission Report on Development. 2009. "Overcoming Fragility in Africa: Forging a New European Approach." January 1, 2009. https://ec.europa.eu/europeaid/node/44159_en.

Express Tribune. 2016. "Former UNDP Director Takes Aim at Pakistan's Elite in Scathing Final Interview." August 29, 2016. http://tribune.com.pk/story/1171773/former-undp-director-takes-aim-pakistans-elite-scathing-final-interview/.

FAO (Food and Agriculture Organization of the United Nations). 2005. "Flood Management and Mitigation in the Mekong River Basin: Technical Session I; Introduction to Flood Management." Regional Office for Asia and the Pacific, Food and Agriculture Organization of the United Nations. http://www.fao.org/docrep/004/ac146e/AC146E01.htm.

Farah, E., R. Gandhi, and S. Robidoux. 2019. "State Fragility in Mali." CIFP Fragile Sates Project, Carleton University, Ottawa. https://carleton.ca/cifp/wp-content/uploads/Mali-2019-Fragile-States-Policy-Brief.pdf.

Fattah, K. 2014. "Yemen's Insecurity Dilemma." *Washington Report on Middle East Affairs* 33 (2): 32–33.

Fatton, R. 1995. "Africa in the Age of Democratization: The Civic Limitations of Civil Society." *African Studies Review* 38 (2): 67–99.

Faust, J., J. Grävingholt, and S. Ziaja. 2013. "Foreign Aid and the Fragile Consensus on State Fragility." German Development Institute Discussion Paper no. 8/2013. http://www.die-gdi.de/uploads/media/DP_8.2013.pdf.

Fauvet, P. 1984. "Roots of Counter Revolution: The 'Mozambique National Resistance.'" *Review of African Political Economy* 29:108–21.

Fawthorp, T. 2011. "Asia's Opium Resurgence." *Diplomat*, February 22, 2011. http://thediplomat.com/2011/02/asias-opium-resurgence/1/.

Feeny, S., A. Posso, and J. Regan-Beasley. 2015. "Handle with Care: Fragile States and the Determinants of Fragility." *Applied Economics* 47 (11): 1073–85.

Ferreira, I. A. R. 2017. "Measuring State Fragility: A Review of the Theoretical Groundings of Existing Approaches. *Third World Quarterly* 38 (6): 1291–1309.

Fisk, K., and A. Cherney. 2016. "Pathways to Institutional Legitimacy in Postconflict Societies: Perceptions of Process and Performance." *Governance* 30 (2): 263–81.

Florquin, N., and S. Pézard. 2005. "Insurgency, Disarmament, and Insecurity in Northern Mali, 1990–2004." In *Armed and Aimless: Armed Groups, Guns, and Human Security in the ECOWAS Region*, edited by N. Florquin and E. G. Berman, 47–77. Geneva: Small Arms Survey.

Flyvbjerg, B. 2006. "Five Misunderstandings about Case Study Research." *Qualitative Inquiry*, 12 (2): 219–45.

Forbes, D., and C. Cutler. 2005. "Laos in 2004: Political Stability, Economic Opening." *Asian Survey* 45 (1): 161–65.

François, M., and I. Sud. 2006. "Promoting Stability and Development in Fragile and Failed States." *Development Policy Review* 24 (2): 141–60.

Frankel, J. 2010. "The Natural Resource Curse: A Survey." NBER Working Paper no. 15836 (March 2010). National Bureau of Economics Research. https://www.nber.org/papers/w15836.

Freedom House. 2016. *Freedom in the World 2016: Anxious Dictators, Wavering Democracies: Global Freedom under Pressure*. Washington, DC: Freedom House.

Fukuyama, F. 2006. Foreword to Huntington, *Political Order in Changing Societies*.

Furness, M. 2014. "Let's Get Comprehensive: European Union Engagement in Fragile and Conflict-Affected Countries." German Development Institute Discussion Paper no. 5/2014. http://www.die-gdi.de/uploads/media/DP_5.2014.pdf.

Ganguly, S. 2008. "Pakistan after Musharraf: The Burden of History." *Journal of Democracy* 19 (4): 26–31.

Gautam, M., and R. Faruqee. 2016. *Dynamics of Rural Growth in Bangladesh: Sustaining Poverty Reduction*. Washington, DC: World Bank Group.

George, A., and A. Bennett. 2005. *Case Studies and Theory Development in the Social Sciences*. Cambridge, MA: MIT Press.

Gerring, J. 2007. *Case Study Research: Principles and Practices*. Cambridge: Cambridge University Press.

Gilley, B. 2006. "The Meaning and Measure of State Legitimacy: Results for 72 Countries." *European Journal of Political Research* 45 (3): 499–525.

Ginsburg, T. 2008. "Lessons from Democratic Transition: Case Studies from Asia." *Orbis* 52 (1): 91–105.

Gisselquist, R. 2015. "Varieties of Fragility: Implications for Aid." *Third World Quarterly* 36 (7): 1269–80.

Goldstone, J. 2009. "Pathways to State Failure." *Conflict Management and Peace Science* 25 (4): 285–96.

Goldstone, J. A., and J. Ulfelder. 2004. "How to Construct Stable Democracies." *Washington Quarterly* 28 (1): 9–20.

Grammaticas, D. 2000. "Bomb Blast in Laos Capital." BBC News, July 31, 2000. http://news.bbc.co.uk/2/hi/asia-pacific/859457.stm.

Grare, F. 2013. "Pakistan's Foreign and Security Policies after the 2013 General Election: The Judge, the Politician and the Military." *International Affairs* 89 (4): 987–1001.

Grävingholt, J., S. Ziaja, and M. Kreibaum. 2012. "State Fragility: Towards a Multi-Dimensional Empirical Typology." German Development Institute Discussion Paper no. 3/2012. http://www.die-gdi.de/uploads/media/DP_3.2012.pdf.

———. 2015. "Disaggregating State Fragility: A Method to Establish a Multidimensional Empirical Typology." *Third World Quarterly* 36 (7): 1281–98.

Grimm, S. 2014. "The European Union's Ambiguous Concept of 'State Fragility.'" *Third World Quarterly* 35 (2): 252–67.

Grimm, S., and J. Leininger. 2012. "Not All Good Things Go Together: Conflicting Objectives in Democracy Promotion." *Democratization* 19 (3): 391–414.

Grimm, S., N. Lemay-Hébert, and O. Nay. 2014. "'Fragile States': Introducing a Political Concept." *Third World Quarterly* 35 (2): 197–209.

References

Gros, J. 1996. "Towards a Taxonomy of Failed States in the New World Order: Decaying Somalia, Liberia, Rwanda and Haiti." *Third World Quarterly* 17 (3): 455–71.

Grubbs, W., and N. Yahnke. 2017. "Out of Sight, out of Mind." http://drones.pitchinteractive.com/.

Gurtner, F. J. 1999. "The CFA Franc Zones and the Theory of Optimum Currency Area." *Africa Spectrum* 34 (1): 33–57.

Gurr, T. R., and J. Birnir. 2010. "Chronology for Hmong in Laos." Minorities at Risk Project, University of Maryland Center for International Development and Conflict Management. Last updated June 8, 2016. http://www.mar.umd.edu/chronology.asp?groupId=81201.

Haddad, M., and S. Bollier. 2012. "Interactive: Fractured Yemen." Al-Jazeera, June 5, 2012. http://www.aljazeera.com/indepth/interactive/2012/06/20126510233575914.

Hall, M. 1990. "The Mozambican National Resistance Movement (Renamo): A Study in the Destruction of an African Country." *Africa* 60 (1): 39–68.

Hanlon, J. 1984. *Mozambique: The Revolution under Fire*. London: Zed Books.

———. 2004. "Do Donors Promote Corruption? The Case of Mozambique." *Third World Quarterly* 25 (4): 747–63.

Hanlon, J., and M. Mosse. 2010. "Mozambique's Elite: Finding Its Way in a Globalized World and Returning to Old Development Models." United Nations University World Institute for Development Economic Research Working Paper no. 2010/105.

Haqqani, H. 2004. "The Role of Islam in Pakistan's Future." *Washington Quarterly* 28 (1): 85–96.

Harrison, S. 1981. *In Afghanistan's Shadow: Baluch Nationalism and Soviet Temptations*. Washington, DC: Carnegie Endowment for International Peace.

Hasan, A. D. 2016. "Balochistan: Caught in the Fragility Trap." United States Institute of Peace brief, June 27. https://www.usip.org/publications/2016/06/balochistan-caught-fragility-trap.

Hegre, H., H. Strand, S. Gates, and H. M. Nygard. 2011. "The Conflict Trap." Paper presented at the American Political Science Association 2011 annual meeting.

Hetland, Ø. 2008. "Decentralisation and Territorial Reorganisation in Mali: Power and the Institutionalisation of Local Politics." *Norsk Geografisk Tidsskrift* [Norwegian journal of geography] 62 (1): 23–35.

Hindu. 2016. "Bangladesh Executes Jamaat Chief Nizami for War Crimes." May 11, 2016. https://www.thehindu.com/news/international/south-asia/bangladesh-hangs-jei-chief-for-1971-war-crimes/article8581571.ece.

Hirschman, A. O. 1986. *Rival Views of Market Society and Other Recent Essays*. New York: Viking Penguin.

Horowitz, D. L. 1985. *Ethnic Groups in Conflict*. Berkeley: University of California Press.

———. 1993. "Democracy in Divided Societies." *Journal of Democracy* 4 (4): 18–38.

Horowitz, S. 2005. *From Ethnic Conflict to Stillborn Reform: The Former Soviet Union and Yugoslavia*. College Station: Texas A&M University Press.

HRW (Human Rights Watch). 1994. "Human Rights in Yemen during and after the 1994 War." *Human Rights Watch/Middle East* 6 (1): 1–31. https://www.hrw.org/sites/default/files/reports/YEMEN94O.PDF.

———. 2015. "Saudi Arabia: Mass Expulsions of Migrant Workers." Human Rights Watch. May 9, 2015. https://www.hrw.org/news/2015/05/09/saudi-arabia-mass-expulsions-migrant-workers.

———. 2017. "Bangladesh: End Disappearances and Secret Detentions." Human Rights Watch. July 6, 2017. https://www.hrw.org/news/2017/07/06/bangladesh-end-disappearances-and-secret-detentions.

Hume, C. R. 1994. *Ending Mozambique's War: The Role of Mediation and Good Offices.* Washington DC: US Institute of Peace Press.

Huntington, S. P. 1968. *Political Order in Changing Societies.* New Haven, CT: Yale University Press.

———. 1993. *The Third Wave: Democratization in the Late Twentieth Century.* Norman: Oklahoma University Press.

Hyden, G. 1980. *Beyond Ujamaa in Tanzania: Underdevelopment and an Uncaptured Peasantry.* Madison: University of Wisconsin Press.

ICG (International Crisis Group). 2003. "Yemen: Coping with Terrorism and Violence in a Fragile State." International Crisis Group Middle East Report no. 8. https://www.crisisgroup.org/middle-east-north-africa/gulf-and-arabian-peninsula/yemen/yemen-coping-terrorism-and-violence-fragile-state.

IISS (International Institute for Strategic Studies). 2000. "Unrest in Laos: Growing Regional Concerns." *Strategic Comments* 6 (7): 1–2.

IMF (International Monetary Fund). 2013. "Republic of Mozambique: Staff Report for the 2013 Article IV Consultation, Sixth Review under the Policy Support Instrument, Request for a Three-Year Policy Support Instrument and Cancellation of Current Policy Support Instrument." IMF Country Report no. 13/200, June 10, 2013. http://www.imf.org/external/pubs/ft/scr/2013/cr13200.pdf.

Imperato, P. J. 1989. *Mali: A Search for Direction.* Boulder, CO: Westview Press.

Independent Evaluation Group. 2013. *World Bank Group Assistance to Low-Income Fragile and Conflict-Affected States: An Independent Evaluation.* Washington, DC: World Bank.

Ingram, S. 2000. "Five Dead in Laos Border Clash." BBC News, July 3, 2000. http://news.bbc.co.uk/2/hi/asia-pacific/817335.stm.

Institute for Economics and Peace. 2016. *Global Peace Index 2016: Ten Years of Measuring Peace.* Sydney: Institute for Economics and Peace. http://visionofhumanity.org/app/uploads/2017/02/GPI-2016-Report_2.pdf.

IRIN (Integrated Regional Information Networks). 2010. "Laos: New MDG to Tackle UXOs." IRIN News, November 12, 2010. http://www.irinnews.org/report/91072/laos-new-mdg-tackle-uxos.

Islam, M. M. 2013. "The Toxic Politics of Bangladesh: A Bipolar Competitive Neopatrimonial State?" *Asian Journal of Political Science* 21 (2): 148–68.

Ismail, A. A. 2016. "The Political Economy of State Failure: A Social Contract Approach." *Journal of Intervention and Statebuilding* 10 (4): 513–29.

Jackson, R., and C. Rosberg. 1982. *Personal Rule in Black Africa.* Berkeley: University of California Press.

Jackson, R. H. 1990. *Quasi-States: Sovereignty, International Relations, and the Third World.* Cambridge: Cambridge University Press.

Jalan, J., and M. Ravallion. 2002. "Geographic Poverty Traps? A Micro Model of Consumption Growth in Rural China." *Journal of Applied Econometrics* 17 (4): 329–46.

Jamal, H. 2009. "Income Inequality in Pakistan: Trends, Determinants, and Impact." United Nations Development Program in Pakistan Policy Brief no. 2. http://www.pk.undp.org/content/pakistan/en/home/library/poverty/publication_2.html.

Jensen, M., and W. Meckling. 1976. "Theory of the Firm: Managerial Behavior, Agency Costs and Ownership Structure." *Journal of Financial Economics* 3 (4): 305–60.

Joiner, C. A. 1987. "Laos in 1986: Administrative and International Partially Adaptive Communism." *Asian Survey* 27 (1): 104–14.

Jones, S., and F. Tarp. 2016. "African Lions: Understanding Mozambique's Growth Experience through an Employment Lens." Brookings Institute, April 25, 2016. https://www.brookings.edu/research/african-lions-understanding-mozambiques-growth-experience-through-an-employment-lens/.

Kabeer, N., S. Mahmud, and J. G. I. Castro. 2012. "NGOs and the Political Empowerment of Poor People in Rural Bangladesh: Cultivating the Habits of Democracy?" *World Development* 40 (10): 2044–62.

Kaplan, S. 2008. "Fixing Fragile States." *Policy Review* 152:63–77.

———. 2013. "Power and Politics in Pakistan." Norwegian Peacebuilding Resource Center Expert Analysis. https://www.files.ethz.ch/isn/163808/07f02d6b2e01427f1eceedc9cf4f4e14.pdf.

———. 2014. "Identifying Truly Fragile States." *Washington Quarterly* 37 (1): 49–63.

Kapstein, E. B., and N. Converse. 2008. *The Fate of Young Democracies*. Cambridge: Cambridge University Press.

Keister, J. 2014. "The Illusion of Chaos: Why Undergoverned Spaces Aren't Ungoverned, and Why That Matters." Cato Institute Policy Analysis no. 766.

Keita, K. 1998. "Conflict and Conflict Resolution in the Sahel: The Tuareg Insurgency in Mali." *Small Wars and Insurgencies* 9 (3): 102–28.

Kerkvliet, B. J. 2009. "Everyday Politics in Peasant Societies (and Ours)." *Journal of Peasant Studies* 36 (1): 227–43.

Khan, A. 2005. *Politics of Identity: Ethnic Nationalism and the State of Pakistan*. New Delhi: SAGE Publications.

Khan, M. R., and F. Ara. 2006. "Women, Participation and Empowerment in Local Government: Bangladesh Union Parishad Perspective." *Asian Affairs* 29 (1): 73–92.

Khan, N. A. 2016. "Challenges and Trends in Decentralised Local Governance in Bangladesh." Institute of South Asian Studies Working Paper no. 222. Singapore: National University of Singapore.

Khandker, S. R., M. A. Baqui Khalily, and H. A. Samad. 2016. "Beyond Ending Poverty: The Dynamics of Microfinance in Bangladesh." Washington, DC: World Bank Group.

Khandker, S. R., and G. B. Koolwal. 2010. "How Infrastructure and Financial Institutions Affect Rural Income and Poverty: Evidence from Bangladesh." *Journal of Development Studies* 46 (6): 1109–37.

Kharas, H., and A. Rogerson. 2012. "Horizon 2025: Creative Destruction in the Aid Industry." Overseas Development Institute. July 2012.

Khasru, B. Z. 2010. *Myths and Facts: Bangladesh Liberation War; How India, U.S., China, and the U.S.S.R. Shaped the Outcome*. New Delhi: Rupa.

Ki-moon, B. 2012. "Report of the Assessment Mission on the Impact of the Libyan Crisis on the Sahel Region, 7 to 23 December 2011." Letter to the President of the United Nations Security Council, January 17, 2012. ReliefWeb, January 27, 2012. https://reliefweb.int/report/mali/report-assessment-mission-impact-libyan-crisis-sahel-region-7-23-december-2011-s201242.

Kingwell, M. 2007. "What Fragility Can Teach Us." *Globe and Mail*, October 27, 2007, F7.

Knox, C. 2009. "Dealing with Sectoral Corruption in Bangladesh: Developing Citizen Involvement." *Public Administration and Development* 29:117–32.

Knutsen, C. H., and H. M. Nygård. 2015. "Institutional Characteristics and Regime Survival: Why Are Semi-Democracies Less Durable than Autocracies and Democracies?" *American Journal of Political Science* 59 (3): 656–70.

Kohli, A. 1990. *Democracy and Discontent: India's Growing Crisis of Governability*. Cambridge: Cambridge University Press.

Kraay, A., and D. McKenzie. 2014. "Do Poverty Traps Exist? Assessing the Evidence." *Journal of Economic Perspectives* 28 (3): 127–48.

Lamb, R. 2014. "Rethinking Legitimacy and Illegitimacy: A New Framework for Assessing Support and Opposition across Disciplines." Washington, DC: CSIS and Rowman & Littlefield.

Lambach, D., E. Johais, and M. Bayer. 2015. "Conceptualising State Collapse: An Institutionalist Approach." *Third World Quarterly* 36 (7): 1299–315.

Larémont, R. R. 2011. "Al Qaeda in the Islamic Maghreb: Terrorism and Counterterrorism in the Sahel." *African Security* 4 (4): 242–68.

Le Billon, P. 2001. "The Political Ideology of War: Natural Resources and Armed Conflicts." *Political Geography* 20:561–84.

Leftwich, A. 2010. "Beyond Institutions: Rethinking the Role of Leaders, Elites and Coalitions in the Institutional Formation of Developmental States and Strategies." *Forum for Development Studies* 37 (1): 93–111.

Leftwich, A., and C. Wheeler. 2011. *Politics, Leadership and Coalitions in Development: Findings, Insights and Guidance from the DLP's First Research and Policy Workshop, Frankfurt 10–11 March 2011*. DLP (Developmental Leadership Program). June 2011. http://www.dlprog.org/publications/politics-leadership-and-coalitions-in-development-findings-insights-and-guidance.php.

Lemay-Hébert, N. 2009. "Statebuilding without Nation-Building? Legitimacy, State Failure and the Limits of the Institutionalist Approach." *Journal of Intervention and Statebuilding* 3 (1): 21–45.

Lemay-Hébert, N., and X. Mathieu. 2014. "The OECD's Discourse on Fragile States: Expertise and the Normalisation of Knowledge Production." *Third World Quarterly* 35 (2): 232–51.

Levi, M., and A. Sacks. 2009. "Legitimating Beliefs: Sources and Indicators." *Regulation and Governance* 3 (4): 311–33.

Levi, M., A. Sacks, and A. Tyler. 2009. "Conceptualizing Legitimacy, Measuring Legitimating Beliefs." *American Behavioral Scientist* 53 (3): 354–75.

Levitsky, S., and M. V. Murillo. 2009. "Variation in Institutional Strength." *Annual Review of Political Science* 12:115–33.

References

Levitsky, S., and L. A. Way. 2002. "The Rise of Competitive Authoritarianism." *Journal of Democracy* 13 (2): 51–65.
Lipset, S. M. 1959. "Some Social Requisites of Democracy: Economic Development and Political Legitimacy." *American Political Science Review* 53 (1): 69–105.
Lode, K. 1997. "The Peace Process in Mali: Oiling the Works?" *Security Dialogue* 28 (4): 409–24.
Lottholz, P., and N. Lemay-Hébert. 2016. "Re-reading Weber, Re-conceptualizing State-Building: From Neo-Weberian to Post-Weberian Approaches to State, Legitimacy and State-Building." *Cambridge Review of International Affairs* 10 (29): 1467–85.
Lust, E., and D. Waldner. 2015. *Unwelcome Change: Understanding, Evaluating, and Extending Theories of Democratic Backsliding*. Washington, DC: United States Agency for International Development. http://pdf.usaid.gov/pdf_docs/PBAAD635.pdf.
Lustick, I. 1979. "Stability in Deeply Divided Societies: Consociationalism versus Control." *World Politics* 31 (3): 325–44.
Mahmud, W., S. Ahmed, and S. Mahaj. 2008. "Economic Reforms, Growth, and Governance: The Political Economy Aspects of Bangladesh's Development Surprise." Commission on Growth and Development Working Paper no. 22. Washington, DC: World Bank. http://documents.worldbank.org/curated/en/763541468013237841/Economic-reforms-growth-and-governance-the-political-economy-aspects-of-Bangladeshs-development-surprise.
Malik, A. H. 201. "A Comparative Study of Elite-English-Medium Schools, Public Schools, and Islamic Madaris in Contemporary Pakistan: The Use of Pierre Bourdieu's Theory to Understand 'Inequalities in Educational and Occupational Opportunities.'" EdD thesis, Department of Sociology and Equity Studies in Education, University of Toronto. https://tspace.library.utoronto.ca/bitstream/1807/34798/1/Malik_Akhtar_H_201211_EdD_thesis.pdf.
Malik, I. H. 1996. "The State and Civil Society in Pakistan: From Crisis to Crisis." *Asian Survey* 36 (7): 673–90.
Manning, C. L. 2002. *The Politics of Peace in Mozambique: Post-conflict Democratization, 1992–2000*. Westport, CT: Greenwood.
Mansfield, E. D., and J. Snyder. 2007. "The Sequencing 'Fallacy.'" *Journal of Democracy* 18 (3): 5–10.
Marquez, X. 2016. "The Irrelevance of Legitimacy." *Political Studies* 64 (1): 19–34.
Marshall, M., and B. R. Cole. 2014. *Global Report 2014: Conflict, Governance, and State Fragility*. Vienna, VA: Center for Systemic Peace. https://www.systemicpeace.org/vlibrary/GlobalReport2014.pdf.
———. 2010. "Polity IV Country Report 2010: Pakistan." Vienna, VA: Center for Systemic Peace. http://www.systemicpeace.org/polity/Pakistan2010.pdf.
Marshall, M., and J. Goldstone. 2007. "Global Report on Conflict, Governance and State Fragility 2007: Gauging System Performance and Fragility in the Globalization Era." *Foreign Policy Bulletin* 17 (1): 3–21.
Mata, J. F., and S. Ziaja. 2009. *Users' Guide on Measuring Fragility*. Bonn and Oslo: German Development Institute and United Nations Development Programme. http://www.la.undp.org/content/dam/undp/library/Democratic%20Governance/OGC/usersguide_measure_fragility_ogc.pdf.

Mazarr, M. J. 2013. "The Rise and Fall of the Failed-State Paradigm: Requiem for a Decade of Distraction." *Foreign Affairs* 93 (1): 113–21.

McLoughlin, C. 2015. "When Does Service Delivery Improve the Legitimacy of a Fragile or Conflict-Affected State?" *Governance* 28 (3): 341–56.

McMann, K. M. 2016. "Developing State Legitimacy: The Credibility of Messengers and the Utility, Fit, and Success of Ideas." *Comparative Politics* 48 (4): 538–56.

Means, G. P. 1996. "Soft Authoritarianism in Malaysia and Singapore." *Journal of Democracy* 7 (4): 103–7.

Menocal, A. R., V. Fritz, and L. Rakner. 2008. "Hybrid Regimes and the Challenges of Deepening and Sustaining Democracy in Developing Countries." *South African Journal of International Affairs* 15 (1): 29–40.

Messner, J. J., N. Haken, K. Hendry, P. Taft, K. Lawrence, S. Pavlou, and F. Umaña. 2013. *Failed States Index Data 2013: The Book*. Washington, DC: Fund for Peace. http://library.fundforpeace.org/cfsir1306.

Mezzera, M., and S. Aftab. 2009. *Pakistan State-Society Analysis*. The Hague: Netherlands Institute of International Relations. https://www.clingendael.org/sites/default/files/20090300_cru_pakistan_mezzera.pdf.

Migdal, J. 1988. *Strong Societies and Weak States: State-Society Relations and State Capabilities in the Third World*. Princeton, NJ: Princeton University Press.

———. 2001. *State in Society: Studying How States and Societies Transform and Constitute One Another*. Cambridge: Cambridge University Press.

Minorities at Risk. 2010. "Data: Chronology for Hmong in Laos." Minorities at Risk Project, University of Maryland Center for International Development and Conflict Management. Last updated July 16, 2010. http://www.mar.umd.edu/chronology.asp?groupId=81201.

Minter, W. 1989. *The Mozambican National Resistance (Renamo) as Described by Ex-Participants*. Chicago: Ford Foundation and Swedish International Development Agency.

Mitchell, K. 2010. "Ungoverned Space: Global Security and the Geopolitics of Broken Windows." *Political Geography* 29 (5): 289–97.

Moniruzzaman, M. 2009a. "Party Politics and Political Violence in Bangladesh." *South Asian Survey* 16 (1): 81–99.

———. 2009b. "Parliamentary Democracy in Bangladesh: An Evaluation of the Parliament during 1991–2006." *Commonwealth and Comparative Politics* 47 (1): 100–126.

Moss, T., G. Pettersson, and N. van de Walle. 2006. "An Aid-Institutions Paradox: A Review Essay on Aid Dependency and State Building in Sub-Saharan Africa." Center for Global Development Working Paper no. 74. https://www.cgdev.org/publication/aid-institutions-paradox-review-essay-aid-dependency-and-state-building-sub-saharan.

MRG (Minority Rights Group International). 2015. "MRG Mali: Peoples." World Directory of Minorities and Indigenous Peoples. http://minorityrights.org/country/mali/.

Mulgan, R. 2011. "Accountability." In Badie, Berg-Schlosser, and Morlino, *International Encyclopedia of Political Science*, 1–15. http://sk.sagepub.com/reference/download/intlpoliticalscience/n1.pdf.

Munslow, B. 1988. "Mozambique and the Death of Machel." *Third World Quarterly* 10 (1): 23–36.

References

Mushtaq, M. 2009. "Managing Ethnic Diversity and Federalism in Pakistan." *European Journal of Scientific Research* 33 (2): 279–94.

Naudé, W., A. Santos-Paulino, and M. McGillivray. 2011. "Fragile States: An Overview." In Naudé, Santos-Paulino, and McGillivray, Fragile States. DOI: 10.1093/acprof:oso/9780199693153.001.0001.

Naudé, W., A. Santos-Paulino, and M. McGillivray, eds. 2011. *Fragile States: Causes, Costs, and Responses*. Oxford: Oxford University Press.

Nay, O. 2013. "Fragile and Failed States: Critical Perspectives on Conceptual Hybrids." *International Political Science Review* 34 (3): 326–41.

Nazneen, S. and S. Tasneem. 2010. "A Silver Lining: Women in Reserved Seats in Local Government in Bangladesh." *IDS Bulletin* 41:35–42.

Nelson, M. J. 2009. "Pakistan in 2008: Moving beyond Musharraf." *Asian Survey* 49 (1): 16–27.

Norris, P., R. W. Frank, and F. Martínez i Coma. 2014. *Advancing Electoral Integrity*. New York: Oxford University Press.

North, D. 1990. *Institutions, Institutional Change and Economic Performance*. Cambridge: Cambridge University Press.

———. 1995. "The New Institutional Economics and Third World Development." In *The New Institutional Economics and Third World Development*, edited by J. Harriss, J. Hunter, and C. M. Lewis, 17–26. London: Routledge.

———. 2005. *Understanding the Process of Economic Change*. Princeton, NJ: Princeton University Press.

North, D., J. J. Wallis, S. B. Webb, and B. R. Weingast. 2007. "Limited Access Orders in the Developing World: A New Approach to the Problems of Development." World Bank Policy Research Working Paper no. 4359. Washington, DC: World Bank Group. http://econweb.umd.edu/~wallis/MyPapers/Limted_Access_Orders_in_the_Developing_WorldWPS4359.pdf.

O'Donnell, G., and P. C. Schmitter. 1986. *Transitions for Authoritarian Rule: Comparative Perspectives*. Baltimore: Johns Hopkins University Press.

OECD (Organisation for Economic Co-operation and Development). 2007. "Principles for Good International Engagement in Fragile States and Situations." OECD, April 2007. https://www.oecd-ilibrary.org/development/international-engagement-in-fragile-states_9789264086128-en.

———. 2010. *The State's Legitimacy in Fragile Situations: Unpacking Complexity*. Paris: OECD Publishing.

———. 2011. *Statebuilding in Situations of Conflict and Fragility: Policy Guidance*. DAC Guidelines and Reference Series. Paris: OECD Publishing.

———. 2013. Mozambique. OECD. http://www.oecd.org/countries/mozambique/.

———. 2015. *States of Fragility 2015: Meeting Post-2015 Ambitions*. Paris: OECD. http://dx.doi.org/10.1787/9789264227699-en.

Olson, M. 1993. "Dictatorship, Democracy, and Development." *American Political Science Review* 87 (3): 567–76.

O'Meara, D. 1991. "The Collapse of Mozambican Socialism." *Transformation* 14:82–103.

Omeje, K. 2008. "Challenges to State Legitimacy and Institutional Channels of Political Participation in Africa." *Africa Insight* 37 (4): 183–91.

Ottaway, M. 1988. "Mozambique: From Symbolic Socialism to Symbolic Reform." *Journal of Modern African Studies* 26 (2): 211–26.

———. 2003a. *Democracy Challenged: The Rise of Semi-Authoritarianism.* Washington, DC: Carnegie Endowment for International Peace.

———. 2003b. "Promoting Democracy after Conflict: The Difficult Choices." *International Studies Perspectives* 4(3): 314–22.

Oxfam America. 2010. "Oxfam Fact Sheet: Pakistan Floods." Oxfam America. https://www.oxfamamerica.org/static/media/files/pakistan-floods-factsheet.pdf.

Panday, P. K. 2013. *Women's Political Participation in Bangladesh: Institutional Reforms, Actors and Outcomes.* New York: Springer.

Panday, P. K., and G. Rabbani. 2011. "Good Governance at the Grass-Roots: Evidence from Union Parshads in Bangladesh." *South Asian Survey* 18 (2): 293–315.

Parkinson, J. 2003. "Legitimacy Problems in Deliberative Democracy." *Political Studies* 51 (1): 180–96.

Parnini, S. N. 2006. "Civil Society and Good Governance in Bangladesh." *Asian Journal of Political Science* 14 (2): 189–211.

Patrick, S. 2010. "Are 'Ungoverned Spaces' a Threat?" CFR Expert Brief. Council on Foreign Relations. https://www.cfr.org/expert-brief/are-ungoverned-spaces-threat.

Paul, B. P. 2010. "Does Corruption Foster Growth in Bangladesh?" *International Journal of Development Issues* 9(3): 246–62.

Perez, H., and P. Le Billon. 2013. "Foreign Aid, Resource Rents, and State Fragility in Mozambique and Angola." *Annals of the American Academy of Political and Social Science* 656 (1): 79–96.

Pew Research Center. 2013. "On Eve of Elections, a Dismal Public Mood in Pakistan." Pew Research Center. http://www.pewglobal.org/2013/05/07/on-eve-of-elections-a-dismal-public-mood-in-pakistan/.

Pézard, S., and M. Shurkin. 2013. *Toward a Secure and Stable Northern Mali: Approaches to Engaging Local Actors.* Santa Monica, CA: RAND Corp.

Phillips, S. 2007. "Evaluating Political Reform in Yemen." Carnegie Endowment for International Peace Papers. February 14, 2007. http://carnegieendowment.org/files/cp_80_phillips_yemen_final.pdf.

Phiri, M. Z. 2012. "The Political Economy of Mozambique Twenty Years On: A Post-conflict Success Story?" *South African Journal of International Affairs* 19 (2): 223–45.

Pop-Eleches, G., and G. B. Robertson. 2015. "Structural Conditions and Democratization." *Journal of Democracy* 26 (3): 144–56.

Pospisil, J., and A. R. Menocal. 2017. "Why Political Settlements Matter: Navigating Inclusion in Processes of Institutional Transformation." *Journal of International Development* 29 (5): 551–58.

Prichard, W. 2010. "Taxation and State Building: Towards a Governance Focused Tax Reform Agenda." IDS Working Paper no. 341. Institute of Development Studies. https://www.ids.ac.uk/publications/taxation-and-state-building-towards-a-governance-focused-tax-reform-agenda/.

Pritchett, L., and F. de Weijer. 2010. "Fragile States: Stuck in a Capability Trap?" World Development Report Background Paper. November 5, 2010. Washington, DC: World Bank.

References

Pritchett, L., M. Woolcock, and M. Andrews. 2010. "Capability Traps? The Mechanisms of Persistent Implementation Failure." Center for Global Development Working Paper no. 234. https://www.cgdev.org/publication/capability-traps-mechanisms-persistent-implementation-failure-working-paper-234.

———. 2013. "Looking Like a State: Techniques of Persistent Failure in State Capability for Implementation." *Journal of Development Studies* 49 (1): 1–18.

Przeworski, A., M. Alvarez, A. Cheibub, and F. Limongi. 1996. "What Makes Democracies Endure?" *Journal of Democracy* 7 (1): 39–53.

———. 2000. *Democracy and Development*. Cambridge: Cambridge University Press.

Przeworski, A., and F. Limongi. 1997. "Modernization: Theories and Facts." *World Politics* 49:155–83.

Pye, L., and S. Verba. 1965. *Political Culture and Political Development*. Studies in Political Development, vol. 5. Princeton, NJ: Princeton University Press.

———. 1971. "The Legitimacy Crisis." In *Crises and Sequences in Political Development*, edited by L. Binder and J. La Palombara, 135–58. Studies in Political Development, vol. 7. Princeton, NJ: Princeton University Press.

Rana, E. A., and A. N. M. Wahid. 2017. "Fiscal Deficit and Economic Growth in Bangladesh: A Time-Series Analysis." *American Economist* 62 (1): 31–42.

Reeve, R. 2013. "Sahel to High Water: Drug Trafficking in West Africa." *HIS Jane's Intelligence Review* 25 (7): 44–49.

Reuters. 2012. "Factbox: Ansar Dine; Black Flag over Northern Mali." Reuters, July 3, 2012. http://blogs.reuters.com/faithworld/2012/07/03/factbox-ansar-dine-black-flag-over-northern-mali/.

Riaz, A. 2014. "Bangladesh's Failed Election." *Journal of Democracy* 25 (2): 119–30.

Rizvi, H. A. 1991. "The Military and Politics in Pakistan." *Journal of Asian and African Studies* 26 (1–2): 27–42.

Robinson, D. 2003. "Socialism in Mozambique? The 'Mozambican Revolution' in Critical Perspective." *Limina: A Journal of Historical and Cultural Studies* 9:131–51.

Roder, W. 1997. "Slash-and-Burn Rice Systems in Transition: Challenges for Agricultural Development in the Hills of Northern Laos." *Mountain Research and Development* 17 (1): 1–10.

Rosser, A. 2006. "Lao People's Democratic Republic." *IDS Bulletin* 37 (2): 27–39.

Rostow, W. W. 1960. *The Stages of Economic Growth: A Non-Communist Manifesto*. Cambridge: Cambridge University Press.

Rotberg, R. I. 2003. *State Failure and State Weakness in a Time of Terror*. Washington, DC: Brookings Institution Press.

———. 2004. *When States Fail: Causes and Consequences*. Princeton, NJ: Princeton University Press.

———. 2012. *Transformative Political Leadership: Making a Difference in the Developing World*. Chicago: University of Chicago Press.

Rothchild, D. 1986. "Hegemonial Exchange: An Alternative Model for Managing Conflict in Middle Africa." In *Ethnicity, Politics and Development*, edited by D. Thompson and D. Rover, 65–104. Boulder, CO: Lynne Rienner.

Roy, A. 2010. "Mali: Instrumentalisation de la 'société civile.'" *Alternatives sud* 17:111–18.

Ruud, A. E., and M. M. Islam. 2016. "Political Dynasty Formation in Bangladesh." *South Asia: Journal of South Asian Studies* 39 (2): 401–14.

Sachs, J. 2005. *The End of Poverty: Economic Possibilities for Our Time*. New York: Penguin Press.

Sachs, J., and A. Warner. 1995. "Natural Resource Abundance and Economic Growth." NBER Working Paper no. 5398. National Bureau of Economic Research. http://www.nber.org/papers/w5398.

Savada, A. M. 1995. *A Country Study: Laos*. Washington, DC: Federal Research Division, Library of Congress.

Schedler, A. 1998. "What Is Democratic Consolidation?" *Journal of Democracy* 9 (2): 91–107.

———. 2006. *Electoral Authoritarianism: The Dynamics of Unfree Competition*. Boulder, CO: Lynne Rienner.

Schofield, J. 2011. "Diversionary Wars: Pashtun Unrest and the Sources of the Pakistan-Afghan Confrontation." *Canadian Foreign Policy Journal* 17 (1): 38–49.

Schwarz, R., and M. de Corral. 2013. "Not a Curse at All: Why Middle Eastern Oil States Fail and How It Can Be Prevented." *Journal of Intervention and Statebuilding* 7 (3): 402–22.

Scott, J. 1976. *The Moral Economy of the Peasant: Rebellion and Subsistence in Southeast Asia*. New Haven, CT: Yale University Press.

Seawright, J., and J. Gerring. 2008. "Case Selection Techniques in Case Study Research: A Menu of Qualitative and Quantitative Options." *Political Research Quarterly* 61 (2): 294–308.

Shah, A. 2003. "Pakistan's 'Armoured' Democracy." *Journal of Democracy* 194 (4): 26–40.

———. 2008. "Pakistan after Musharraf: Praetorianism and Terrorism." *Journal of Democracy* 19 (4): 16–25.

Shaw, S. 2013. "Fallout in the Sahel: The Geographic Spread of Conflict from Libya to Mali." *Canadian Foreign Policy Journal* 19 (2): 199–210.

SIGAR (Special Inspector General for Afghanistan Reconstruction). 2017. "Quarterly Report to the United States Congress." January 30, 2017.

Sisson, R., and L. E. Rose. 1991. *War and Secession: Pakistan, India, and the Creation of Bangladesh*. Oakland: University of California Press.

Smillie, I., and J. Hailey. 2001. *Managing for Change: Leadership, Strategy and Management in Asian NGOs*. London: Earthscan.

Smith, A. D. 2013. "Will Mali's Poll Bring Unity and Peace?" *BBC News*, July 25, 2013. http://www.bbc.co.uk/news/world-africa-23449457.

Stasavage, D. 1999. "Causes and Consequences of Corruption: Mozambique in Transition." *Journal of Commonwealth and Comparative Politics* 37 (3): 65–97.

Steinmo, S. 2008. "What Is Historical Institutionalism?" In *Approaches in the Social Sciences*, edited by Donatella Della Porta and Michael Keating, 118–38. Cambridge: Cambridge University Press.

Stern, M., and J. Öjendal. 2010. "Mapping the Security-Development Nexus: Conflict, Complexity, Cacophony, Convergence?" *Security Dialogue* 41 (1): 5–29.

Stewart, F. 2009. "Horizontal Inequality: Two Types of Trap." *Journal of Human Development and Capabilities* 10 (3): 315–40.

Stewart, F., and G. Brown. 2009. "Fragile States." CRISE Working Paper no. 51. Oxford: Centre for Research on Inequality, Human Security, and Ethnicity.

References

St. John, R. B. 2006. "The Political Economy of Laos: Poor State or Poor Policy?" *Asian Affairs* 37 (2): 175–91.

Storholt, K. H. 2001. "Lessons Learned from the 1990–1997 Peace Process in the North of Mali." *International Negotiation* 6 (3): 331–56.

Strand, H., H. Hegre, S. Gates, and M. Dahl. 2012. "Democratic Waves? Global Patterns of Democratization." Paper prepared for the 3rd International Conference on Democracy as Idea and Practice, Oslo, January 12–13, 2012. https://www.uio.no/english/research/interfaculty-research-areas/democracy/news-and-events/events/conferences/2012/papers-2012/Strand-Hegre-Gates-Dahl-wshop7.pdf.

Stuart-Fox, M. 1986. *Laos: Politics, Economics, and Society*. Boulder, CO: Lynne Rienner.

———. 1997. *A History of Laos*. Cambridge: Cambridge University Press.

———. 2006. "The Political Culture of Corruption in the Lao PDR." *Asian Studies Review* 30 (1): 59–75.

Sumner, A. 2012. "Where Do the World's Poor Live?" IDS Working Paper. Institute of Development Studies. https://www.ids.ac.uk/files/dmfile/Wp393.pdf.

Suykens, B. 2017. "The Bangladesh Party-State: A Diachronic Comparative Analysis of Party-Political Regimes." *Commonwealth and Comparative Politics* 55 (2): 187–213.

Takeuchi, S., R. Murotani, and K. Tsunekawa. 2011. "Capacity Traps and Legitimacy Traps: Development Assistance and State Building in Fragile Situations." In *Catalyzing Development: A New Vision for Aid,* edited by H. Kharas, W. Jung, and K. Makino, 127–54. Washington, DC: Brookings Institution Press.

Talbot, I. 2002. "The Punjabization of Pakistan." In *Pakistan: Nationalism without a Nation?*, edited by C. Jaffrelot, 51–62. London: Zed Books.

Tasnim, F. 2012. "How Vigilant Is the Vibrant Civil Society in Bangladesh? A Survey-Based Analysis." *Journal of Civil Society* 8 (2): 155–83.

Tavares, J. 2003. "Does Foreign Aid Corrupt?" *Economic Letters* 79 (1): 99–106.

Telegraph. 2011. "Yemen's President Saleh Wounded in Palace Attack." *Telegraph,* June 3, 2002. http://www.telegraph.co.uk/news/worldnews/middleeast/yemen/8554795/Yemens-President-Saleh-wounded-in-palace-attack.html.

Thayer, C. A. 2000. "Laos in 1999: Economic Woes Drive Foreign Policy." *Asian Survey* 40 (1): 43–48.

———. 2004. "Laos in 2003: Counterrevolution Fails to Ignite." *Asian Survey* 44 (1): 110–14.

Thelen, K. 1999. "Historical Institutionalism in Comparative Polictics." *Annual Review of Political Science* 2 (1): 369–404.

Thompson, M. R. 2012. "Asia's Hybrid Regimes." *Asian Affairs* 43 (2): 204–20.

TI (Transparency International). 2013a. "Corruption by Country/Territory: Mali." Transparency International. Accessed October 23, 2013. https://www.transparency.org/country/MLI.

———. 2013b. "Mozambique." Transparency International. http://www.transparency.org/country#MOZ.

Tikuisis, P., and D. Carment. 2017. "Categorization of States beyond Strong and Weak." *Stability: International Journal of Security and Development* 6 (1): 12. http://doi.org/10.5334/sta.483.

Tikuisis, P., D. Carment, and Y. Samy. 2013. "Prediction of Intrastate Conflict Using State Structural Factors and Events Data." *Journal of Conflict Resolution* 57 (3): 410–44.

Tikuisis, P., D. Carment, Y. Samy, and J. Landry. 2015. "Typology of State Types: Persistence and Transition." *International Interactions* 41 (3): 565–82.

Tudor, M. 2014. "Renewed Hope in Pakistan?" *Journal of Democracy* 25 (2): 105–18.

Turper, S., and K. Aarts. 2017. "Political Trust and Sophistication: Taking Measurement Seriously." *Social Indicators Research* 130 (1): 415–34.

UCDP (Uppsala Conflict Data Program). 2014. "UCDP Conflict Encyclopedia: Laos." Department of Peace and Conflict Studies, Uppsala University. http://ucdp.uu.se/#country/812.

UNDHA (United Nations Department of Humanitarian Affairs). 1996. "Lao Situation Report No. 2." Relief Web. October 3, 1996. http://reliefweb.int/report/lao-peoples-democratic-republic/lao-situation-report-no2.

UNDP (United Nations Development Programme). 2013. "Mozambique: Human Development Indicators." UNDP Human Development Reports. http://hdr.undp.org/en/countries/profiles/MOZ.

———. 2016. *Human Development Report 2016: Human Development for Everyone*. New York: United Nations Publications.

UNDP Pakistan. 2014. "Education: Governance Conundrum." *Development Advocate Pakistan* 1 (2). http://www.pk.undp.org/content/pakistan/en/home/library/development_policy/development-advocate-pakistan--volume-1-issue-2.html.

Uphoff, N. 1989. "Distinguishing Power, Authority and Legitimacy: Taking Max Weber at His Word by Using Resources-Exchange Analysis." *Polity* 22 (2): 295–322.

USAID (United States Agency for International Development). 2005. *Measuring Fragility: Indicators and Methods for Rating State Performance*. Washington, DC: USAID. https://pdf.usaid.gov/pdf_docs/PNADD462.pdf.

Vanhanen, T. 1990. *The Process of Democratization: A Comparative Study of 147 States 1980–1988*. New York: Crane Russak.

———. 2000. "A New Dataset for Measuring Democracy, 1810–1998." *Journal of Peace Research* 37 (2): 251–65.

Vines, A. 1991. *Renamo: Terrorism in Mozambique*. Bloomington: Indiana University Press.

———. 2013. "Renamo's Rise and Decline: The Politics of Reintegration in Mozambique." *International Peacekeeping* 20 (3): 375–93.

Vixathep, S., P. Onphanhdala, and P. Phomvixay. 2013. "Land Distribution and Rice Sufficiency in Northern Laos." Kobe University Graduate School of International Cooperation Studies (GSICS) Working Paper no. 27. https://econpapers.repec.org/paper/kcswpaper/27.htm

Weatherford, S. M. 1992. "Measuring Political Legitimacy." *American Political Science Review* 86 (1): 149–66.

Weaver, C. 2008. *Hypocrisy Trap: The World Bank and the Poverty of Reform*. Princeton, NJ: Princeton University Press.

Weiner, M. 1971. "The Macedonian Syndrome: An Historical Model of International Relations and Political Development." *World Politics* 23 (4): 665–83.

WFP (World Food Programme). 2006. "Risk and Vulnerability Analysis: Lao PDR." World Food Programme. https://www.wfp.org/sites/default/files/Annual%20Report%202006%20%28lowrez%29.pdf.

References

———. 2011. "Fighting Hunger Worldwide: Overview on Mozambique." World Food Programme. http://www.wfp.org/countries/Mozambique/Overview.

Wigell, M. 2008. "Mapping 'Hybrid Regimes': Regime Types and Concepts in Comparative Politics." *Democratization* 15 (2): 230–50.

Wing, S. D. 2013. "Mali: Politics of a Crisis." *African Affairs* 112 (448): 476–85.

World Bank. 2007. *Aid That Works: Successful Development in Fragile States*. Directions in Development. Washington, DC: World Bank. https://openknowledge.worldbank.org/handle/10986/6636.

———. 2011. *World Development Report 2011: Conflict, Security and Development*. Washington, DC: World Bank. https://openknowledge.worldbank.org/handle/10986/4389.

———. 2013. "Mozambique." World Bank. http://www.worldbank.org/en/country/mozambique/overview.

———. 2014. *The World Bank Group Goals: End Extreme Poverty and Promote Shared Prosperity*. Washington, DC: World Bank Group. https://openknowledge.worldbank.org/handle/10986/20138.

———. 2016a. "Helping Bangladesh Reach Middle Income Country Status." World Bank, April 7, 2016. http://www.worldbank.org/en/news/feature/2016/04/07/World_Bank_Group_s_New_Country_Partnership_Framework_helps_Bangladesh_Reach_Middle_Income_Country_Status.

———. 2016b. "Pakistan." World Bank. http://data.worldbank.org/country/pakistan.

———. 2017a. "Agriculture, Value Added (Annual % Growth): Laos, 1985–1990." World Development Indicators. https://data.worldbank.org/indicator/NV.AGR.TOTL.KD.ZG?locations=LA.

———. 2017b. "Arable Land (% of Land Area): Laos, 2009." World Development Indicators. https://data.worldbank.org/indicator/AG.LND.ARBL.ZS?locations=LA.

———. 2017c. "GDP Growth (Annual %): Laos, 1985–2000." World Development Indicators. https://data.worldbank.org/indicator/NY.GDP.MKTP.KD.ZG?locations=LA.

———. 2017d. "GDP Growth (Annual %): Mali, 1980–1990." World Development Indicators. http://data.worldbank.org/data-catalog/world-development-indicators.

———. 2017e. "Inflation, Consumer Prices (Annual %): Laos, 1990–1998." World Development Indicators. https://data.worldbank.org/indicator/FP.CPI.TOTL.ZG?locations=LA.

———. 2017f. "Lao PDR to Improve Water Resources Management." World Bank, July 26, 2017. http://www.worldbank.org/en/news/press-release/2017/07/26/lao-pdr-to-improve-water-resources-management.

———. 2017g. "Net ODA Received (% of GNI): Laos, 1998." World Development Indicators. https://data.worldbank.org/indicator/DT.ODA.ODAT.GN.ZS?locations=LA.

———. 2017h. "Net Official Development Assistance Received (Constant 2011 US$): Mali, 1980–2012." World Development Indicators. https://data.worldbank.org/indicator/DT.ODA.ODAT.KD?locations=ML.

———. 2017i. "Personal Remittances, Received (% of GDP): Laos, 1995–2000." World Development Indicators. https://data.worldbank.org/indicator/BX.TRF.PWKR.DT.GD.ZS?locations=LA.

———. 2017j. "Logistic Performance Indicators: Laos." https://lpi.worldbank.org/international/aggregated-ranking.

———. 2017k. "GDP Per Capita: Bangladesh." https://data.worldbank.org/indicator/NY.GDP.PCAP.CD?locations=BD.

Wright, J. 2009. "How Foreign Aid Can Foster Democratization in Authoritarian Regimes." *American Journal of Political Science* 53 (3): 552–71.

Zakaria, F. 1997. "The Rise of Illiberal Democracy." *Foreign Affairs* 76 (6): 22–43.

Zaman, R. U. 2012. "Bangladesh: Between Terrorism, Identity and Illiberal Democracy—The Unfolding of a Tragic Saga." *Perceptions* 17 (3): 151–77.

Index

The letter "f" following a page number denotes a figure; the letter "t" denotes a table.

Afghanistan, 6, 39–41, 46–49, 54, 65, 76, 90–92, 106–8, 182
Africanization, 116
aid, 2–3, 11–13, 17–18, 25, 47, 177–78, 188–90; Bangladesh, 148; Laos, 112, 130–31, 133, 136, 139, 141, 143; Mali, 112–15, 121–26, 143–44, 184; Mozambique, 173–74, 185; Pakistan, 82, 104, 107–8, 183; USAID, 11; Yemen, 87, 89, 92
aid, developmental, 82, 123
aid, foreign, 2, 13–14t, 25, 34, 64, 76, 146, 155, 166–67, 170, 172; Bangladesh, 146, 155; Laos, 131, 136, 139, 141, 143; Mozambique, 146, 166–67, 170, 172; Pakistan, 108–9; Yemen, 92
aid, humanitarian, 89, 148
aid, military, 109, 183
aid darling, 17, 25, 34, 113, 172
aid dependent, 30, 112, 114, 125, 143, 185
aid orphan, 25, 34
aid programs, 1, 107, 139, 178, 183
ALC (authority-legitimacy-capacity), 3–5, 13–14, 26, 37–43, 46–49, 56, 61, 79–80, 89, 177, 182; Bangladesh, 80, 147–49; Laos, 128f, 80, 139; Mali, 114–15f, 80, 117; Mozambique, 56, 145, 163, 80; Pakistan, 41, 80, 95–96f; Yemen, 41, 80, 84f–85
Algeria, 55t–56, 61, 117, 119, 126
All-India Muslim League, 97
al-Qaeda, 39, 87–92, 101, 107, 113, 119; AQAP (al-Qaeda in the Arabian Peninsula), 88–89, 91; AQC (al-Qaeda Central), 119; AQIM (al-Qaeda in the Islamic Maghreb), 119–20, 126
ANC (African National Congress), 164
Ansar al-Sharia, 88
Ansar Dine, 117, 119–20
anti-Americanism, 108
Arab Spring, 27, 73, 79, 90
armed forces. *See* military (armed forces)
Asian financial crisis, 127, 131–32, 139

authoritarianism, 69–73, 91, 144, 146, 149, 156, 160, 184; bureaucratic, 82, 101, 105, 181
authoritarian management, 46, 75
authoritarian regimes, 2, 70, 74
Awami League, 150–55

backsliding, 20, 27, 68–69, 71–72
Bahanga, Ibrahim Ag, 118–19
Baluchistan, 100, 102, 107–8
Bamako, 116–17, 119, 121, 144
Bangladesh, 145–61, 175, 181, 186; ALC (authority-legitimacy-capacity), 147–49; Awami League, 150–55; BNP (Bangladesh Nationalist Party), 150–55; conflict, 98, 145–46, 180–81; exited state, 29–30, 55t, 80, 149–51, 156–58, 173, 180–81, 185; fragility, 145–49; Jatiya Party, 151–54
Bhutto, Benazir, 99–101, 106, 153
Bhutto, Zulfiqar Ali, 98
bin Laden, Osama, 107
BNP (Bangladesh Nationalist Party), 150–55
Bouphavanh, Bouasone, 133–34
Burkina Faso, 33, 114, 121
Burundi, 33, 40–41, 49t, 54–55t

capability trap, 19, 21, 45, 50, 51f, 53, 58, 60–61, 178–79
capacity trap, 45–46, 75
Central African Republic, 12, 33, 39, 41t, 43
Chad, 40t–41t, 43, 49t, 54–55t, 117
China, 25, 108, 131–33, 136, 139–41, 144
Chissano, Joaquim, 165–68
CIFP (Country Indicators for Foreign Policy), 5, 35, 37–38, 47, 80
civilianization, 106, 149–50, 152, 185
Cold War, 39, 66, 130, 169–70
conditionality, 11, 178, 188
conflict, 3–6, 38–39, 44–45, 48, 52–54, 58t–62, 177–81; Afghanistan, 54 (*see also* Afghanistan); armed, 73, 77, 113, 136; Bangladesh, 145–46, 180–81; Burundi, 33, 54; civil, 6, 170;

Index

conflict (cont.)
　ethnic, 6, 16, 97, 99, 102; intensity, 5, 14t, 50–52, 54, 59–60, 178, 180; internal, 29, 82, 97; Laos, 127–38, 141, 180–81; Mali, 112–26, 134, 180–81; Mozambique, 61, 145–46, 163–65, 169–71, 180–81, 185; Pakistan, 29, 81–82, 94–103, 105–8, 180–81; regional, 120, 145; risk of, 4, 19; Syria, 6; Tuareg, 114, 117–18, 123; Yemen, 54, 85–91, 109, 180–81
conflict trap, 19, 24, 34, 44, 49–54, 59–62, 178
Congo, Democratic Republic of, 9, 12, 33, 40–41, 43, 46, 49t, 54–55, 182
corruption, 2, 7, 9, 12, 14, 17, 19, 30, 34, 48, 74, 79, 177, 182; Afghanistan, 182; Bangladesh, 146, 150–51, 153–54, 156–58, 186; Laos, 13–34, 142; Mali, 123–24, 144; Mozambique, 172–75, 186; Pakistan, 48, 99, 104–5; Yemen, 92–93, 109
Corruption Perceptions Index, 48
Côte d'Ivoire, 40t, 43, 71
CPIA (Country Policy and Institutional Assessment), 33, 35–36
Cristina, Orlando, 165

democracy, 4, 6, 20, 23, 69–73, 180, 189–90; Bangladesh, 145–46, 153, 156–57, 160, 186; level of, 11, 14t; Mali, 113, 117, 122, 125, 143; Mozambique, 168–71; Pakistan, 97, 101, 103, 105; Yemen, 82, 91. See also democratization
democratization, 3–4, 69–73, 168, 176, 188; Bangladesh, 156, 188; Mali, 117, 120, 188; Mozambique, 181, 188; Pakistan, 105; Yemen, 91, 181
departicipation, 67–68, 105, 174
disengagement, 67–68, 105, 186–87

economy, 3, 65, 67–68, 185; Bangladesh, 146–48, 150–51, 154–58, 173–75; informal, 65, 68; Laos, 128, 130–31, 135; Mali, 114–16, 122, 124–25, 143; market-based, 130, 166; Mozambique, 166–67, 169, 172–75; Pakistan, 102, 106; political, 106, 109–10, 142, 175; Yemen, 82, 86–87, 183. See also GDP (gross domestic product); growth, economic; rent economy
Egypt, 72, 77, 89
elite bargaining, 67–68, 73, 125, 157, 168, 170
elite behavior, 27, 64–65, 69, 72, 75, 177, 180
elite capture, 2, 22, 61, 77–79, 101, 103, 105, 110, 178, 180, 182
elites, 27, 63–80, 177, 180, 182, 184–87, 190; Bangladesh, 149–51, 156–57, 160–61, 173–75; Laos, 128, 134, 136, 138–42, 184; Mali, 29, 113, 116, 118, 120–22, 125–26; Mozambique, 166–68, 170, 172–74, 185; Pakistan, 81, 101–6, 109–10, 187; political, 42, 75, 105; regional, 65, 67, 90–91, 118, 126; rent seeking, 29, 120, 122, 142, 172, 177, 187; Yemen, 81, 90–91, 93, 109
Equatorial Guinea, 55–56
Ershad, General Hussein Mohammad, 150–54
Ethiopia, 40t, 48–49t, 54–55t
ethnic tensions, 6, 16, 97, 99, 102
exited states, 61–62, 179–80
extremists, 83, 108, 155

failed state, 36, 39; failing state, 2, 36, 39, 41, 177. See also FSI (Fragile States Index)
FATA (Federally Administered Tribal Areas), 6, 94, 96, 101, 107
FE (fixed effects), 52–53, 58, 60
FI (Fragility Index), 5, 14, 33, 35, 38, 49, 51–52. See also FSI (Fragile States Index)
fragility, correlates of, 38, 49, 52, 58t, 60
fragility, drivers of, 36, 49, 76, 79, 168; Bangladesh, 156, 158; Laos, 134; Mali, 120; Mozambique, 181; Pakistan, 81, 101; Yemen, 81, 84, 89
fragility, exit from, 27–33, 46, 55–64, 68, 77–81, 176, 179–81, 185–87; Bangladesh, 149, 156–58, 173, 180–81, 185; Laos, 127, 139, 184; Mozambique, 145, 161–62, 170, 173, 180–81, 185. See also exited states
fragility trap, 1–3, 11–19, 24–28, 30–35, 37–38, 41–66, 71, 76–82, 176–90; Afghanistan, 5, 47, 49 (see also Afghanistan); Bangladesh, 181; Laos, 112; Mali, 112, 181; Mozambique, 61, 181; Pakistan, 49, 55, 95, 110, 180–81; Yemen, 29, 49, 55, 81–82, 89–90, 109–10, 180–81, 183
France, 88, 112–13, 115–16, 120–21, 129, 136, 141, 165, 169
Frelimo (Marxist Frente de Libertação de Moçambique), 163–72, 185
FSI (Fragile States Index), 33, 35–37, 48. See also FI (Fragility Index)
Fund for Peace, 15, 33, 48

Ganda Koy, 123
GASP (Salafist Group for Preaching and Combat), 119
GDP (gross domestic product), 11–12, 14t, 94; Bangladesh, 146, 154, 156, 157; growth, 83, 124, 135, 139, 154; Laos, 135, 139; Mali, 124; Pakistan, 94; per capita, 12, 14t, 51–52t, 58t, 83, 146; percentage of, 14t, 156; Yemen, 83.

Index

See also economy; growth, economic; rent economy
gender, 5, 12, 22, 39–40t, 75, 104; empowerment, 11, 14t, 186; imbalances, 150; performance on, 49, 56
Ghali, Iyad Ag, 117, 119
governance, 5, 7, 20–21, 23, 40t–41, 44–45, 66, 82, 188–90; Bangladesh, 156, 158–61; decentralized, 92, 154, 160; effective, 5, 7, 21, 23, 74, 76; good, 12, 21, 23, 37, 46; Libya, 123–24; Mali, 121–22; poor, 34, 56, 78, 147, 159, 190; slow-growth-poor-governance equilibrium trap, 34; World Bank Worldwide Governance Indicators, 7, 9, 23, 46, 50
governance trap, 45
Grameen Bank, 159–61, 174
growth, 7, 12, 25, 136, 180–81, 184; Bangladesh, 146, 150, 155–58, 173, 175, 185; GDP, 124, 135, 139; impacts on, 19, 25; income, 13, 43, 51; Laos, 113, 134–36, 139–40, 144, 184; low, 19, 34, 177; Mali, 114, 124–26; models, 18, 189; Mozambique, 146, 162, 166–73, 185; Pakistan, 82, 94–95, 103–5, 110, 184; population, 85; rapid, 71, 156; rates, 43, 157–58; sustainable, 62, 65; Yemen, 83–85, 184
growth, economic, 12, 18–19, 25, 30, 44, 59, 65, 70, 74, 181, 186, 189; Bangladesh, 146, 155–57, 173, 185; Laos, 113, 134, 140; Mali, 126; Mozambique, 146, 170–73, 185; Pakistan, 94, 104–5. *See also* economy; GDP (gross domestic product); rent economy
Guatemala, 55t–57, 61
Guebuza, Armando, 168
Guinea, 40t–41, 43, 71
Guinea-Bissau, 33, 40t–41t, 55t
Gulf Cooperation Council, 88

Hadi, Abd-Rabbu Mansour al-, 88–90
Hasina, Sheikh, 152–56
Hmong Insurgency, 127, 131–33, 135–38, 144
Houthi, 85, 89; movement, 90, 110; northern, 83, 110; rebels, 88–90
Hudood Ordinance, 98
human development, 5, 39–41, 49, 56, 65, 91, 186; Bangladesh, 157, 174; Human Development Index, 12, 14t, 83, 95; indicators, 12, 109, 157; Pakistan, 104; Yemen, 109
Hussein, Saddam, 87
hybridity, 65, 69, 72, 114, 124, 188

IMF (International Monetary Fund), 121, 166–67, 172

"in" and "out" states, 31, 55t–56, 181
income, 12–13, 22, 43, 49–51, 58, 65, 71; Bangladesh, 146, 158; Laos, 138, 141, 184; levels, 18, 43, 51, 158; low, 12, 19, 24, 36, 43–44, 48, 56, 146; middle, 24–25, 48, 56, 82, 94, 146; Pakistan, 94, 104; per capita, 12, 18–19, 43, 50–54, 56, 58, 60; Yemen, 85, 87. *See also* LICUS (low income country under stress); MIFF (middle-income failed and fragile state)
India, 25, 94, 97–100, 105–7, 155
inequality, 12–13, 24, 46, 68, 70–71, 75, 82, 97, 104, 110, 187; economic, 2, 6, 96; horizontal, 23, 76, 158
insecurity, 2, 17, 34, 101, 103, 177. *See also* instability; security; stability
instability, 52, 72–73, 101; regional, 16; political, 73, 78, 85; drivers of, 27, 34, 73. *See also* insecurity; security; stability
Iraq, 25, 40t–41, 46, 66, 87, 93
IS (Islamic State), 89, 108
Islamist, 83, 88–89, 91, 110, 113, 120, 126; Islamization, 102
isomorphic mimicry, 20, 25, 29, 45, 72, 120, 171, 177–78

Jatiya Party, 151–54

Kashmir, 94–95, 98–100
Keita, Modibo, 116
Kenya, 40t, 69
Khan, Gen. Ayub, 98
Khan, Maj. Gen. Akbar, 98
Khmer Rouge, 136
Kidal Region, 113, 120, 126
Konaré, Alpha Oumar, 117–18, 123

Laos, 28, 55t, 112–13, 127–44; agriculture, 129–31, 134–36; ALC (authority-legitimacy-capacity), 128f, 80, 139; conflict, 127–38, 141, 180–81; environment, 113, 130, 134–35; fragility, 29, 112, 127, 134, 139, 184; independence, 129–30; Laos-Thailand border, 127–28, 130–33, 136–37; LCMD (Lao Citizens Movement for Democracy), 133, 137; LPRP (Lao People's Revolutionary Party), 128–30, 132–40, 142, 144, 184; RLG (Royal Lao Government), 129; stability, 112, 128, 142–43
LCMD (Lao Citizens Movement for Democracy), 133, 137
legitimacy trap, 21, 23, 46, 50–51f, 60, 75, 149, 178

liberalization, 68, 70, 72–73, 121–22, 131, 140, 142–43, 166–67, 169–70, 188; economic, 69, 73, 122, 131, 142–43, 165, 189
Libya, 40t, 89, 117–19, 123–24; Libyan Civil War, 118, 123
LICUS (low income country under stress), 36, 39
LPRP (Lao People's Revolutionary Party), 128–30, 132–40, 142, 144, 184

Machel, Samora, 164–65, 171
Malawi, 6, 55t–56
Mali, 112–26, 143–44; ALC (authority-legitimacy-capacity), 114–15f, 117, 120; conflict, 112–26, 134, 180–81 (see also al-Quaeda: al-Qaeda in the Islamic Maghreb; Tuareg: Tuareg Rebellion); fragility, 28–29, 40t, 112–15, 120, 134, 184; MNLA (National Movement for the Liberation of Azawad), 119–20, 126; MUJAO (Movement for Oneness and Jihad in West Africa), 119–20
Maputo, Province of, 164–66, 172
Marshall-Goldstone State Fragility Index, 35
MDG (Millennium Development Goals), 12–13, 42. See also SDG (Sustainable Development Goals)
Mekong River, 133, 135–36, 141, 144
microfinance, 158–61
MIFF (middle-income failed and fragile state), 25, 81–82
migrants, Tuareg, 117, 119, 122, 124. See also Tuareg
military (armed forces), 64, 71, 82, 86, 97–98; aid, 109, 183; Bandladesh, 145–46, 149–52, 155–57, 160–61, 185; coup, 20, 94; expenditure and spending, 6, 14t, 78, 85, 91–92; intervention, 113, 120; Laos, 132, 138, 142–43; leaders, 78, 88, 185; Mali, 113, 120–21, 123–24, 126; Mozambique, 164–66, 170; Pakistan, 98–103, 105–6, 108–9, 187; regime, 74, 106, 187; support, 14, 164; tensions, 98, 108, 150; Yemen, 85–88, 91–92
Minh, Ho Chi, 129
MNLA (National Movement for the Liberation of Azawad), 119–20, 126
Mozambique, 28–30, 145–46, 161–75; ALC (authority-legitimacy-capacity), 56, 145, 163, 80; ANC (African National Congress), 164; conflict, 61, 145–46, 163–65, 169–71, 180–81, 185; fragility, 40t, 55t–57, 145, 161–62, 173, 185; Frelimo (Marxist Frente de Libertação de Moçambique), 163–72, 185; ONUMOZ (United Nations Operation in Mozambique), 69; Renamo (Resistência Nacional Mozambicans), 57, 163–73; Rome General Peace Accords, 165, 168, 170
MQM (Muhajir Qaumi Movement), 99
mujahideen, 87, 107, 119
MUJAO (Movement for Oneness and Jihad in West Africa), 119–20
Mujibur, Sheikh Rahman, 146, 150, 152
multidimensional approach, 11, 35, 37–38, 41; multidimensionality, 12, 43
Musharraf, Pervez, 95–96, 100–101, 103, 106–7

natural resource curse, 44, 49
natural resource trap, 44, 49
NGO (nongovernmental organization), 125, 135, 159, 160–61, 174
Nicaragua, 55t–56

ODA (Official Development Assistance), 34, 141
OECD (Organisation for Economic Co-operation and Development), 2, 6, 10, 33–34, 38, 42, 78, 155. See also OECD DAC
OECD DAC (Organisation for Economic Co-operation and Development, Development Assistance Committee), 2, 45
OLS (Ordinary Least Squares), 52–53
ONUMOZ (United Nations Operation in Mozambique), 69

Pakistan, 81–82, 94–111; ALC (authority-legitimacy-capacity), 41, 80, 95–96; conflict, 29, 54, 81–82, 94–103, 105–8, 180–81; FATA (Federally Administered Tribal Areas), 6, 94, 96, 101, 107; fragility, 28–29, 40t–41t, 49t, 55t, 81–82, 94–96, 101, 103, 110; middle-income, 25, 48, 94; PML-N (Pakistani Muslim League, Nawaz), 99, 105, 108; PML-Q (Pakistani Muslim League, Quaid e Azam Group), 101; PPP (Pakistan People's Party), 98–99, 101
Pao, Maj. Gen. Vang, 138
Papua New Guinea, 25
Pathet Lao, 129, 136
patronage, 92, 109, 122, 158; network, 125–26, 168; system, 82, 91–93, 110, 125, 183; politics, 89
PDRY (People's Democratic Republic of Yemen/South Yemen), 84, 86, 92–93, 181
Phomvihane, Kaysone, 132, 139–40, 142
PML-N (Pakistani Muslim League, Nawaz), 99, 105, 108
PML-Q (Pakistani Muslim League, Quaid e Azam Group), 101

Index

poverty, 12–13, 16, 19, 24, 26, 37, 44, 60, 177, 178; absolute, 49–50, 54, 167; Bangladesh, 154, 158–61; extreme, 12, 24–25, 159; Laos, 140; levels of, 25, 70, 154, 173; line, 24, 85, 109; Mozambique, 167, 173; Yemen, 85, 109. *See also* poverty trap

poverty trap, 18–19, 43–44, 49–54, 58, 60, 178. *See also* poverty

PPP (Pakistan People's Party), 98–99, 101

praetorianism, 105–6

premature load bearing, 20, 25, 45, 120, 143

principal-agent theory, 64

public goods, 10, 42, 75, 187; core, 5, 7; provision of, 7, 13, 44, 71, 78–79, 182, 187

public loyalty, 5, 21, 74, 182

Punjab, 100, 102–3

Qaddafi, Muammar, 117, 119, 124

Rahman, (Zia) Ziaur, 150–51, 153. *See also* Zia, Khaleda

RE (random effects), 52–53

reform, 19, 45, 64, 67, 72–74, 177, 179, 182–83, 187; Bangladesh, 160–61, 185; democratic, 122, 125, 128, 142–43, 160, 166, 175, 188; economic, 2, 77, 122, 125, 128, 141–42, 166, 169; Laos, 113, 128, 134, 139, 142–43, 184; Mali, 114, 120, 122, 125, 184; Mozambique, 167, 171–72, 185; Pakistan, 104, 110; political, 122, 125, 128, 142–43, 160, 166, 175, 188; Yemen, 83, 86, 93

Renamo (Resistência Nacional Moçambicans), 57, 163–73

rent economy, 82, 115, 124–26, 128, 134, 143, 182–83

rent seeking, 22, 61, 64–65, 78–79, 178, 180, 182, 190; Bangladesh, 156–57, 175; Laos, 142; Mali, 29, 115, 120, 122; Mozambique, 171–72, 174–75, 185; Pakistan, 187

resources, 2, 11, 13, 44–45, 25–26, 73–78, 177, 182–83, 186–89; aid, 2, 17, 126; allocation and distribution of, 45–46, 64–66, 71–72, 79, 121, 125–26, 168, 174, 182, 185, 188–89; Bangladesh, 155; dependence, 45, 184; economic, 2, 7, 104; extraction, 45, 142; Laos, 134–36, 141–42; Mali, 121, 124–26; Mozambique, 162, 172–74; natural, 8, 18, 44, 49, 77, 85, 102, 121; Pakistan, 100, 102–4, 150; use of, 11, 45, 189; Yemen, 83, 85, 183, 186

rights: civil liberties, 8, 12, 14, 22, 56, 76, 99–100; human, 14t, 22, 65, 95, 131; political, 8, 12, 14t, 22, 56; property, 2, 17, 34, 37, 128, 177; Universal Declaration of Human Rights, 22

RLG (Royal Lao Government), 129
Rome General Peace Accords, 165, 168, 170
rule of law, 5, 7, 12, 21, 26, 46, 65, 67, 92, 158
Rwanda, 39, 46, 55

Saleh, Ali Abdullah, 82–83, 85–93, 109–10, 183–84
Sanaa, 85, 88–89
Saudi Arabia, 87–90, 92
SDG (Sustainable Development Goals) 13, 42. *See also* MDG (Millennium Development Goals)
security, 5–7, 34–35, 42, 45–47, 65–66, 74–75, 189–90; Bangladesh, 153, 155; and crime, 39–41, 56; food, 174; Laos, 127, 133; Mozambique, 165, 168; Pakistan, 95–96, 101–2, 108; security-development nexus, 15; security/stability stream, 38–39, 89, 95; state, 27; Yemen, 83, 88–89. *See also* insecurity; instability; stability
Senegal, 55t, 116
sequencing, 3–4, 27–28, 32, 163, 183
Sharif, Nawaz, 99–101, 108
Shia, 90, 99, 102
Shiite, 92, 100
Sierra Leone, 39–40t
Sindhi, 100, 102–3
Somalia, 12, 33, 39–41, 49t, 53–55, 65, 182
Songhai, 123
South Africa, 76, 164–65, 170–72; apartheid, 76, 164
South Sudan, 12, 33, 39–41, 49t, 53–55t
stability, 21, 29, 38, 43, 46, 67, 69, 73, 76, 84, 90–91, 95, 98; economic, 5, 7; political, 5, 7, 14t, 29, 34, 46; security/stability stream, 38–39, 89, 95. *See also* insecurity; instability; security
state building, 6–7, 11, 38, 45, 65
state-society legitimacy, 22, 61, 74
state-society relations, 23, 66, 74, 173, 185–86; Bangladesh, 159; elites, 27, 61, 63, 65, 72, 180; Pakistan, 97
sub-Saharan Africa, 33, 56, 76, 78
Sudan, 33, 39–41, 43, 46, 48–49, 55t. *See also* South Sudan
Sunni, 90, 99–100, 102

Taliban, the, 39, 47, 101, 107
terrorism, 6, 7, 14t, 90, 99, 103, 106, 171; GWOT (Global War on Terrorism), 15, 29, 81, 85, 87–88, 107, 183; terrorist activities, 82, 85, 108; terrorist networks and groups, 6, 47, 107, 109, 144

Thailand, 127–33, 136–38, 140–41, 144
Touré, Amadu Toumani, 113, 117–18, 120, 123–24
transitions, 1, 4, 27, 32, 35, 69–72, 90; Bangladesh, 147–48, 156–58, 181; democratic, 70–71, 78, 108, 125, 156–57, 170, 185, 190; fragile state, 14, 28, 63, 70; Mali, 113–14, 117, 125; Mozambique, 168–70, 181; political, 70–71, 78, 108, 125, 156–57, 170, 185, 190; successful, 3, 4, 14, 30
Traoré, Moussa, 114, 116–18, 121–22
trapped countries. *See* trapped states
trapped states, 1–2, 12, 17, 19, 24, 28, 31, 33, 35, 38, 47–64, 71, 76–78, 176–90
Tuareg, 114, 116–24, 126, 144; rebels, 118–19; Tuareg Rebellion, 114, 117–18, 123
typology, 28, 32, 55t, 63; countries, 27, 32, 38, 55t, 58

UCDP (Uppsala Conflict Data Program), 50
Uganda, 40t, 48–49t, 54–55t
UN (United Nations), 107, 113, 120, 168–70; ONUMOZ (United Nations Operation in Mozambique), 69; SDG (Sustainable Development Goals) 13, 42; UNDP (United Nations Development Programme), 12, 110; United Nations Security Council, 87, 165
undergoverned spaces, 61, 68, 79, 89–90, 122, 134, 144, 180, 182, 184, 186

variable, 13, 21, 28, 50–51; accountability, 50, 54, 58; authority, 85; capacity, 58; conflict, 52, 58; effectiveness, 50, 54; legitimacy, 52–53, 85
Vietnam, 129–31, 134, 136, 138, 140–41; Viet Minh, 129–30; Vietnam War, 136, 138, 141

violence, 2, 5, 7–8, 17, 22, 34, 67, 76, 79; Bangladesh, 146, 151, 154–55, 185; cycle of, 31, 187; Laos, 135, 138; large-scale, 30, 178; Mali, 119, 123; Mozambique, 146, 164, 171, 185; organized, 48, 154; Pakistan, 95–96, 99–103, 108; political, 7, 16, 155, 177; sectarian, 95–96, 99–103, 108 (*see also* conflict: Pakistan); Yemen, 85, 187
Vong, King Sisavang, 129

war crimes, 108
World Bank, 35–36, 38, 48, 56, 82, 141, 156, 166–67, 172, 177; CPIA (Country Policy and Institutional Assessment), 33, 35–36; World Bank Worldwide Governance Indicators, 7, 9, 23, 46, 50

YAR (Yemen Arab Republic/North Yemen), 86, 92–93, 181
Yemen, 29, 81–94; ALC (authority-legitimacy-capacity), 41t, 80, 84f; civil war, 81–85, 89–92, 109; conflict, 54, 85–91, 109, 180–81; fragility, 28, 40t–41, 43, 49t, 55t, 81–84, 89–90, 109, 183; PDRY (People's Democratic Republic of Yemen/South Yemen), 84, 86, 92–93, 181; state, middle-income, 25, 48, 82; YAR (Yemen Arab Republic/North Yemen), 86, 92–93, 181; YSP (Yemen Socialist Party), 93

Zia, Khaleda, 153–54, 156. *See also* Rahman, (Zia) Ziaur
Zia-ul-Haq, President/General Muhammad, 95, 98, 100, 103–4